The Publishing
and Review
of Reference Sources

Forthcoming topics in *The Reference Librarian* series:

- Reference Services Today: From Interview to Burnout, Number 16
- International Aspects of Reference Services, Number 17
- Current Trends in Information: Research and Theory, Number 18
- Reference Services Administration and Budget, Number 19
- Reference Services and Public Policy, Number 20
- Information and Referral, Number 21
- Information Brokers and Consultants, Number 22

Published:

Reference Services in the 1980s, Number 1/2
Reference Services Administration and Management, Number 3
Ethics and Reference Services, Number 4
Video to Online: Reference Services and the New Technology, Numbers 5/6
Reference Services for Children and Young Adults, Numbers 7/8
Reference Services and Technical Services: Interactions in Library Practice, Number 9
Library Instruction and Reference Services, Number 10
Evaluation of Reference Services, Number 11
Conflicts in Reference Services, Number 12
Reference Services in Archives, Number 13
Personnel Issues in Reference Services, Number 14
The Publishing and Review of Reference Sources, Number 15

The Publishing and Review of Reference Sources

Edited by
Bill Katz and Robin Kinder

School of Library & Information Science
State University of New York at Albany

The Haworth Press
New York • London

The Publishing and Review of Reference Sources has also been published as *The Reference Librarian*, Number 15, Fall 1986.

© 1987 by The Haworth Press, Inc. All rights reserved. No part of this book may be reproduced or utilized in any form or by any means, electronic or mechanical, including photocopying, microfilm and recording, or by any information storage and retrieval system, without permission in writing from the publisher. Printed in the United States of America.

The Haworth Press, Inc., 12 West 32 Street, New York, NY 10001
EUROSPAN/Haworth, 3 Henrietta Street, London WC2E 8LU England

Library of Congress Cataloging-in-Publication Data

The Publishing and review of reference sources.

  Published also as the Reference librarian, no. 15, fall, 1986.
  Bibliography: p.
  1. Reference books—Evaluation. 2. Reference books—Publishing. 3. Book reviewing. 4. Reference services (Libraries) I. Katz, William A., 1924– . II. Kinder, Robin.
Z1035.1.P83   1986   028.1'2   86-22910
ISBN 0-86656-571-X

The Publishing and Review of Reference Sources

The Reference Librarian
Number 15

CONTENTS

INTRODUCTION

Publishing, Reviews and the Reference Process   3
    Bill Katz

REVIEWS AND EVALUATION OF REFERENCE WORKS

Evaluation Reference Books in Theory and Practice   9
    Norman Stevens

    Reviewing Experience   11
    What Is a Reference Book?   11
    Theory   13
    Practice   15
    A Final Comment   19

The Reference Reviewer's Responsibilities   21
    James Rettig

    Ivory Tower vs. Reviewer   23
    Four Keys to Reviews   24
    Importance of Evaluation   26
    A Delicate Responsibility   28
    Publishers and Reviews   30
    Information Is Not Enough   32

How to Be a Book Critic: A Guide for Librarians   35
    Richard Grefrath

  Procedure   36
  To Review or Not| to Review   42
  How to Break Into Reviewing   43
  The Rewards of Book Reviewing   45

Dear Encyclopedia Critic   47
    Ken Kister

Evaluation of Reference Sources Published or to Be Published   55
    Jovian Lang, OFM

  Publishers Seek to Fulfill Needs   55
  Online Reference Services   56
  State of Reference Reviewing   57
  Evaluating Reference Tools   58
  Criteria for any Reference Tool   58
  Summary   62
  Criteria for Periodicals on Reference   62
  Criteria for Non-Print Materials on Reference   63
  Conclusion   63

Reference Book Reviewing Tools: How Well Do They Do the Job?   65
    James H. Sweetland

  Method   65
  General Coverage   66
  Currency of Coverage   67
  Review Content   68
  Recommendations by Reviewers   69
  Overall Agreement Among Reviews   70
  Number of Items in a Review   71
  Conclusion   72

Book Reviewing in Sociology   75
    Sharon Quist

  Influential Factors   76
  Prestige   77

Publish or Perish	77
Location of Reviews	78
Scholarly vs. Popular Social Science	80
Comparison of Reviewing Sources	80
Indexing Practices	82
Popular Social Science	83
Conclusion	83

REVIEWS AND EVALUATION: TWO PROPOSALS

Publication of Reference Tools for Special Collections   **89**
    Daniel Traister

New Reference Sources on Women: An Analysis and Proposal   **109**
    Helen B. Josephine
    Deborah K. Blouin

Criteria	110
Outstanding Sources	110
Inadequate Sources	112
New Reference Sources in Women's Studies	113
Statistics	114
Encyclopedias	115
Yearbooks	117
Databases	117
Conclusion	120

REFERENCE PUBLISHING

Communication Between Publishers and Librarians: Cooperation or Conflict?   **125**
    Martin Grayson
    Carol Stuckhardt

The Librarian Is the Key	126
How Do We Communicate With Librarians?	128
Where Do We Go From Here?	129

The Buzz Industry and the Book Industry   **131**
    Fred Ruffner

Recognizing Our Roots	131

Computer Miracles	132
Computer Technology—A Means, Not an End	133
Books—An Endangered Species?	134
On Co-Existence	135
From Beech Trees to Books	137

On the Writing of Reference Books: Real and Ideal; In Which the Author Discourses on Motivation, Process, Publication, Reviews and Rewards — **139**
Marda Woodbury

Drifting Into Writing	140
The Grant Story	143
Advice to Authors	145

Reference Books From a Scholarly Publisher — **147**
Marilyn Brownstein
Nora Kisch
Mary R. Sive

Developing Reference Books	148
Greenwood's Reference Program	149
Editorial Procedures	150
Production Procedures	151
Promotion and Marketing Procedures	152

From Book Idea to Contract: Writing Reference and Professional Books — **155**
Pat Schuman

Developing a Book	158
Book Proposal Checklist	159
Choosing a Publisher	160
The Book Contract	162

Who Are the Whos: The Uses of Biographical Reference Sources for Social Demography — **169**
Adele Hast

Overview of Elite Studies	169
Business Elites	170

Women Elites	172
Other Elite Studies	173
Variables Analyzed	173

Small Press Reference Books — 177
Kay Ann Cassell

How to Locate the Material	178
Review Sources and Listings	179
Distribution	181
Small Press Arts Reference Books: A Case Study	181
Addresses	183

Major Business Reference Works — 185
Thomas P. Slavens

Standard and Poor's Guides	186
And From Moody's	188
The Predicasts Group	190
Marketing Directory	191
Who Has What	192

Publishing Reference Works in the Electronic Age: Information Delivery Through Multiple Channels — 195
Phyllis B. Steckler

Print	196
Online Publishing	196
Distributed Database Publishing	197
Electronic Publishing at Oryx Press	198

Online Searching—Reference Librarians and Reference Publishers Meet the Challenge Together — 201
Jon Clayborne

Cost Discourages	202
Staff Training	203
Perceptions	205
Reactions	206

Old Books—New Technologies   **209**
      Davie Biesel

    Let's Be Inventive   210
    Advantages   211
    Let's Imagine   213
    Carr on CD   214

The Medium Must Match the Message   **217**
      Kathy Niemeier

    Developing the MegaDatabase   218

Ready Reference Using Online Databases   **225**
      Barbara E. Anderson

    Online Databases and Ready Reference   226
    What Cannot Be Found Online (Yet)   234
    Online Bibliographic Databases as Ready Reference
      Sources   234
    Summary   235

The Reference Services From Mead Data Central: Combining Index Terms and Free Text Searching for Saturation Retrieval   **237**
      Sharon K. Peake

    Advantages of the Reference Service   238
    Online User Aids   240
    The Basis for Growth   241
    Other Services from Mead Data Central   242

Optical Disk—The Electronic Library Arrives   **251**
      Sandra Sinsel Leach

    The Technology   251
    The Environment   253
    The Products   255
    Datext Inc.'s Corporate Information Database   258
    IPS Are Maintaining Flexibility   258
    The Effects of Optical Disk Technology   263
    Keeping Up With Optical Disk Developments   265

Online Services at the Reference Desk:
New Technologies vs. Old Problems 269
Mary Boulanger

Gateway and Front-End Software 270
End User Products 271
CD-ROM Systems 272
Videodisks 273
Implications for Reference Services 274
Summary 275

PUBLISHING POLICIES AND REFERENCE SOURCES

Keeping the Lid On: Approaches to the Control of Costs in Reference Book Purchasing in an Academic Library 281
Heather S. Miller

The Reference Book Situation 282
Approaches to Control 297
Conclusion 301

Reference Publishing and Changing Distribution Techniques 303
Sharon C. Bonk

Reference Books 306
Distribution Technologies 308

The Effect of Publishing Policies on Reference Service in the Large Academic Library 317
Constance A. Fairchild

The Problem of Spin-Offs 318
Keyword Indexing vs. Traditional Subject Headings 319
Format Problems 320
Microforms 321
Summary 322

What Is Reference Publishing? A Dialogue 323
Robert Franklin

EDITOR

BILL KATZ, *School of Library & Information Science, State University of New York at Albany*

ASSOCIATE EDITORS

RUTH A. FRALEY, *Chief Law Librarian, Office of Court Administration, Albany, NY*
ROBIN KINDER, *Darien Library, Darien, CT*

EDITORIAL BOARD

JAMES BENSON, *Professor, Graduate School of Library Service, University of Alabama, University*
SANFORD BERMAN, *Head Cataloger, Hennepin County Library, Edina, MN*
FAY M. BLAKE, *Professor, School of Library and Information Studies, University of California, Berkeley*
LARRY EARL BONE, *Director of Libraries, Mercy College, Dobbs Ferry, NY*
FRANCES NEEL CHENEY, *Professor Emeritus, Department of Library Science, George Peabody College, Vanderbilt University, Nashville, TN*
D. E. DAVINSON, *Assistant Director, Academic Affairs, Leeds Polytechnic, England*
RICHARD DeGENNARO, *Director of Libraries, University of Pennsylvania, Philadelphia*
BARBARA FELICETTI, *President Info/motion, Kingston, MA*
RICHARD W. GREFRATH, *Instructional Services Librarian, University Library, University of Nevada, Reno*
NORMAN HORROCKS, *Director, School of Library Service, Dalhousie University, Halifax, Nova Scotia*
ILSE MOON, *Library Consultant, Sarasota, FL*
BERRY GARGAL RICHARDS, *Director, Lehigh University Libraries, Bethlehem, PA*
PAT ROM, *Director of Information Services, Library, Hunter College, New York, NY*
SAMUEL ROTHSTEIN, *Professor, School of Librarianship, The University of British Columbia, Vancouver*
JOSEPH F. SHUBERT, *Assistant Commissioner for Libraries and State Librarian, New York State Library, Albany*
PATRICIA SILVERNAIL, *Assistant University Librarian, University of Oregon, Eugene, OR*
PEGGY SULLIVAN, *Dean, College of Professional Studies, Northern Illinois University*
ROBERT S. TAYLOR, *Dean, School of Information Studies, Syracuse University, Syracuse, NY*
B. C. VICKERY, *Director, School of Library Archive and Information Studies, University College London, England*
A. J. WALFORD, *Editor of* Guide to Reference Material, *Walford, Herts, England*
MARTHA E. WILLIAMS, *Professor, Information Retrieval Research Laboratory, University of Illinois at Urbana-Champaign, Urbana*
MARDA WOODBURY, *President, Research Ventures, Berkeley, CA*

The Publishing and Review of Reference Sources

INTRODUCTION

Publishing, Reviews and the Reference Process

Bill Katz

This issue of *The Reference Librarian* is dedicated to an examination of facets of reference publishing and reviewing. It is a fitting topic. None of us would function without at least the publisher, and few could manage to select without the aid of conscientious reviewers.

Reference works make up five to six percent of the output of new titles by American publishers each year, which is to say from 1500 to 2000 books can dutifully be labelled as titles one looks to for answers rather than involved reading. These days the net must be cast wider to include databases and CD-Rom, as well as other technological wonders, yet regardless of physical form the reference tool is just that—a place to turn to, to find answers.

How, though, does a publisher decide which type of reference book is needed? What are the processes involved in securing authors/editors? What steps are taken in the actual production of the reference work, and how is it distributed and marketed? Once the book is published, how well (if at all) is it reviewed? How do editors and reviewers determine what is, or is not to be considered? How well do the critics evaluate reference works? These, and related questions, are addressed by authors in this issue. It is suggested that the reference librarian with a better understanding and appreciation of publishing and reviewing will be in a position to evaluate not only individual titles, but types of reference works and the needs of individual users. In other places, other articles, efforts have been made to link the publisher and the reviewer, to show that certain publishers inevitably receive more and better reviews than others. The connection is tenuous, if only because of the numerous variables, and in the final analyses the librarian should judge each publisher, each title, each review on its own. To attempt to discover some magic quantitative formula which neatly links the review/publisher to allow automatic selection is nonsense.

Equally silly is the notion that publishers of reference works are only in it for the money. Obviously, they all hope to be able to pay the mortgage and buy ice cream, but even a casual glance at the articles by the various publishers in this issue will reassure the idealist and quell the misgivings of the cynic. All are deeply concerned with the needs of librarians, and all are ever-anxious to find new ways, new approaches, indeed, new books, to meet those needs. Either directly or by implication they deplore the sometimes less-than-interested response of librarians to requests on how this or that reference work might be improved, or for ideas of what is needed in a given area. At the same time, the publisher applause is deafening when it comes to appreciation of those librarians who do let publishers know what is required, what should be modified.

What is most heartening about the articles, from both publishers and librarians, is the voice of the individual in the land of reference services. True, conglomerates are not strangers to the reference publishing scene, but for the most part the individual editor remains a voice and not an echo of the conglomerate's insatiable quest for dollars. Even more encouraging is the number of small, well defined publishers of reference works who essentially are one- or two-person business concerns. For every conglomerate there seems to rise a half-dozen or so independents. (The point is stressed over and over again in the articles, but see particularly Kay Cassell's discussion of the small press and its place in the reference scene.)

The new technologies, from online to CD-Rom, are having a revolutionary effect on publishing and on reference services. While one hardly sees the demise of the printed book, one can certainly envision the time when reference books, and other lesser-used items in the library, may very well be available only at a computer. The technological ramifications of all of this is gone into in some detail by several authors, e.g., Steckler, Niemeir, Anderson et al. While it took almost 400 years to modify Gutenberg's initial invention to allow mass production of books, it is now taking less than a decade to completely change the publishing and reference scene. And while most of it is for the good, there is a bit of hype, a bit of a nightmare in the whole which is considered by several writers.

If there is any consensus among this diverse group of librarians and publishers it is the interdependence of one upon the other, and the sometimes almost anguished plea by both for understanding, one of the other. It seems the American Library Association and local library associations would do well to devote not only sections, but meetings to the relationship between publisher and reference librarian. Such understanding has always been necessary, but today it is an absolute requirement. This is not theory. This is fact.

As Norman Stevens points out in his study of the art of reviewing, "the theory and the practice of evaluating reference books is quite different." He, as others in the section, then goes on to explore the theory (from the text book outline of accuracy, appropriateness, etc.) and the practice. He concludes, "it is not possible to teach the art of evaluating reference books." One suspects much the same is true of an appreciation of different publishers. True skill, the true art comes not from assigning quantitative formulas, but from reading, reading and more reading. This supports Retting's appreciation of the reviewer and review which builds to the final question of the qualitative nature of the review. It is the question put by the reader. "Does this review help me to decide whether I should add this item to the library reference collection?"

All of this is fine, but Grefrath notes that one still needs direction in writing a review and he proceeds to the nitty gritty steps. These are practical, even to the point of admitting that "Occasionally you should decline the invitation to review a book." His lead is carried to specifics by Kister, the "Dear Abby of Encyclopedias." He demonstrates the kind of queries librarians are likely to receive about the sets from the public. He gives some witty and timely answers, as does Jovian Lang about the workings of the RASD, Reference Sources Committee for Small and Medium-sized Libraries. He, as the committee on which he serves, offers some excellent criteria "for any reference tool" evaluation.

Yes, but just how good is the reviewing scene these days? Comparing the major review media, Sweetland concludes the major sources—from *Choice* to *Library Journal*—are up and down. His final words of advice seem worth repeating: "Read several reviews, and be careful. The best advice to the reviewers, and to their editors remains—try harder to do the job." This is echoed by Quist who studies reviews in sociology and decides knowledge of the "workings of the reviewing process" may be the most important.

In-depth reviewing is not possible in most cases, but as Traister observes it is essential when one considers standard bibliographical works. It is essential to know certain types of information in order that the special library may function. The author then goes on to a detailed criticism of much library press publishing. Josephine and

Blouin consider another aspect of bibliography. How well are women considered in standard reference sources? They then suggest needed publications.

Turning to publishers, several of the basic leaders in the field explain reference publishing from their point of view: Fred Ruffner at Gale; Jon Clayborne of H.W. Wilson Co.; Martin Grayson and Carol Stuckhardt from John Wiley and Sons; Marda Woodbury of Research Ventures, Brownstein of Greenwood; Hast of Marquis Who's Who are representative of the industry. Kay Ann Cassell speaks for the small presses while Tom Slavens outlines the major business reference sources. Each, of course, has a different point of view, but all are concerned with libraries and particularly involved with trying to bridge the gap of understanding between the two. Grayson summarizes the situation with the direct question: "How do we communicate with librarians?" The implication here, and elsewhere, is that librarians, in turn, should make more of an effort to discuss their needs with the publishers.

Phyllis Steckler of Oryx Press takes a turn suggested by the other publishers, the turn to technology as does Dave Biesel of Sharpe. Niemeir of Information Access observes, "The medium must match the message," and the revolution in the storage and the access of information has strongly influenced not only publishing but reference services.

Online databases are the concern of Anderson, speaking for Dialog, and this discussion is considered as well by Peake of Mead Data Central. Librarians, as noted by both Leach and Boulanger, have a somewhat different view of the technology of the online search. What is noteworthy in this group of articles is the recognition by both publishers and librarians of the interdependence of the new technology and the skills of the librarian.

"Everyone knows what a reference book is," says Miller, but from the point of view of librarians the new technology, the standard print methods are secondary in terms of the increasing number of reference works and their mounting costs. What's the librarian to do to control the problem? A solution, all admit, is a dream, but one keeps trying. Bonk takes an objective view of the "economic ups and downs of the industry" and how this, and the different formats, influence distribution. Finally, Fairchild sums it all up with an overview of "the effect of publishing policies on reference service."

REVIEWS AND EVALUATION OF REFERENCE WORKS

Evaluating Reference Books in Theory and Practice

Norman Stevens

The evaluation of reference books, whether in terms of an initial decision to acquire them or a subsequent decision as to their utility, is an important element of our professional work. The important skill of evaluation is one that is taught in library schools as a core component of the instructional program. Like other basic skills, however, this one is refined and sharpened as we become practicing librarians. That mature skill is, I suspect, a matter of individual development and style. It is clearly one area where the science that has been taught to a student becomes an art as it is developed by the practitioner over time. Is there anything to be gained from an examination of the distinction between the skill and the art of evaluating reference books? I think so. This essay is an attempt to undertake such an exam in the hope that it will help others think about how they have developed their techniques, and will help instruct students and newcomers in the transformation of the skill that they have been taught into an art. The theory and the practice of evaluating reference books are quite different. The difference deserves our consideration.

These thoughts are not based on either research or a careful examination of what others may have said on the subject. There appears to have been little written on this subject although, as usual, I have not conducted an exhaustive literature search. Although carefully taught that a literature search is an essential first step of any attempt to write on a subject, I now blithely ignore that instruction. I have made extensive continuing use of the library literature over time and have, I feel, a good sense of what exists or does not exist that might guide me in writing on a subject. More

The author is Acting Director of University Libraries, University of Connecticut, Storrs, CT 06268 and a frequent contributor to the literature of evaluation of library-oriented monographs.

importantly I have something distinctive to say, based on my experience, that is shaped by that experience and by my thoughts, not by what somebody else may have said or done. Read this piece with the understanding that it represents a personal point of view.

For that reason it is important to explain why any real reference librarian should heed the words of an administrator, who has never worked as a practicing reference librarian, on this subject. Like all librarians I was taught the theory of evaluating books, and especially reference books, in my library school education which took place at the Graduate School of Library Service at dear old Rutgers in the mid-1950s. While, on the whole, that instruction was excellent, I must confess that my basic reference course was less than satisfactory. Taking to heart, and to a greater degree than I am sure anyone would have thought advisable, the notion that Rutgers, at that time, was interested, as it clearly was, in teaching its students the broad concepts of librarianship rather than practical skills our instructor, among other things, spent at least one class period discussing the importance of the verb in the reference question! Nevertheless in that and in other courses we were taught to examine, evaluate, and produce written annotations of books including reference books. Shortly thereafter I taught the basic reference course once or twice; as a novice I carefully modified and followed a precise outline that taught how to evaluate a reference book.

That all seems, as it is, far away. During the course of my career I have developed additional skills in the evaluation of reference books. In both my professional and my personal life I make constant use of reference materials to assist me with the location of information. Hardly a day goes by that I don't use a reference book. In doing so I have, without consciously setting out to do so, developed some particular ways of evaluating the books that I use. Frequent use alone, much of which is casual, hardly refines one's skills. Those who taught me at Rutgers, especially Paul S. Dunkin, encouraged me to develop a professional writing career. In the course of my writing career I have done a substantial number of reviews of reference books in the field of librarianship. Those reference works, which as one would expect typically follow a well-organized traditional format, offer only a limited opportunity to learn. I have also, since 1978, reviewed reference books in a variety of fields for *American Reference Books Annual*; I have, at this point, written more than 100 brief reviews for *ARBA*. That reviewing has involved a catchall range of subjects with an emphasis on antiques and collectibles, sports, New England, the South Pacific, as well as any number of obscure subjects.

REVIEWING EXPERIENCE

The important thing about that reviewing experience is not just the skills it has helped developed in attempting to evaluate reference books in a way that is meaningful to others, but the opportunity it has given me to review a range of reference books on various subjects, many of which result in the production of reference books that by no stretch of the imagination can be said to follow standard practices. There are a lot of strange reference books out there! I have even written an article, for an obscure publication called *Collectrix*,[1] on evaluating reference books on antiques and collectibles from the point of view, on the one hand, of a professional librarian and reviewer and, on the other hand, a collector using those same books. I thus have been in a position to take a set of practical skills that I was taught, to refine those skills initially by teaching them to others in a formal sense, and then to transform those skills into an art both through the actual use of reference books and the formal evaluation of reference books. This analysis of the theory and practice of evaluating reference books is based on that experience.

WHAT IS A REFERENCE BOOK?

In considering even such a simple question as what is a reference book it is clear that there is a considerable distinction between theory and practice. That distinction needs to be examined before delving into the distinctions in the theory and practice of evaluating whatever a reference book may be.

The ALA Glossary of Library and Information Science provides the best standard theoretical definition. It defines a reference book as: (1) A book designed by the arrangement and the treatment of its subject matter to be consulted for definite items of information rather than to be read consecutively. (2) A book whose use is restricted to the library building.[2] Those are fine theoretical distinctions but, alas, they fail in practice. Some people, like me, may prefer to read what appear to be reference books all the way through for enjoyment. By contrast a recent study by Patricia and Gordon

Sabine, conducted for Fred Kilgour of OCLC, on *How People Use Books and Journals* concludes, among other things, that of the people they interviewed eight out of ten reported that they usually read only small parts, rather than the entire text, of the books and journals they use.[3] In addition many books may not leave a library that we would hardly consider reference books. If an academic library does not circulate bound periodicals, as many do not, and if users are consulting those journals only for small parts of an article, does that make a bound periodical a reference book?

There are more practical, if not more useful, definitions. One that I use is that anything sent to me by *ARBA* for review is a reference book. Another, slightly more cynical, definition is that a reference book is: any book found in the reference department of a library especially if it does not circulate and has the word reference, or some variation such as R or Ref., over the call number in the catalog and/or on the book; and most especially a book that can be found only by asking a reference librarian because the book is so valuable that it is kept in a special location that is not clearly indicated by the catalog, and may even be hidden from sight, either to protect it from theft or to allow the staff to appear to have some mystical powers of retrieval.

The real difficulty though is that today even such practical definitions are no longer totally satisfactory. There is, perhaps, no good precise way to define a reference book. There are some works, such as major encyclopedias, that are clearly reference books; there are other works, such as in most cases the current best-selling novels, that are clearly not reference books. There is, however, a large indeterminate area in which it is difficult to determine by any simple theoretical or practical definition whether or not something is a reference book. What is a reference book in one library is not in another. What may be used as a reference book by one person may not be by another. What is a reference book today is not tomorrow. The reality is that there are a large number of publications which must be evaluated as reference books on a continuing basis by individual libraries and librarians both in the decisions that are made about the location of the book within the library and the way in which it is used to provide information. That broader vague definition means, among other things, that the simpler evaluative skills that may be taught (e.g., does the book have an index) are not always adequate or appropriate. In the context of that definition the evaluation of reference books, whether in theory or practice, becomes a more complex task.

THEORY

While the theory of evaluating reference books does have its complexities, on the whole it is possible to outline and describe in fairly simple terms the kinds of questions that should be raised in the evaluation of any reference book. Those questions, which are fairly standard, have not changed much over time. The approach taught in the 1950s is not much different from that of earlier times and, for the most part, that same approach still stands the would-be evaluator in good stead. In theory by thinking carefully about the following eighteen points, or as many of them as are appropriate in a particular case, it should be possible to make an evaluative judgment about a particular reference work.

Accuracy. A reference book, in particular, is of little value if the information which it contains is not accurate. It is not always, of course, easy to determine how accurate information may be but simple tests based on one's own knowledge, especially if you have any expertise in the subject, and a comparison with information found in other sources are reasonable ways of judging accuracy.

Appropriateness. Some perfectly good reference books are not appropriate for a particular library or for attempting to locate a particular kind of information. Beyond that there are questions to be asked about whether or not the arrangement, the content, and, in general, the approach is appropriate for the subject.

Arrangement. A good reference book presents its information in an orderly fashion and is organized and arranged in such a way as to facilitate use.

Authority. The qualifications of the author, contributors, and the publisher are sometimes an important aspect of evaluating the quality of a work. If they are recognized experts in a field, and have written and/or published other works on the subject, which have been well received, then perhaps it may be presumed that they know something about the subject.

Bibliography. Almost, but not quite, every subject has had previous work published about it. A good reference tool provides adequate bibliographic information about previous work on the same, or related, subjects that will help guide users who wish to pursue a subject further.

Comparability. It is always important to consider what similar or related reference books already exist and to compare a new reference book with those previous works. Such a comparison is a good way to check such things as accuracy and arrangement as well as to obtain a general sense of the utility of one reference work in contrast to another.

Completeness. It is important to know, and here too a comparability test can be of value, whether or not the material that should be included in a particular reference book is there and whether or not the subject, as defined by the author, has been covered completely and thoroughly.

Content. It is above all the content of the book, and a general impression of the content and its overall value, that is likely to be the primary consideration in evaluating any reference book.

Distinction. A truly outstanding reference work has some quality about it that gives it a character of its own which is not shared by any other reference work. That distinction is the indescribable quality that not only sets the work apart but makes it an obvious purchase or the obvious source to be used for answering certain kinds of reference questions on a regular basis.

Documentation. Knowledge about the source of the information contained in a reference book and how and where that information was obtained, is a vital consideration. A reference book that provides no documentation and contains no information by which one can test its accuracy and reliability is automatically suspect.

Durability. With today's professional interest in preservation one might think that every book, and especially every reference book, should be printed on acid-free paper. That is not necessarily the case but every reference book should be evaluated in terms of whether its physical make-up is durable enough for the intended use and likely life of the work.

Ease-of-use. Even an organized book, and sometimes even a well-organized book, may not be easy to use. Since, for the most part, reference books are intended to provide ready access to particular pieces of information, the ability to find the information contained in a reference work easily and readily is another important quality.

Illustrations. Not all reference books need illustrations but many do as an effective way of describing a particular aspect of a subject or complementing written information. The first question is whether a particular reference work should or should not, and does or does not, contain illustrations. Only then, assuming that there are illustrations, should the question of whether or not the illustrations are adequate, representative, and well-selected be considered.

Index. An index is often considered a *sine qua non* of a reference book and, in many cases, that is certainly true but a bad and/or incomplete index, or one that simply duplicates the basic arrangement of the text and provides no additional access points, is worse than no index at all.

Level. Almost any subject can be dealt with in various ways depending upon the age, education, and level of understanding of the intended audience. The approach that a reference work takes to a subject, including such things as the language used, and the relationship of that approach to the intended audience's capabilities and needs is worth some thought.

Reliability. Reliability is accuracy on a larger scale. It is not simply a question of whether or not the information presented is correct but also a question of whether or not a particular reference work can be relied upon as a standard primary source of information on a subject. The simple test of reliability is whether or not the user is likely to find the information on a subject he/she is most often looking for in a particular tool.

Revisions. Information, as we too well know, changes over time. Few reference books endure without some regular provision for updating and revision. On the other hand revision for the sake of revision, and perhaps incidentally the ability to sell a new edition more often than is really needed, is of no real value.

Uniqueness. The last, and perhaps the truest, test of the value of any reference work is its uniqueness. An outstanding reference work somehow provides information, or access to information, in a fashion that is unlike what is found in any other reference work on the same subject and that somehow gives the work a character all of its own.

PRACTICE

All of those elements of evaluating reference books must be placed eventually in a perspective that relates to a particular situation whether in selection for use in an individual library or selection for use in seeking particular information. Selection for purchase needs to take into account such additional factors as price, available funds, relationship to existing sources in the library, and the needs of the library and its users. In addition the appropriate use of reviews and/or guides to reference books are important elements to assist in that kind of evaluation and choice. In evaluating a reference work for use other factors such as the information sought, the needs and abilities of the user, the sources available, and the librarian's own understanding of the reference collection and individual reference works need to be considered. Taking all of those factors into account the moderately complex task of evaluating reference works on a theoretical basis is simpler—largely because there is a specific list of elements to be considered—than the actual practice of evaluating reference works where professional judgment is involved and where other elements that cannot be easily categorized somehow always come into play.

It is possible to describe and teach the theoretical skills of evaluating reference books; it is even possible to give students and beginning professional librarians hands-on experience in practicing those skills under supervision. It is not possible, in any meaningful sense, to teach the art of evaluating reference books. That is a quite different level of skill that is learned only through extended practice. It is, in most respects, a highly individual aspect of professionalism. One can speak and write of the maturity that comes with experience. It is more difficult, if not impossible, to describe in any detail the elements of that experience, or to explain how to achieve that maturity. The balance of this essay is an effort to describe, in general terms, some of the techniques that one practiced reviewer and user of reference books has developed and uses. Such a description may, one might hope, assist others in thinking about how they approach the evaluation of reference books and in sharpening their skills.

The reviewing of reference books, whether of excellent professional tools or inconsequential guides to collecting gizmos, requires an ability not only to describe, usually in a very brief space, the content and purpose of a work but to place that work in a perspective that will be meaningful to others using that review as they attempt to select, or understand, a particular reference work. One begins by looking at, even if only in a casual and non-specific manner, all of the eighteen elements of a theoretical evaluation that have been described above. Not all of those elements carry equal weight in respect to a single work and, in some cases, a number of them may not apply at all. Judgment in determining what elements do apply and what weight is to then be given to them is especially critical. A reviewer must look at the purpose of the work and the extent to which the work, through its content and organization, meets that purpose. The strengths and weaknesses of a particular work, its quality, and its character are the elements that are apt to emerge as most significant to a reviewer. While a sense of balance, and the conveyance of that sense of balance in the actual review is important, most of all the experienced reviewer seeks to arrive, after a careful examination of a reference book, at a judgment that involves an overall impression as to the quality and value of the book. Is it good or bad? Does it serve a need? Can it be recommended? The answer to those questions then shapes the content and the wording of the review. In the perhaps vain hope that a review will influence an author and/or publisher in the production of future works, or will assist librarians in thinking about the ways in which they evaluate and select reference works, the experienced reviewer of reference works often uses a particular review to address a larger issue that warrants attention. A reference work, for example, that is almost entirely derivative from a larger reference work by the same publisher—unfortunately an increasingly common practice—should invoke a commentary on that practice and the pitfalls it presents to the unwary reference librarian. The reviewer must seek to convey a meaningful overall impression of the work and its potential and real value. That is by no means an easy task especially since there is both an enormous proliferation of reference materials and, in particular, an increasing abundance of items that have marginal utility in a library. Reference books are meant to be used and, for that reason, they must also be judged from the standpoint of the user. Not all reference books have as their primary audience a library. Many are intended primarily for a specific, and often unsophisticated audience, looking for some simple basic information to help them with their pursuits. It is as important to praise the well-meaning amateur who has produced a less than perfect reference book intended to serve individuals interested in a subject, as it is to condemn the slick commercial publisher who is producing what may appear to be a high quality publication but is, in fact, producing something only because there is an apparent library market for a work that has limited practical utility for either the library or its users. Above all the reviewer must review a reference book fairly and honestly and must seek to be sympathetic to the author and the publisher while, at the same time, considerate of the interests and needs of libraries and potential users. Praise for the sake of praise, or for some ulterior motive, is to be avoided just as much as is criticism for the sake of criticism, or for some base motive. In particular the tempting opportunity that often presents itself to write clever, but damaging and unhelpful, comments is to be avoided at all costs. A good evaluative review for publication requires a careful examination of the book, a careful consideration of its value, a careful organization of one's thoughts, a careful presentation of one's views, and a careful choice of one's words.

Others will have to deal with the evaluation of reference books from the standpoint of a reference librarian seeking to learn his/her craft and helping others to find information. That is a role that I have played only incidentally and never as a regular assignment.

From the standpoint of a user, however, the evaluation of reference tools is quite another matter and one on which I am more qualified to comment. As a reviewer one has high standards and seeks to carefully evaluate the quality of a book. As a user one has lower expectations that are more directly result oriented. The questions that are important to the user of any reference book are straightforward. Does it answer my question? Does it tell me something I didn't already know? Does it guide me to the location of other information? Does it improve my understanding of a subject? A number of the standards used to evaluate a reference book may be of little significance to a user or may only require a lower level of compliance. Physical format may be important, for example, but even if a user purchases a reference book it is with the knowledge that he/she will give it more limited use than a library and expect it only to meet his/her needs during a finite lifetime. Organization and ease-of-use are also important, especially to those using a reference book for the first time and who will use it only occasionally. For works that are used more extensively over time a user expects to be able to comprehend and make use of even unduly complicated or poorly arranged material. Documentation is less important than accuracy. A user may not necessarily be troubled by the lack of any indication as to the sources of information but if such a work is found to contain one or two errors one naturally tends to feel that the entire work cannot be relied upon except as trial and error proves it out. Most of all a user, and especially an owner, of certain reference books should have a tolerance for faults that would lead a reviewer and/or a librarian to criticize it severely. The question of a reference book's real value and utility is incidental or unimportant. The only real question is does the book please the user and does it suit the user's needs which may, after all, be somewhat limited. In addition almost any reference book can be examined, or even read, simply for the pleasure of learning a little something about a new subject, and seeing how an author has chosen to inform an audience about a subject. Lower standards and lower expectations make evaluating reference books for personal use a much greater pleasure, and subject to much less anguish over precision, than evaluating them in any professional capacity. Almost any reference book can be enjoyed when we deal with it as a user rather than as a professional.

A FINAL COMMENT

Reference books, no matter how that term is defined, make a significant contribution to our professional and often to our personal life. Reference books provide a structured way of obtaining information that can serve our own professional and personal needs as well as those of library users. For that reason, especially given the quantity of reference books that already exists and is regularly being augmented by a substantial volume of current publishing, the evaluation of reference books is a critical professional activity. The development of the skills necessary to the effective evaluation of reference books is something of importance to every professional librarian. Evaluative skills can be taught in library schools, developed in an initial professional position, and refined during one's professional career. As that refinement occurs the skill becomes an art. The experienced evaluator of reference books, whether practicing that art in an individual library or as a reviewer in professional publications, makes an important contribution to our work. The serious art of evaluation for professional purposes needs to be balanced by the more joyful evaluation that can occur as one uses reference books for personal purposes.

REFERENCES

1. Norman D. Stevens. "Evaluating Reference Books" *Collectrix* 7: 30–2, 41–2, 1984 (Fall).
2. *The ALA Glossary of Library and Information Science*. Chicago, ALA, 1983. p. 188.
3. Patricia and Gordon Sabine. "How People Use Books and Journals," Dublin, OH, OCLC, 185.

The Reference Reviewer's Responsibilities

James Rettig

Nobody goes to school for the purpose of learning how to review reference books. Nobody teaches would-be reference book reviewers how to review reference books. Perhaps in a reference course in library school, a student has to write one review; however this is not adequate experience to teach one much about how a reference work ought to be reviewed properly.

Despite this lack of preparation for the part, librarians starting out in tenure track positions in today's publish-or-perish world of academic libraries are rather routinely advised to cut their teeth on reviewing in preparation for what is presented as the "real" work of conducting and publishing research. Reviews are presented as no more than a way station along the track whose only valid terminus is research based on the narrow model of the social sciences. Nonetheless, reviewing is promoted as a useful way to learn how to write for publication in the field's journals. At the same time these librarians are advised to get into reviewing, they are often told that their reviews, because they are "*just* book reviews," will carry very little weight when those librarians are judged for promotion and tenure. The message is very ambiguous; it can readily be interpreted as "It is important to do reviews, but the reviews themselves are not important."

The prevalence of this sort of advice in academic libraries probably accounts for the predominance of academic librarians among reviewers in the major reference book review media. *Choice* is, of course, aimed at the academic library audience so it makes sense that its reviewers are drawn from the audience. Even though *American Reference Books Annual*, *RQ*, *Library Journal*, and

---

The author is the well-known editor/author of the "Current Reference Books" section in *Wilson Library Bulletin*; and he serves as the head of the Reference Department at the Main Library of the University of Illinois at Chicago, Box 8198, Chicago, IL 60680.

© 1987 by The Haworth Press, Inc. All rights reserved.

ALA's *Reference Books Bulletin* aim at much broader audiences, their reviewers come mostly from the ranks of academic librarians. In private conversation review editors vent their frustration over the lopsidedness of their reviewers pools. Lacking the publish-or-perish motivation, librarians in other types of libraries are less likely to volunteer to review reference books. Those librarians who rely on reference book reviews for guidance in selecting reference materials for their collections should be grateful for this. The field does not need more reference book reviewers who see the task as a mere warm-up exercise or who attempt reviewing because they feel pressured into it. The academic libraries presently supply a surfeit of such reviewers.

One would expect that, although its members are drawn mostly from academic, especially university, libraries, there is a corps of very capable reviewers producing the hundreds of reference book reviews that are published annually in *Choice*, *LJ*, ARBA, *RBB*, and *RQ*. The truth is that within that corps there are very capable reviewers. This is only part of the truth. The full truth is that there are also a number of reviewers who, having been advised, in effect, that the process of reviewing is important but that the product is not, produce slipshod, superficial evaluations. They are told to review, but not taught *how* to review. They are told the process is important, not for the profession, but for themselves, that they should undertake it so they learn the discipline of meeting deadlines, so they overcome the fear of the blank page, so they gain confidence from seeing their names in print for the first time. The advice to librarians starting out in tenure track positions that they begin their publishing career as reviewers has benefited the individuals more than it has benefited the readers of reviews, the compilers and editors of reference books, or the publishers of reference works. Academic librarians who give such advice often give it without considering the consequences, not only of the advice, but also of the way in which the advice is given. They can easily instill in their junior colleagues a condescending attitude towards reviews as a genre and towards reviewers. The senior librarians who create this attitude do not do it maliciously; however, whatever their motives, their damaging effect is the same. Many of the people who are encouraged to write reviews do not feel as much responsibility towards the task as they ought to.

IVORY TOWER VS. REVIEWER

From its ivory tower vantage point, a promotion or tenure committee can easily dismiss a reference book review as a piece of ephemera and nothing more. While reviews generally do not have lasting value, they are extremely important to a number of people at the time they are published. As has been noted, the author of a review may not be one of these persons; in many cases the importance of the review to the author was in learning something about writing for publication, not in the resulting publication itself. Every reference book review is important to the author, editor, or compiler of the book reviewed; to the publisher of the book; to the editor of the journal in which the review is published; and to the readers of that review who must use it in making a decision whether or not to purchase the book reviewed for their reference collections. This is the world of commerce and day-to-day library reference service that rarely intersects with the narrow concerns of academic library promotion or tenure committees. These committees concentrate on a candidate's publication record in which reviews play at best an insignificant role. The reviews are dismissed first because they are ephemeral and second because they supposedly do not involve research.

If the senior academic librarians who so glibly recommend reviewing to their junior colleagues would adopt a less condescending attitude towards reviews as a genre, they might come to appreciate how similar a good reference book review is to a good research report. To meet his many responsibilities to his many constituencies, a good reference book reviewer must gather data, test these data, and synthesize the conclusions drawn from testing these data before writing up the results in the form of a review. Unfortunately these similarities are not acknowledged and although individual libraries and library associations offer workshops on how to publish articles and on how to conduct research, they do not offer workshops on reviewing. The good reviewers have taught themselves how to write good reviews. They have done this by recognizing that the ephemeral nature of their reviews does not diminish their responsibilities. An examination of those responsibilities will show how, in order to meet them fully, a reviewer must go through the same process as the author of a research study. Perhaps then, academic librarians who recommend that their junior colleagues volunteer their services as reviewers will value the product as much as the process and become as involved in teaching those junior colleagues how to write good reviews as they are in teaching them how to publish articles. Librarianship needs reviews as well as research articles. Librarianship cannot afford condescending attitudes by librarians in one type of library toward those in other types. Nor can it afford condescending attitudes by authors of one type of publication towards authors of other types. Librarians should be equally concerned about cultivating the abilities of the authors of both reviews and articles.

A reviewer of a reference work, whether the work under review is in traditional codex format, in microform, in an interactive online format, or on a compact disk, has one overriding responsibility to all of his constituencies, the book's author, its publishers, the editor of the journal which will publish the review, and the audience which will read the review. That is the responsibility to be knowledgeable. All of the reviewers' more particular responsibilities to each of these constituencies follow from this responsibility to be knowledgeable. The reviewer must have a good knowledge of how reference tools are used in practice and an expansive knowledge of the universe of existing reference tools as deep as it is broad. The reviewer also needs a good working general knowledge and ought to have special knowledge of one or more disciplines. The reviewer has the further responsibility to demonstrate his knowledgeableness in his reviews. A reviewer must not be ostentatious about this, making a show of knowledge for its own sake. Instead the reviewer must apply whatever knowledge is called for to review the book in hand properly.

FOUR KEYS TO REVIEWS

A reviewer demonstrates this knowledgeableness in four ways in a review. The first three can be found executed to varying degrees of success in most reference reviews. A review written from a sound knowledge base describes, compares, and evaluates. The fourth way a reviewer demonstrates knowledgeableness is through making a commitment based on the description, comparison, and evaluation of the work under review.

A reviewer has the responsibility of describing the book accurately and clearly, informing the reader of the review about the book's purpose, its scope, and the nature of its contents. The reviewer and the review editor share the responsibility of providing an accurate bibliographic description of the book under review: its author's, editor's, or compiler's name; the title; the publisher; the publisher's complete address in the case of new or obscure publishers; imprint date; length; availability in paperback; and price, including advertised discounts. This factual information is easy to come by since publishers almost always provide it in press releases accompanying review copies. A reviewer can, if he dares, also accept a publisher's statements about the purpose, scope, and nature of a book. However, since publishers' publicity people write releases to promote the sale of books, hyperbole and misrepresentation are always strong possibilities. For this reason most of the reference reviewing sources do not forward the publisher's promotional materials to the reviewer along with the book.

Instead of depending upon the publisher's promotional brochure or press release, a reviewer should make himself knowledgeable about a book's purpose, scope, and nature by examining the book itself. Teachers of reference routinely advise their students of the value of reading prefaces of reference books as an effective way to become acquainted with them. It is probably the least heeded advice given in library schools. Reviewers, however, must heed it, for reading a book's preface or introduction can be very informative. The preface states the author's concept of the book—what it attempts to do, how it does that, why it is needed. Statements on these points allow the reviewer to test the book in terms of these statements. For example, if the preface to a national directory of college and university faculty claims it is comprehensive, the reviewer can check the contents against faculty rosters in several college catalogs published comfortably before the directory's cut-off date. If the directory omits numerous names listed in those rosters or if omissions follow some pattern, the claim of comprehensiveness has been called into question. The reviewer must point this out in the review. Given the compiler or author's statement of the purpose of the book, the reviewer can ask it questions which it ought to be able to answer if it does indeed fulfill that purpose. For example, a dictionary of new English words which claims to explain the origins of the words it defines ought to include an entry on and explain the development of the word "Yuppie."

Such testing allows the reviewer to describe not only a book's parts and their internal organization and interactions, but also the nature and scope of its contents. From such testing the reviewer can answer key questions about the work: What is it? By what means does it attempt to accomplish its purpose? How well does it accomplish that purpose? These must be addressed in the review.

The reviewer also has a responsibility to determine whether or not other works of similar scope or purpose exist. If so, the review should include a comparison of the work under review with the existing work or works. This permits testing of the accuracy of the work's contents. A reviewer should conduct additional testing against other sources, ideally against primary sources. For example, the reviewer of a directory of microcomputer bulletin boards should logon to a modem-equipped microcomputer and dial into appropriate local bulletin boards to check the accuracy of the directory's listings. A reviewer of a bibliography should spot check citations to judge the bibliography's accuracy.

Comparisons measure the unique contribution of the work under review in terms of whether or not it provides more convenient access to the information common to it and one or more additional reference works, whether or not it is more inclusive or more selective than others, whether or not it is appropriate for a purpose or audience different from the others.

IMPORTANCE OF EVALUATION

Ideally, evaluation permeates a review from beginning to end. In description, in comparison, in statements reporting a work's degree of accuracy, a review should convey to its readers an ever clearer sense of just how good the work under review is. Unfortunately too many reviewers gloss over this responsibility by concluding a review with the unqualified word "Recommended," allowing the tail to wag the dog. All too often the reader cannot, based on the evidence presented in the review, explain *why* a particular book is "Recommended." To evaluate a reference work properly, a reviewer must take into consideration how it can or is likely to be used in everyday reference work. For example, if its format is such that the work will require special handling and will thereby be stored apart from most other materials in its subject area, readers of the review deserve to be warned about this. Since reference works are for use, such a consideration could negate a positive evaluation of content or organization. Each relevant aspect of a work—its purpose, contents, format, organization, intended audience, access devices—must be evaluated both in terms of its appropriateness in a given work and in terms of its usefulness. A reviewer demonstrates that he or she is knowledgeable through an accurate, fair description of the work under review, through assessments of its accuracy based on comparisons with related works and primary sources, and through evaluation of its parts and their organization based on tests of performance in simulated reference situations. The reviewer also demonstrates knowledgeableness by committing himself in making a recommendation about a reference work. That recommendation sums up the rest of the review. Negative recommendations should be made very clearly, even when qualified. A positive recommendation need not be as explicit. For example, it does not have to tell librarians for what sort of library or libraries a book that passes all of its tests is appropriate. The reader of a review should not have to wonder what the reviewer thinks of the item reviewed. The descriptive, comparative, and evaluative information given, along with the reviewer's statement of overall assessment, should be adequate to allow each reader of a review to answer the reader's question which prompted him or her to read the review: Should I add this new item to my library's reference collection?

It is true that going through this thorough process—necessary whether the product runs two hundred words or two thousand—will enable a would-be scholar to gain confidence and experience in writing for publication. More importantly, however, the process will result in a truly useful reference book review. All of the constituencies a reviewer serves—reference book authors, publishers, review editors, reference book selectors—have a stake in high quality reference book reviews. By producing them, reviewers serve the needs of all these groups. Not every constituent will be pleased by every high quality review. For example, a negative review will please the selectors who know they should not purchase a book; that same review will displease the work's author or editor who presumably sent it to the publisher confident that it was a useful contribution to reference literature. The purpose of reference reviews is not to make everyone feel good, but to provide all of these constituencies with critical commentary enabling them to do their respective jobs more effectively than they could in the absence of that critical commentary. The linchpin responsibility of every reviewer, producing a high quality review, serves the best interests of all of these groups. Meeting this responsibility encompasses numerous other responsibilities to each group.

A DELICATE RESPONSIBILITY

The reviewer's responsibilities to the author, editor, or compiler of the work under review are probably the most delicate. Reviewers and reference book authors rarely meet, yet the communication between them, generally one-sided, resembles that between a teacher and a student or a counselor and a client. The difference is that it goes on in public. The reviewer should take his part very seriously; nevertheless, it is very open to being misconstrued by the author. A reviewer has a responsibility to a reference book's author to be informed, that is, to acquaint himself with the book under review adequately enough to judge it. The same means which enable the reviewer to describe the work satisfactorily in the review can be used to fulfill this responsibility. The reviewer does not have to be an expert on the work's subject, but must be or must quickly become well informed enough about its contents to be able to judge them.

The reviewer has the further responsibility to the author to be fair. A time honored tradition, observed especially frequently in the pages of the large weekly general purpose book reviewing journals, seems to give reviewers license to use a review as an occasion to expound upon the topic of a book rather than to analyze and evaluate the book itself. This is not fair to the book and its author. A good reference book review always focuses on the book under review even if along the way the reviewer expresses some opinions about the book's topic. A reviewer should not hide his or her verbal talents; indeed these should and must be mustered to the cause of writing a good, useful review. Yet the reviewer must be careful lest flashy verbal pyrotechnics rather than the book itself become the review's raison d'être. The point of a reference book review is to show the book, not to show off the reviewer. Analogies, anecdotes, and comparisons must relate to the assessment of the book. The reviewer can judge these by removing them; if the review is just as effective without an analogy, then the analogy should be dropped rather than divert attention from the business of the review. A reference book review can be entertaining, but if any of the entertainment value of a review is directly or indirectly at the expense of the book's author, there must be grounds for it in the book itself and these must be brought out in the review.

A reviewer's final responsibility to the author is to be critical. As an expert on reference works in general and/or on the reference literature of a particular subject, the reviewer is in a position not only to judge the new book, but also to make suggestions for its improvement. The nature of these suggestions will depend upon the book. They can focus on its scope, its organization, its accuracy, its timeliness, its indexing, its illustrations, some other aspect, or even the lack of one or more of these. This responsibility increases if the work under review is a serial and the suggestions can therefore be used to improve future issues. Even if it is not a serial, the work might someday be revised and updated; this responsibility is always present.

The reviewer also has responsibilities to the publisher of the work under review. The publisher shares in the reviewer's responsibilities to the work's author. However, the reviewer has additional responsibilities to the publisher that he does not have to the author. Despite the numerous caveats cited above, if the review editor supplies it, the reviewer has the responsibility to read the promotional material the publisher supplies with the book. Much of the purpose of the testing process discussed above is to find a reference work's failings. The publisher understandably does not point these out in the promotional material. Instead the publisher emphasizes the work's strengths. Presumably the testing process will uncover these. Yet the information given in the press release can speed this process of confirming or negating the publisher's claims on behalf of a book. A book's successes are as important to all concerned with a review as are the book's shortcomings. A reviewer must approach a book with an open mind; he or she should not assume either guilt or innocence. A good review rests on proof of a book's quality or its absence of quality.

A reviewer must not, of course, submit a libelous review. Nevertheless, a reviewer has the responsibility not to be afraid of a publisher. The delicacy characterizing the reviewer-author interaction is absent from the reviewer-publisher interaction. Hurt authors will sometimes write to reviewers or to review editors complaining of mistreatment at a reviewer's hands. In this reviewer's experience, these authors often betray a lack of understanding of the audience for whom most reference book reviews are written and published. The authors complain that their work was not discussed in terms of the very specialized audience for which it was written (e.g., rare book librarians and antiquarian book dealers). These authors should not have permitted their publishers to send their works out for review to general purpose reference review sources if they did not want them reviewed for a very general audience of reference book selectors. However, the publishers must know what they are doing in such cases. It is an adage in publishing circles that a negative review is better than no review, something an author hurt by critical comments written by a reviewer fulfilling his responsibilities to his audience may reject—at least until the semi-annual royalties statement and payment arrive.

PUBLISHERS AND REVIEWS

Publishers rarely complain about a negative review. As professionals, they recognize the risk involved every time a book is sent out for review. The author has invested a great deal of intellectual and emotional (and perhaps financial) capital in his book; a publisher invests its financial capital in the book. Yet it diversifies its investments by publishing a great number of books knowing that some will run in the red. Every publisher develops a list that will keep staff working and include enough successful titles to turn an overall profit. Publishers promote the winners; they do not waste effort trying to resurrect the dead or revive the seriously wounded. Unless they write libelous reviews, reference book reviewers should not be afraid of publishers.

Although not as delicate as their relationship with authors, reviewers can have a more intimate relationship with publishers. The most experienced, most prolific reviewers have a responsibility to exchange information with publishers. They can pass on general advice (for example, on improving the design or format of an ongoing series) which, if heeded, can improve reference works yet to come, a benefit to authors, publishers, reference book selectors, and ultimately to patrons who will use those works. From publishers' editorial and marketing personnel, reviewers can learn about upcoming projects that will be worthy of review and, perhaps, note in a review of a new work the imminent publication of a similar work. This cautions libraries to hold off making a purchase decision until a comparison can be made between the new work and the yet-to-be-published work. Because each one is an expert on the reference literature of a particular field or fields, reviewers can also suggest to publishers needed reference works. The publishers have the resources to bring these into being. Much good to all parties involved with reference works can come from frequent, frank communication between reference reviewers and reference publishers.

Every reviewer has special responsibilities to his or her editor. The editor presumably carefully exercises his responsibility to make prudent assignments to reviewers. This means the editor should match reviewers' subject expertise with appropriate books and pace assignments at agreed-upon intervals. If the editor has erred and assigned a book for which the reviewer lacks subject expertise or if the editor has made too many assignments in so short a period that the reviewer cannot meet them, the reviewer has the responsibility to explain the situation to the editor immediately so that the book or books in question can expeditiously be assigned to another reviewer. In the unusual circumstance that the reviewer has already done or received an assignment to do a signed review of a title for another journal, he should tell the second editor this immediately so the book can be reassigned.

Most of a reviewer's responsibilities to his or her editor can be summarized by saying that the reviewer has a responsibility to treat the editor with courtesy. The reviewer has the responsibility to meet the deadline assigned for submission of the review. That review should adhere, in so far as possible given the work under review, to the editor's printed guidelines sent at the time the review assignment is made. The guideline most difficult to observe is that governing maximum length. Editors vary in their willingness to stretch these limits. It is in everyone's best interests that editors allow them to be stretched as far as their pages will possibly accommodate; very short reviews are very unhelpful. The copy submitted should be "clean" —i.e., the reviewer should proofread and correct it before dropping it in the mailbox. The reviewer should also verify all information given in the review header by checking it against the book itself since the journal's staff cannot do this once the review copy has been sent to the reviewer. If the journal requires the use of a special form or copy paper, the review should be submitted on this form.

One could use "to describe, to compare, to evaluate" to summarize every reference book reviewer's responsibilities to his audience. But that would be substituting platitude for something open to examination. Readers of reviews have every reason to expect these attributes in reference reviews. But these are minimal; a reviewer has greater responsibilities to his audience.

INFORMATION IS NOT ENOUGH

It is not enough for a reviewer to produce an informative review; it should also be interesting, something the reader, after beginning it, wants to continue reading to its end. This can be done without violating the canon of fairness to author and book. A reviewer can make a review interesting by putting the spirit of the book itself into that review. It is not enough to tell what a book is and does; a good reference review conveys a sense of the book itself, of its manner, its style, its tone, its biases. Liberal use of examples is the tried-and-true (and, ironically, neglected) way of doing this. Most reference book reviews these days stint on examples. They are the poorer for this foolish frugality, as are the reviews' readers who must base judgments on abstractions unanimated by particulars.

By being interesting as well as informative, a reviewer goes a long way towards meeting the responsibility to be clear. Even if the final judgment on a book is noncommittal, even if it is such a mixture of the good and the bad that it is impossible to take a definitive stand, it must be clear to the reader *why* this is impossible. After reading a review, a selector ought to understand what is good or bad about a reference work. Except perhaps in belletristic writing, clarity is every writer's responsibility. Reference reviewers carry a special responsibility to their audience to be clear so that readers can use reviews to make decisions.

A reviewer's final responsibility to his audience is to not be afraid of controversy. Every reference librarian knows the profession's collective wisdom about the inestimable value of certain reference works. Perhaps the profession would be better served if it could have a system of rating reference works in the same way as sports records are kept. Athletes are fond of telling interviewers that "records are made to be broken." With few exceptions, reference works can be said to be published to be improved upon. Few would have thought it possible to exceed the accomplishment embodied in the Mansell catalog of pre-1956 imprints. However, even before the Mansell catalog was completed, OCLC had in large part done precisely that. A reviewer should not be afraid to declare a new work superior to an old and revered standard or to point out how a new work has chipped away at such a monument's niche. If the universe of reference works were not a dynamic one in which spectacular success and phenomenal failure and every degree between is always possible, there would be no need for new works nor any need for reviews of them. Like an umpire or a referee, every reviewer has to call them the way he sees them regardless of the possible reaction of the crowd.

Although reference book reviews by and large are ephemeral, the process of writing them to meet the many responsibilities every reference reviewer bears resembles the process of writing a research article. The product of a reference review hides most of the steps of the process made explicit in an article in its discussion of methodology and its citations of other sources. Nevertheless, those academic librarians who tout reviewing as a good preparation for writing research articles probably do not know how right they are. If they examined the situation carefully and compared the responsibilities borne by authors of both types of works and the process each must follow to fulfill those responsibilities, they would have a greater respect for reference book reviewing and a greater regard for reference book reviews. Reference reviewing demands the same intellectual powers as "approved" forms of writing, even if over a shorter period. The reviewers who produce good reviews are the ones who recognize and take seriously their many responsibilities as reviewers.

Good reference book reviewing is not by any means universal. Where good reviewing exists, however, it deserves greater recognition, especially in academe. Academic librarians must come to see that a good review is as important as the process of writing a review. Not until academic librarians give both the process of reviewing and the product of that process their due will good reference book reviewing become more common. Librarians who undertake reference reviewing only to learn the writing process fail to fulfill their many responsibilities to reference book authors, publishers, journal editors, and readers. Those who advise them to undertake reference reviewing for this limited and selfish purpose are equally culpable.

How to Be a Book Critic: A Guide for Librarians

Richard Grefrath

"There are as many opinions as there are people," according to an ancient Roman playwright.[1] Since the book critic owns but one opinion from out of the sea of opinions, it sometimes seems strange that a critical review will wield such awesome authority over the heads of acquisitions librarians and subject bibliographers. Yet, it is true. As a book critic from *Library Journal*, I know that my reviews will reach over 20,000 subscribers, and will probably be read by a significant multiple of that figure since the journal is extensively routed among librarian colleagues. And many book reviews from library periodicals are reprinted or indexed in *Book Review Digest*, *Book Review Index*, and elsewhere, further extending the readership. And what book critic's heart does not leap up upon seeing his own review excerpted in an advertisement, often with the periodical's byline instead of his own name: to have one's own opinions become *"Library Journal* says . . . "! This is a tremendous responsibility, which most reviewers take very seriously.

It hardly needs to be observed that, in the often frantic world of modern librarianship, no librarian can read all prospective purchases before deciding which to buy. The book review section of library periodicals provides an obviously valuable service by presenting synopses and evaluations of books by informed critics. It is that very purpose, to provide a book selection tool for fellow librarians, which should be taken to heart by any librarian who serves as a critic. This is not the occasion to exploit the book under review as a springboard to declaim one's world view, nor is it appropriate to unfairly criticize in an attempt to enhance one's own stature at the expense of the author's.

When I compose a book review I like to think of it in the same

---

The author is Instructional Services Librarian, The University Library, University of Nevada, Reno, NV 89557.

light as helping students at the Reference Desk. A person comes to you for advice: "What's the best newspaper for historical documentation?" "What's the best book on The Beatles?" Whether it's a student at the Reference Desk or a reader of your book reviews, the situation is the same. Time constraints and lack of subject expertise prompt the person to seek the advice of an expert in the field—namely you! Which is to say, reference librarians are natural book critics: all day they recommend particular books, and in doing so implicitly pick each particular book over many other possibilities.

Historically, distinctions have been made between "book reviewing" and "book criticism," the former being a mere synopsis of the book, and the latter being a critical evaluation. This needn't concern us, since that distinction has rarely been insisted upon for many years. I use both terms to describe a synopsis with critical evaluation.

PROCEDURE

Examine the Book

It's no mystery that librarians are especially analytical when it comes to books, but how does one transform opinions formed about a book into a book review for a library periodical?

First, read the book thoroughly. Most books require detailed reading (and re-reading important sections) lest the critic take the author to task for non-existent omissions. Of course, sometimes partial skimming is acceptable, if the item is an index or reference book containing lists, like the Beach Boys discography *Surf's Up!* which I once reviewed. It's simply not necessary to read every single entry in a list of over 300 recordings to be able to make a judgement about the book's value to libraries; one's brains would be scrambled halfway through the attempt. But still, it's better to err on the side of thoroughness: the public is naturally suspicious, as Jean Shepherd observed while recalling his school days: "Already I had mastered the art of manufacturing an entire book report from two paragraphs selected at random, plus a careful reading of the dust jacket, a system which still earns a tidy living for many a professional reviewer."[2]

While reading the book, observe the obvious: What is the book about? Neglect here can be a serious oversight, as I discovered after submitting a review of a book about the Siege of Khe Sanh during the Vietnam War. The editor telephoned me and explained that the review was unacceptable because she couldn't tell what the book was about (other than "the Siege of Khe Sanh") from my review. I had made the mistake of skipping the "synopsis" part of the review in order to quickly launch into a discussion of issues raised in the book, a classic case of putting the cart before the horse. I penitently rewrote the review.

What is the book's scope and audience? Scholars? Teenagers? Is the coverage comprehensive or selective? Don't make the greenhorn's mistake of condemning the book because the title doesn't precisely reflect the contents. Novice critics delight in exposing such inconsistencies, but think for a moment: did anyone criticize the *New Grove Dictionary of Music and Musicians* because it's not a "dictionary" at all but really a multivolume encyclopedia? Our librianly souls may yearn for more standardization of terminology, but there are weightier matters to consider.

Is there an index? Is it a poor one, the kind that gives "Reagan, Ronald" followed by hundreds of undifferentiated page references? Be careful: if you review from "uncorrected galley-proofs" (the preliminary texts that appear prior to actual publication, used for publicity and reviewing purposes) the index is generally not included. Illustrations are usually absent from galley proofs also. In these cases all you can really do is criticize the book if it *doesn't* have an index. If illustrations are included they're well worth evaluating. Do they truly enhance the text or are they simply window-dressing?

Librarian critics hardly need to be reminded about the importance of a bibliography. Is it selective? Annotated? Often a short list of best books on a subject (if annotated, even better) will be much preferable to a voluminous list of nearly everything on the subject.

What about writing style? Is it entertaining or boring? Reviewers should not be puritannical in expecting that the more academic the topic, the more tedious should be the prose. Some reviewers feel a moral obligation to alert everyone to the presence of vulgar language, as if they're providing a bookman's version of the MPAA movie ratings. Perhaps this can be a factor in children's books, but a critic's primary responsibility is probably not to be a guardian of morality.

Now you've read the book, having paid close attention to basic structure, scope, and synopsis. But before turning on the typewriter, pause for a mulling-over period. Be sure to set aside several days for this, during which you can re-read parts of the book, and if necessary perform some background research. Maybe most important, sleep on it, since

> What at night seems oh so scenic
> May be cynic by and by.[3]

Legwork/Research

After reading and carefully examining the book, next comes the legwork stage. How does this book compare to others on the same or similar topics, or by the same author? A vital question, in order to put the book in the proper context, and one which sometimes involves considerable research. Some years ago I reviewed the Mackenzie biography of H. G. Wells, and while "literature" was my specialty, I was anything but an expert on H. G. Wells. Accordingly, I needed to read the then important biographies of Wells, together with critical commentary on them, in order to determine how the Mackenzie work stacked up in comparison.

Relating the book being reviewed to others is especially important for libraries which can't afford to buy every book on the subject (and nowadays that includes most libraries). It takes background research, a firm grip on the subject matter, not to mention some measure of courage, to be able to state "This is the best work yet on the topic." But after all, you're the expert, be bold!

Take some time to verify the accuracy of questionable information. The preliminary galley-proofs that are used for pre-publication reviewing often contain spelling errors, which (the publisher always promises) will be corrected in the final published version, a vow one must take on faith.

Obviously the same generosity cannot be extended to spelling errors in the final product, if that's what you're reviewing from. Recently I reviewed a rock & roll reference book which cited Governor "Jimmie" Carter of Georgia more than once. I knew that "Jimmy" was correct when he was President, but perhaps he used "Jimmie" before that when Governor? Not so, according to a check of *The New York Times Index* and three biographies of the gentleman from Plains. An obvious error like that can be a tip-off: Are there other, more serious inaccuracies?

Galley-proofs and review copies generally come with a publicity information sheet, giving the name and phone number of the contact person at the publisher in charge of marketing that particular title. Don't hesitate to call the contact person if you need to. Often I find myself calling to clarify number of pages, lack of an index or illustrations, and other technical matters. Sometimes the credentials of the author are of interest (especially if they're not given and you can't find any biographical information on the person) and this too the marketing coordinator will supply. But be very careful not to comment about your opinions of the book. Book review editors rightly insist that you not send a copy of your review to the publisher, who will eventually obtain a copy through channels around the time it's published. The version you submit may well not be the final published version anyway after editorial revisions. In the spirit of this forbidden practice, it is definitely not cricket to say "I like the book" on the telephone, even if you're just trying to be cordial. If asked, you can simply say you're not permitted to discuss the matter.

The final bit of legwork is a questionable maneuver, but after I've made up my mind and the review is taking shape inside my head, I like to read a review or two of the book by other critics. This usually isn't possible with *Library Journal* reviews; since they ordinarily send pre-publication galleys in order to have your review published right at the same time the book is published, so no reviews have come out yet while you're composing yours. But through the years I've come to admire the work of book critics like Jim Rettig of the *Wilson Library Bulletin*, as well as many of the fine critics at *Library Journal* and *American Reference Books Annual*, and I'm naturally curious to know what they have to say. Some book review editors specifically insist that your review is to be written independently of other reviews, but I think I'm acting in good faith if I only read other reviews after the mulling-over period is completed and my opinions are formed. This is like asking a colleague's views, in order to avoid the occasional situation where you overlook something crucial. Of course, the practice of composing a review by piecing together other reviews is to be roundly condemned.

Composing the Review

The big moment has arrived: the review is composed in your mind, now you must transcribe it to paper. Here every critic has his own approach: some like to dash out a draft and then extensively revise it, others carefully craft each word from the outset with a minimum of revision. There are afficionados of the word-processor, as well as write-it-all-out-longhand advocates. Regardless of the approach, there are several considerations to remember. Whatever library periodical you're reviewing for will supply you with a "guidelines" sheet. These are generally excellent and detailed, with many helpful suggestions.

While your review should be objective and fair, it need not be sterile. Try to allow your own character to come across, since your review is the result of personal opinion, not an algebraic formula. The best librarian book critics have a distinctive voice, whether it's Paul Feehan on rock & roll, or Ruth Diebold on cookbooks. It's your personality and turn of phrase which make book reviews enjoyable reading and best bring out the book's notable features.

Your own voice should determine the style, but there are certain wretched excesses to avoid regardless. Don't fall prey to the pseudo-intellectual claptrap of such terms as "catharsis," "gestalt," and "plethora." In the same vein, avoid those obnoxious foreign expressions like "vis-à-vis," "sine qua non," and the awful refrain of my college years, "sui generis." It should be obvious to avoid cliches, since they are by definition hackneyed phrases, yet if I read "between a rock and a hard place" one more time I'll scream.

Instead of relying on those sorts of crutches, compose your own colorful style. Your book review editor will restrain your ardor if necessary, as has happened in my own case. In criticizing the over-complimentary gushing of a Jerry Lee Lewis biographer, I said that the book "sounds like it was written by the president of a Jerry Lee fan club." While I thought this was a clever remark, my editor changed it to the book being "much more adulatory"[4] than another under review. This is one reason why you should always keep a file of supporting documentation and copies of reviews you submit. When the published review comes out, compare that version to what you submitted—this will help you get a feel for the stylistic conventions of the journal.

In recent years publishers have compiled detailed guides to eliminating what is viewed as "sexist language." Whether you consider this a socially enlightened development, or an Orwellian exercise in thought control, the fact remains that you won't get away with wording that violates the publisher's code. In a recent review I praised a Vietnam War almanac for having a "military man's perspective," since the author is an infantry Colonel of considerable reputation. Even though the Colonel is indeed a man, and even though the term "military man" has a long literary tradition (including use in a famous conversation in Bernard Shaw's "Don Juan in Hell"), the editor changed "military man" to "military individual."[5] A book critic must learn to be good-natured about such revisions.

There are some cliches unique to book reviewing. To say a book is "useful" is a cliche, and so is starting off your review with the words "This book . . . " At times these are unavoidable. There's no way to keep words like "comprehensive," "extensive," "detailed," and "definitive" from cropping up again and again, since these are factors to consider.

Avoid the cheap shot. For instance, it's easy to adopt a condescending tone toward certain biographees, such as the late Elvis Presley. I once reviewed a book on Presley, and the first thing I decided was to avoid putting down his legion of button-snatching fans, or the excessive drug use which contributed to his demise. Better to appreciate the book and its subject in a larger, social context.

How about the mechanics of composing the review? First, prepare an outline, using notes you've taken along the way, incorporating any research you've conducted on relevant topics. Start with a distinctive, authoritative first line, but don't think you need to sound trumpets to get the reader's attention. You're not composing a publicity release for the publisher's marketing department. Then, discuss and evaluate the book, citing important points only. You will not be able to comment on everything, especially if you're writing a brief *Library Journal* kind of review. Mention the aspects that are outstanding, both good and bad. Average illustrations, an average index, an average bibliography, and competently average prose, none of these are worth mentioning. The fact that there are illustrations, an index, or a bibliography will be noted in the citation that precedes your review.

If you're finding grammatical conventions difficult, consult your favorite composition manual. I like the *Harbrace College Handbook*[6] (which I used myself in college), now in its 9th edition.

Remember, a book review should not require several readings to understand the literal sense. If you prefer interpretation of multiple levels of meaning, perhaps you should be composing poetry?

Aftermath

When your review is completed, usually after some revision, mail it in. That sounds simple, but there's often the temptation to endlessly revise the review, which is usually a bad practice. You'll lose the initial flow of ideas, and the new words you substitute will probably destroy the rhythmic structure of the original prose. And don't sabotage your own career as a book critic by turning in a review past its deadline date. A tardy review may be your last.

Keep a copy of the review with supporting documentation, not only to compare with the final published version, but for your own use if needed to answer any "Letters to the Editor" critical of your review. These occur every week in *The New York Times Book Review*, an angry letter followed by the book critic's rebuttal, yet one seldom sees them in library periodicals. Of course, to avoid the risk and compose only complimentary reviews is cowardice of the worst kind. If you happen to notice an editor's revision which has caused an error, notify the editor immediately. This has only happened to me once, in a review of a book on cinema, where my phrase "shot analyses" (a technical term in filmmaking) became "short analyses" in the published review. After I informed the editor of this, a correction notice was printed in a subsequent issue.

TO REVIEW OR NOT TO REVIEW

Occasionally you should decline the invitation to review a book, if for some reason the validity of your review might be questioned. For instance, I was once asked to review a book to which I had personally contributed, and my name was cited accordingly in the book itself. Obviously, you can't review your own book. What about books by people you know? This is more a tricky matter of judgement. It happens that professional colleagues will be acquainted with each other's work in similar fields, so if you feel that your relationship might affect your judgement of the book, decline the invitation. If you do decline, be sure to explain fully to your book review editor, since having to reassign the review is an inconvenience. But you don't want to contribute a review which might turn out to reflect badly on the journal, were it challenged.

If you decline to review a book because you don't feel competent in the subject area, you'll need to discuss the matter more fully with your editor. There would appear to be a misunderstanding about your areas of expertise.

HOW TO BREAK INTO REVIEWING

Sometimes you'll see an advertisement, like this one from a recent *Library Journal*:

> We are seeking reviewers for books on Oriental and primitive art. If you are qualified to evaluate such titles, we'd like to hear from you. Please write to Judith Sutton, The Book Review.[7]

More likely you'll have to beat the bushes yourself. First, decide in which fields you have special knowledge and experience. Probably your undergraduate major would be a good one, unless your college days were so long ago that you've forgotten everything! If you're an amateur gardener and have collected handbooks on the subject, you might be qualified to review non-technical gardening books. If you're an avid cook and have a shelf of cookbooks from among which you can't help pick favorites, you might be qualified to review cookbooks, and so on.

Peruse the library periodicals available to you to determine which one you would most like to become a part of.

Then select a few fields in which you're strongest, and construct a resume designed to highlight that expertise. Yes, a resume! Seeking assignment as a book critic is much like applying for a full-fledged job. Send the resume, with cover letter explaining your skills and desire to review, together with some sample of your writing. The best sample is a book review in the format of the library periodical's own book reviews. To do this just select a book in your field that hasn't been reviewed by that periodical, compose a review of it as best you can in their format (of course, you won't have their Guidelines for Critics sheet, but your work will be evaluated in that light), and send it in. Better to submit one excellent sample review than a melange of your collected works.

If you're unsuccessful with major library periodicals, then you can work your way up from humbler beginnings. What about the library periodical published by your state or regional library association? Often these publications are hungry for material. You can volunteer your services, or compose a few reviews and submit them. Or you could write a short bibliographic essay exploring a core collection in a particular field, perhaps on a local topic, which has a good chance of being welcomed by the editor of your state/regional library publication. After getting in print locally, submit this work along with your cover letter and resume to the major library periodicals, being sure to compose and include a sample review in their format.

Since the monolithic *Choice* finally saw the light recently and eliminated unsigned reviews, nearly all library periodicals identify the reviewer at the conclusion of the review. Suit yourself, but I would advise against reviewing for any publication that refuses to include your byline. The unsigned review suggests that book reviews are the grossest form of piecework, one book critic being the same as another and therefore not worth identifying. Most of us think otherwise. And it is only fair to identify the author and his institutional affiliation, to enable the reader to relate that to any possible bias involved in judging the book.

Perhaps you'd like to practice reviewing a bit before composing a sample review to submit as evidence of your work. If you like television, a simple way to warm up is to match wits with the writers who compose the blurbs for movie listings in *T.V. Guide*. These one-sentence annotations can be eloquent in their brevity, presenting as they do a plot capsule and evaluation all in one sentence. Find the listing for a movie you're familiar with, and without looking at the blurb, try to write one sentence which includes the crux of the plot together with some assessment of the movie overall. If you can do that, you've accomplished something! Examples from a typical issue:

> *Rabbit, Run* (1970). Disappointing adaptation of John Updike's novel about an ex-athlete (James Caan) with a loveless marriage and a child on the way.
>
> *Casanova's Big Night* (1954). Mild costume romp with Bob Hope as a tailor's meek apprentice who impersonates the notorious Casanova.
>
> *The King of Comedy* (1982). Robert DeNiro is excellent as a deranged would-be comic who kidnaps a talk-show host (Jerry Lewis) for a guest shot on his T.V. show.[8]

Now: how would you sum up *Gandhi* in one sentence? Or *Citizen Kane*? Writing a one-page review is child's play by comparison.

A good next step would be to do the same thing for a *Library Journal* or *Publisher's Weekly* type of short review, which run about a half-dozen sentences. Once you've mastered your evaluation technique and identifying the essence of the plot, it's a simple matter to expound.

THE REWARDS OF BOOK REVIEWING

Rarely is there any payment for composing book reviews for library periodicals, so this is not a lucrative endeavor for the critic. Usually you do get a free copy of each book you review, which is really a marvellous way to build up your personal library in your own areas of special interest. Or you can be magnanimous and donate the books to the library where you work.

In terms of professional advancement, being a book critic is a gold star on your resume, but those who judge such things are sometimes more impressed by full-fledged journal articles.

Personally, I feel a tremendous sense of gratitude toward the book review editors who have invested confidence in my abilities, and through the years have given me the opportunity to develop expertise in specific subject areas which I would not have the time or probably the inclination to do otherwise. Aside from the occasional librarian with only one subject specialty (music librarian, art librarian), most of us have a generalist orientation (reference librarian) or serve a specialist function in terms of library operations (cataloger, systems librarian.) Pursuing an academic discipline to the point where one becomes an authority is a truly rewarding intellectual endeavor, and a rare opportunity for librarians.

Practically speaking, your expertise can be helpful in your library, since patron's questions which fall into the fields of your reviewing specialties can be directed to you for answers.

To review a topnotch book, and thereby be in a position to give credit where credit is due, is a professionally thrilling experience. On the other hand, condemning a book which deserves it is equally satisfying, especially when you consider the many acquisitions librarians who will now receive adequate warning thanks to your review. Librarians are already in a service profession, and librarian book critics doubly enjoy providing an important service to their colleagues across the miles.

A computer can generate a comprehensive list of books on a particular topic. But it takes a human being to critically evaluate a book, and say "This is the best book on the subject." Reviewing books develops the librarian's analytical abilities, so much so that it can safely be said that librarian book critics become better librarians for the experience.

But it is the joy of reading, which brought many of us into librarianship in the first place, which fuels our fires: "The good critic is one who tells of his mind's adventures among the masterpieces" (Anatole France).[9]

REFERENCES

1. "Quot homines tot sententiae: suo' quoique mos." ("There are as many opinions as there are people: each has his own correct way.") Terence, *Phormio*, 454.
2. Jean Shepherd, *In God We Trust: All Others Pay Cash* (NY: Doubleday, 1966), p. 208.
3. Tom Jones and Harvey Schmidt, *The Fantasticks* (NY: Drama Book Specialists, 1964), p. 58.
4. *Library Journal*, 15 November 1981, p. 2239.
5. *Library Journal*, January 1986, p. 73.
6. *Harbrace College Handbook*, 9th edn. NY: Harcourt, Brace Jovanovich, 1984.
7. *Library Journal*, 15 November 1985, p. 89.
8. *T.V. Guide*, 1–7 February 1986, pp. A-91, A-14, A-12.
9. Anatole France, *La Vie Litteraire* (Preface), 1888.

BIBLIOGRAPHY

Drewry, John E. *Writing Book Reviews*. Boston: The Writer INC, 1966.
Gard, Wayne. *Book Reviewing*. NY: Alfred A. Knopf, 1928.
Hackett, Francis. *On Judging Books*. NY: The John Day Co., 1947.
Jones, Llewellyn. *How to Criticize Books*. NY: W. W. Norton & Co., 1928.
Kamerman, Sylvia E., ed. *Book Reviewing*. Boston: The Writer INC, 1978.
Kister, Ken. "Wanted: More Professionalism in Reference Book Reviewing." *RQ*, 19 (Winter 1979), 144–48.
Sissman, L. E. "Reviewer's Dues" (from the author's "Innocent Bystander" column), *The Atlantic*, 234 (no. 1, July 1974), 20–22. [Reprinted with minor revisions as "Book Reviewing" in: (1) *The Writer*, October 1974, 24–26. (2) *The Writer's Handbook*, A. S. Burack, ed. Boston: The Writer INC, 1980, pp. 515–519.]
Swinnerton, Frank. *The Reviewing and Criticism of Books*. Philadelphia: R. West, 1977.
"What Makes a Good Review? Ten Experts Speak." *Top of the News*, 35 (Winter 1979), 146–52.

Dear Encyclopedia Critic

Ken Kister

I have been reviewing encyclopedias for almost two decades, first in *Booklist* as a member of the ALA Reference and Subscription Books Review Committee (now the Reference Books Bulletin Editorial Board), then in three editions of *Encyclopedia Buying Guide* (Bowker, 1976–81), and most recently in *Best Encyclopedias* (Oryx, 1986). During this time numerous questions about encyclopedias have come my way via letters, notes, and telephone calls from interested consumers all over North America, as well as a few from abroad. And I have tried to answer each question as fully and conscientiously as circumstances permit, leading a colleague to dub me the "Dear Abby of Encyclopedias," a unique if somewhat droll distinction.

What is interesting, however, is that the questions I've received over the years constitute an informal record of the collective concerns of serious encyclopedia and reference book consumers during the 1970s and 80s. With that thought in mind, what follows is a representative sampling of the questions, along with my answers (updated when appropriate to reflect present conditions).

Dear Encyclopedia Critic: I'm considering buying an encyclopedia for the kids (six, eight, and nine) to use for homework, but an article I read the other day in the paper says encyclopedias will soon be replaced by computers. Is that true? Perplexed in Maryland

Dear Perplexed: Computers have become an increasingly influential, even dominating, force in our lives during the past ten years or so. But, no, computers will not replace encyclopedias anytime soon. The familiar set of printed books covering basic knowledge

---

Mr. Kister is Reference Librarian, Pinellas Park Public Library, Florida. He is a well known authority on encyclopedias, dictionaries, atlases and darn near every other type of reference work. His latest book is *Best Encyclopedias: A Guide to General and Specialized Encyclopedias* (Phoenix, AZ: Oryx Press, 1986).

© 1987 by The Haworth Press, Inc. All rights reserved.

from A to Z that we call an encyclopedia will continue to be a fixture for the foreseeable future. The computer revolution, however, is creating an entirely new form of encyclopedia that consumers like you should know about and understand—the electronic encyclopedia (also called the automated or online encyclopedia). At present, the electronic encyclopedia is in its infancy. Only two titles of any significance, the *New Encyclopaedia Britannica* and the *Academic American Encyclopedia*, are currently available in electronic form, and usership is quite limited. But by the end of the century, as more and more homes, libraries, schools, and offices become equipped with computer terminals, I look for automated encyclopedias to compete more or less on an equal footing with print encyclopedias. Right now the biggest problem with automated encyclopedias, aside from their lack of wide availability, is cost. The present pricing structure, which is based on computer connect time (similar to long-distance telephone billing), can be quite expensive. An online search for information on, say, the Civil War may cost $25 or $30 or more, depending on the type of question involved and the skill and discipline of the searcher. At that rate, an entire encyclopedia in print form could be acquired for the price of as few as twenty or thirty searches.

Dear Encyclopedia Critic: What's the quickest and easiest way to size up an encyclopedia? I don't have time to go through the elaborate procedure you recommend in your book. In a Hurry in New York

Dear Hurry: Serious consumers should inspect *firsthand* any encyclopedia being considered for purchase. Nothing beats hands-on examination when it comes to judging reference materials, and this is particularly true in the case of encyclopedias, where the expense involved can be quite high. How, you ask, can the busy consumer go about evaluating an encyclopedia without spending an inordinate amount of time? I suggest that you interview—or interrogate—the encyclopedia as if you were Mike Wallace on the trail of a hot story. Ask the encyclopedia for information on two or three subjects about which you are thoroughly knowledgeable. Does the encyclopedia provide accurate information on the subject? Is the material presented clearly? Impartially? Is it reasonably current? Is it easy to find? Then do the same for a subject or two about which you know little or nothing, checking particularly for comprehension and clarity of style. All of this shouldn't require more than an hour or so—time well spent when considering a product that normally costs from several hundred to over a thousand dollars.

Dear Encyclopedia Critic: We had a Britannica salesman here the other night and we now know and believe that there is now a 2-volume index! Yeah! But they also claim a multi-million dollar re-write, to bring their set up-to-date. Could you tell me in advance of your next volume if Britannica has really been brought up-to-date? Army Officer in Germany

Dear Army: Yes, the *New Encyclopaedia Britannica* was overhauled and greatly improved in 1985. The two-volume index (which you have seen) makes information in the set much more accessible. The *World Data* volume (the annual supplement) appears to be intelligently put together. And there has been a general effort to update the encyclopedic text; for example, *Britannica* now includes an article on acquired immune deficiency syndrome (AIDS). But problems remain. Perhaps the most glaring weakness is the set's double alphabet (*Micropaedia* A–Z; *Macropaedia* A–Z), which tends to confuse most users. In addition, the *Britannica* is considerably more expensive than its chief competitors, namely *Collier's Encyclopedia*, *Encyclopedia Americana*, the *World Book Encyclopedia*, and perhaps the *Academic American Encyclopedia*, all of which I would urge you to compare with the *Britannica*. On the other hand, the *Britannica* is the oldest, largest, best known, and most prestigious general encyclopedia in the English language. Good luck in your quest for the best encyclopedia—that is, the one that best meets your needs and those of your family.

Dear Encyclopedia Critic: Some of the drawings in my daughter's copy of the Random House Encyclopedia are filthy, I think any normal adult would agree. I don't think my grandchildren should be looking at pictures of animals having sex and things like that. Would you please write to my daughter and tell her what you think of those drawings. Concerned in Iowa

Dear Concerned: It is true that the first edition of the *Random House Encyclopedia* (published in 1977) contained some controversial illustrations, including a graphic showing the various types of birth control and another depicting various animal species in the act of sexual reproduction. Interestingly, some of these illustrations have been dropped from the revised edition of the encyclopedia (published in 1983). Some critics of the first edition were, like you, unhappy with these illustrations. For example, Walter Clemons in *Newsweek* (October 10, 1977, p. 105) wrote: "Sometimes the artists go crazy: a very peppy drawing of "Sex in the animal world" shows a Disney woodland run amok—bunnies and field mice humping, birds going at it in a tree while earthworms twine below." For my part, however, I found the encyclopedia's illustrations to be both informative and refreshing. You will have to work this one out with your daughter on your own.

Dear Encyclopedia Critic: Are all encyclopedia salesmen crooks? I have had two at my door within the past month and both of them tried using bulldozer methods to get me to buy. If you are interested, I can give you the details so you can warn others about what these guys are up to. Furious in California

Dear Furious: The adage that encyclopedias are "sold not bought" contains more than a grain of truth. Most people perceive encyclopedias, unlike automobiles or toothpaste, to be a discretionary, or luxury, item. Hence, most potential customers must be convinced that an encyclopedia is a desirable investment. The person who normally does the convincing (or tries to) is the encyclopedia representative. And, indeed, because encyclopedias rarely sell themselves, and because encyclopedia salespeople customarily work on commission, hard sell tactics are not uncommon. And sometimes these salespeople cross the line from hard sell to fraudulent and deceptive practices, such as misrepresenting the purpose of their call or using false advertising. Fortunately, however, the most blatant encyclopedia sales abuses have declined measurably in recent years, thanks in large part to aggressive consumer protection action by the Federal Trade Commission (FTC), a regulatory agency of the U.S. government. But shady and illegal sales practices continue to occur, as your experience indicates. I suggest that you report the two incidents you mention in your letter to the regional office of the FTC closest to you. Specifically, contact the Federal Trade Commission, Federal Building, Room 13209, 11000 Wilshire Blvd., Los Angeles, CA 90024; 213-824-7575. Simply state the facts of the case as clearly as you can and include copies of any documents or other evidence in your possession that support your complaint.

Dear Encyclopedia Critic: I have been told that the finest encyclopedia on the market is by a Frenchman named Detero (or something like that), but no one out here seems to know much more about it. Is it known back east? Could I get a copy from you? Eager for Knowledge in Wisconsin

Dear Eager: I suspect you are referring to the great eighteenth-century French *Encyclopédie*, edited by Denis Diderot and Jean le Rond d'Alembert. This vast undertaking, comprising some 70 volumes issued between 1751 and 1772, challenged the established thought of the day and helped pave the way for the French Revolution. Diderot's *Encyclopédie* is doubtless the most famous and influential encyclopedia ever made. But I also suspect that it would have little practical value to you and your family as an everyday reference source. Rather, the set is important today principally as an historical document. (An excellent book on the subject is Robert Darnton's *The Business of Enlightenment: A Publishing History of the Encyclopédie, 1775-1800*, published by Harvard University Press in 1979.) Nevertheless, if you are still interested in obtaining the *Encyclopédie*, various reprint editions are currently available. For particulars, contact Pergamon Press, Maxwell House, Fairview Park, Elmsford, NY 10523; 914-592-7700.

Dear Encyclopedia Critic: You may think this is a strange question, but believe me I'm serious. My husband and I recently split and he took A through L volumes of our encyclopedia, a 1983 Americana that cost us around $800. Is there anything I can do with my half? Divorced in Florida

Dear Divorced: You have a problem for Solomon, not me! Unfortunately, half an encyclopedia is not the equivalent of the proverbial half a loaf. Perhaps you could buy your ex-husband's half, or sell him yours. Otherwise, sell what you have for wastepaper.

Dear Encyclopedia Critic: What do you think of secondhand encyclopedias? Are they good bargains? How fast do encyclopedias date? I'm asking because my neighbor has an old set called American Peoples Encyclopedia that he is willing to sell me for $250 (he says it sold for $750 new). Thrifty in Illinois

Dear Thrifty: First, on the subject of secondhand encyclopedias generally: substantial savings—sometimes more than 50 percent off the original price—can be realized by investing in an older, used encyclopedia. Like most products, encyclopedias begin to lose value the minute they are purchased. The rule of thumb is that an encyclopedia depreciates between 15 and 20 percent the first year and 10 percent each year thereafter. Naturally, a secondhand encyclopedia will not be as current as a new set. How important a consideration should up-to-dateness be when buying an encyclopedia? If the informational needs of those who will be using the set are mainly in the areas of history, literature, music, philosophy, religion, etc., where knowledge is not as volatile and readily discarded as in the sciences, then a used encyclopedia several years old can be a good buy. If, on the other hand, the encyclopedia's users will be consulting it primarily for information in the physical, technical, biological, or behavioral sciences, where knowledge changes very rapidly and currentness is vital, a secondhand encyclopedia makes little sense, no matter how inexpensive it might be. Generally speaking, an encyclopedia over ten years old should be avoided. Concerning *American Peoples Encyclopedia*, a 20-volume set for adults first published in 1948 and phased out in 1976, I would caution you to examine the set very carefully before paying any money for it. A mediocre work, *American Peoples* was last priced at $325, not $750 as your neighbor claims.

Dear Encyclopedia Critic: I am considering buying a brand name encyclopedia. I like the encyclopedia, but is it necessary, in your opinion, to also get the yearbooks? The salesman says they help keep the encyclopedia current, but a friend of mine who has the same encyclopedia says she never touches them. Wondering in New York

Dear Wondering: You are right to question the value of encyclopedia yearbooks. A few years ago, Consumers' Research, Inc. offered this advice on the subject: "Never contract in advance for yearbooks, as these are little used by many purchasers. They are best purchased on a year-to-year basis." I agree with this statement. Despite publisher claims to the contrary, encyclopedia yearbooks rarely have a direct relationship to the parent set, aside from sharing a common title, and they can be quite costly in terms of value received. In many instances, an inexpensive popular annual like the *World Almanac* or *Information Please Almanac* will serve just as well or even better as an updating supplement to a general encyclopedia.

Dear Encyclopedia Critic: A librarian recommended your book on encyclopedias to me. After looking it over I can't help writing to say how unfair your reviews are. You never have anything negative to say about World Book but, oh boy, do you ever rake Encyclopaedia Britannica over the coals. Are you on the take? Suspicious in Massachusetts

Dear Suspicious: I have stated many times in many places that, at the present time, the *World Book Encyclopedia* is, page for page, the best general English-language encyclopedia currently produced. This opinion is based on extensive independent research, only some of which appears in the published review. Like all encyclopedias, *World Book* has limitations, but when judged comparatively against the competition it usually proves superior in most categories. The *New Encyclopaedia Britannica* is another story. The fifteenth edition, first published in 1974 and revised each year since, is innovative in several ways, but between the years 1974 and 1984 it failed to provide adequate access to the vast store of information it contains. In addition, the set's contents were not always reasonably up-to-date. Fortunately, in 1985 the makers of *Britannica* corrected the set's most glaring defects. As an honest critic, it is my job to identify, discuss, and document each encyclopedia's strengths and weaknesses. If my reviews displease you, I can only suggest that you look elsewhere.

Evaluation of Reference Sources Published or to Be Published

Jovian Lang, OFM

Over the past ten years I have been either serving on the RASD, Reference Sources Committee or working on the publication of their *Reference Sources for Small and Medium-sized Libraries*, Third, Fourth and currently the Fifth Edition. From my experience working on these projects I intend to address the readership of this periodical. During this time I must have handled three to four thousand quality reference tools, helping to make decisions whether or not they were to be included on the lists or in the publications. Many times they have been essential tools for libraries larger than the libraries defined in the preface to *Reference Sources for Small and Medium-sized Libraries*.

PUBLISHERS SEEK TO FULFILL NEEDS

Most librarians who deal regularly in reference materials discover that publishers are really trying to fulfill the needs that we have. For them it means a successful book or item that will sell well because librarians recognize the advantage of having such a tool at their fingertips. All of us have at one time or another received questionnaires from publishers searching for a description of a reference tool that would be helpful to librarians. Once they know what the needs are, they search around until they locate a qualified author to work up the material requested.

We might mention at this spot, that certain publishers do "spin-offs." By this we mean that a publisher has the rather large work, from which he can excerpt certain sections for specific audiences. For instance the *Subject Guide to Books in Print* makes

---

The author is on the faculty of the Division of Library and Information Science, St. John's University, Grand Central and Utopia Parkways, Jamaica, NY 11439.

© 1987 by The Haworth Press, Inc. All rights reserved.

it possible to have a specialized list of books in print available for selected audiences, such as *Business and Economics Books and Serials in Print*; *Children's Books in Print*; *Religious Books and Serials in Print*; etc. In most of these instances the publisher will either add material or have a much better subject breakdown in the spin-off, so that the librarians, aware of the particular item, may decide whether their specialty demands the use of such a work. If they already have the major work, they may want to think very seriously about whether the advantages of the special subsection would be worth the cost of the item. However, for subject specialists, these spin-offs may be the answer to their needs.

The committee has expressed concern on many occasions that there seems to be a dearth of true children and young adult reference works. RASD itself recognizes the problem, and has appointed an ad-hoc committee entitled *Reference Services to Children and Young Adults*, to investigate establishing a standing committee on reference services to young adults and children. One would hope they would be able to put the proper pressure on publishers by suggesting the various areas in which tools of this nature should be available for their clientele.

ONLINE REFERENCE SERVICES

In the Fourth Edition, the title changed from *Reference Books . . .* to *Reference Sources for Small and Medium-sized Libraries*. The main reason was that the subcommittee felt formats such as microforms and databases should be included in the list of reference materials. In this technological age, in many instances, it may be less expensive for libraries to have such services available to their clientele than to purchase hard copy. This is particularly true for indexes and other print sources that have basic bibliographic information, and are usually on the major online vendors, such as BRS, DIALOG, and/or SDC. The use of online reference services has increased more and more, and finally some of the companies, recognizing the value of their material and the wide use it is receiving, are bringing some of the prices within range of present libraries budgets. Payment of such services has been handled in a sufficient number of other articles, together with the problem as to whether or not charges should be made to the patron. Most probably there are other articles on this particular topic even in this current issue of *The Reference Librarian*.

STATE OF REFERENCE REVIEWING

Those of us who depend on review columns of reference tools know the variety of sources in which we find such material and are grateful that they exist. For the most part we are interested in up-to-date review columns, those that appear monthly and quarterly, but we will not refuse to look at certain annuals, to double check our needs against the material that has been reviewed. Most review sources make use of a stable of reviewers who are librarians working in reference materials regularly, and therefore are quite knowledgeable in their review activity.

Editors of review columns are dependent upon the publishers for copies of the material. Usually, the reference material is expensive, more so than the majority of other books that are reviewed, so it might be more costly for the publisher to make sure that a sufficient number of such copies are made available to the various columns or editors. Usually, the small presses do not have sufficient money set aside for such publicity, so that it becomes extremely difficult to find reviews of good reference material published by them. I have spent five minutes or more at many such booths at the ALA Conference, trying to convince the owners of small presses that they should make sure that their reference tools be reviewed by those columns that specialize in reference book reviewing.

While working on the committee, our greatest fear would be that we would miss some rather excellent work that had not been reviewed within the time constraint into which we were boxed. In fact, it was so difficult, that we found it necessary to have a certain percentage of books from the previous year reviewed in the following year, because these works, and reviews about them, did not become available until the time limit for the previous year's list was completed. This is one of the big problems in most reviewing: the difficulty of getting the reviews in time and having them published with the least amount of delay. Frequently it seems to be more troublesome in relation to reference materials, probably because it is more demanding to review them well.

One could say that the state of reference reviewing is quite good for the works that actually appear. As I indicated earlier, qualified reviewers do the work, and can readily make distinctions and comparisons that are beneficial to the reference librarians who need to purchase or evaluate the material for their own use. However, we continuously have that problem of not being aware of some rather good reference tools that have not been reviewed, primarily because the publishers are not aware as to the proper method of distribution of their books so that they will have reviews published readily.

EVALUATING REFERENCE TOOLS

Much of the following material I use during my classes in Collection Development. When I have a group of neophytes in front of me in a classroom, future librarians who will be making many decisions about purchasing items that their library needs, I am convinced there ought to be some criteria that can be given to these students, in order that they can easily justify the reasons for the purchases they will be making. To make the idea much more acceptable to them, as a rule I try to draw out from them the criteria that they think any good piece of print or non-print material should have. Having done this for many years, it is not amazing to me to discover that students from year to year will come up with the same criteria. Consequently, I would like to offer the following as suggestions for authors, publishers, and reviewers of reference books as criteria that they should be searching for within the works that they write, publish, or review. Keep in mind also that this is not only my personal view, but that of hundreds of students who were approaching this problem with a fresh mind on the topic. There is no particular priority order among these criteria. All of us have come to the conclusion that we would not expect every book to have every one of these criteria fulfilled. Yet the more a particular work will possess the better it will be.

CRITERIA FOR ANY REFERENCE TOOL

1. *Credibility*. Almost all of these criteria can be expressed synonymously and frequently are. In this instance the material must be believable, easy to accept; through the presentation of the author the reader would be willing to agree with the material being presented, whether it was a matter of a mere listing of facts, or the logic presented through the author's cogent reasoning.

2. *Artistic Quality*. Under this criterion we admit that the work is an esthetic success. In some instances people might think the reference tool is not necessarily beautiful, however if it is properly

done, it certainly ought to attain some degree of artistic quality in, if nothing else, the way in which the material is presented.

3. *Worth.* This norm answers the question: does it have a message? For reference tools particularly, this would be a major concern, even more so than perhaps some of the other criteria. In many instances it may only be that it satisfies the needs for a certain portion of our clientele, but for them the message is very necessary and valuable. This factor is of serious significance when we find that the information presented has great import for a large sector of humanity. In that way its worth becomes more obvious.

4. *Interest Factor.* Many of these criteria have a vital interest with regard to only a sector of our clientele. Were we trying to judge a much more general book, the interest factor would play a very important part. In this case, if the topic is of high interest for the general populace, the material presented in a reference tool will be more beneficial to a large number of people. Nevertheless even if the interest factor pertains to a small specialized group, it is substantial enough to need our constant consideration.

5. *Effects on User.* Most of us have always agreed that a tool of this nature will satisfy many of the users, will fulfill certain needs, and will usually have a good effect on the user. Such reference material fulfills a demand of the user which brings a good deal of satisfaction. Knowledge picked up in the reference tool may even cause a change in some persons' living patterns, the way in which certain job activities are performed, or ideas are ameliorated—all because of data from an excellent reference tool.

6. *Literary Style.* One usually thinks of literary style in conjunction with fiction. However, courses are available at the college level to aid authors to better their literary style for material other than fiction. This fact indicates that there is a need to present material in a reference work in such a way that it will appeal to the reader and not cause difficulties. Good literary style will aid tremendously in conveying the sometimes complicated ideas to the reader.

7. *Readability or Comprehensibility.* Closely allied to the previous number, is the need that a work, and particularly a reference tool, be readily comprehensible to the user. Much material of a reference nature can be complicated and exceedingly difficult to understand. Readability that enables a person who is not necessarily a specialist in the field to understand the material is extremely important, whatever the person's reason might be to access the material. This does not mean that those reference tools that are

intended primarily for the specialist are to try to avoid using the scientific terms that exist. Just be sure that specialized terms are comprehensible since they are necessary to understand the material discussed.

8. *Reputation and Significance of Author or Producer.* By wording this criterion in this way, it is hoped that we protect the person who may be authoring a first work. In that case, reputation may not have preceded him, yet his significance by reason of his presentation may be sufficient to allow evaluators to come to the conclusion that the particular work is worthwhile, should readily be considered along with other material of this nature, and deserves praise and publicity. In some instances, we recognize certain writers as authorities in a field and would hope that their later publications would be at least comparable to their former endeavors. Also, when it comes to publishers, or producers of non-print material, we may know that certain companies specialize in reference material and their work is more than acceptable, almost an indication that since they have published it, it is most likely markedly good. Their editors are so capable at their jobs, that they can bring even a young author to present material in a way that will satisfy the users, whether librarians or the library's clientele.

9. *Originality, Uniqueness.* Perhaps one might expect to find this more frequently in poetry, drama, and novels, nevertheless it certainly has place in non-fiction material. Reference librarians will be looking for the way in which the material is presented, the fact that certain approaches are different in this particular tool from others with which they are familiar, and therefore of a unique and worthwhile nature. This feature is most obvious in certain types of statistical material. So many librarians say that we have a tremendous amount of statistics available, but to find them in the way in which a specific client needs them is not always possible. Any work therefore that can shed a new light on material that we have searched for in the past and been unsuccessful in locating can fit under this criterion.

10. *Durability.* Under this caption we classify material which may last indefinitely, that though eventually it might become outdated, nevertheless, considering the period it covers, the matter will always be of consequence to someone, even if only the historian. Under another aspect, one might relate it to credibility, in the sense that no matter what time a person picks up the material, the information is still there, worthwhile, believable, and usable.

11. *Universality.* Under this canon we would like a particular work to have application to a broad field. In some instances, when we refer only to some very specialized tools, this norm may seem to be less weighty, yet for all of the specialists in that particular area throughout the whole world, this material would certainly be meaningful and necessary. Insofar as we limit the audience, it has universal appeal to that specific audience.

12. *Authenticity.* Usually this gauge will be quite clear from the way the material is presented, the use of many of the former criteria, such as literary style, readability, significance of the author or publisher, its durability—all of these tie into and proclaim its authenticity. In the field of reference, this is a major standard and one which normally will stand out immediately to a knowledgeable librarian or specialist in the field.

13. *Clarity, Adequacy, and Scope.* When we talked above about literary style and comprehensibility, clarity certainly was of immense importance, yet in the reference field this is such a significant aspect, that it seems worthwhile to mention it as a special area of concern. Included with this idea is whether or not the work covers the proper scope and is adequate for the purpose intended. So certain aspects relate to clarity, yet from other viewpoints, a factor to take into consideration is whether or not the work is actually fulfilling its purpose.

14. *Validity.* Under this general caption, we would be stressing such ideas as accuracy, objectivity, the lack of bias, up-to-dateness, usefulness, and appropriateness. We would hope to find many situations where the material is not simply factual, but the presentation of various aspects of the particular topic, usually with different points of view. An example might be one of the most excellent textbooks that I ever used (Child Psychology, by George G. Thompson: Houghton Mifflin, 1952), in which the author presented one after another the various theories many scholars had, giving their viewpoints.

15. *Format.* Many times the manner of presentation is of utmost importance in a reference tool, in order to achieve many of the kinds of things we have been talking about so far. In some instances it may not be as decisive as others, yet the fact that we avert to it as a concern in certain circumstances makes it worth mentioning at this time. We are interested in its physical makeup, the type face and type size for the age level of the intended audience, the binding being durable and attractive, sufficient margins for rebinding, paper

of good quality, probably off-white, and the appropriateness of having illustrations, maps, charts, glossary, bibliographies and appendices. We want to know if the illustrations are simple, artistic, and suited to the content and meaningful to the intended audience. Most essential in any reference tool is the index, so much so, that most librarians will not even consider a work as reference unless it has a satisfactory index.

16. *Thesis.* All our reference tools should have some purpose for their existence, usually stated in the preface or foreword, making it clear what the particular author had in mind. In a sense it sets up a measuring rod against which the authors or reviewers can place the books and decide whether or not they have achieved the purposes intended.

SUMMARY

To reiterate some of the points mentioned above, one could conclude that good reference material should supply knowledge and information in the subject field, be in keeping with the interest, needs, and concepts of the audience in a manner that will render the material within their comprehension, might lead to higher ideals, could very well help in the formation of opinions, extend and improve basic cultural, moral, political, social, and psychological values, build belief in social equality and individual freedom, aid a person in choice of modes of behavior, bolster a person's sense of power and prestige, and all of this accomplished through an excellent literary quality exemplified with simplicity, beauty, humor, imagination, and sincerity.

CRITERIA FOR PERIODICALS ON REFERENCE

In keeping with the criteria discussed above, one could conclude that the content of such periodicals should contain articles of quality, both long and short, depending on the specific topic under discussion. Most probably a certain amount of activities that have been occurring in certain libraries that have proved beneficial, a sufficient number of reviews to satisfy the readership, and advertisements of value for that same group. As to format, it is to be hoped the paper and print will be of size and quality that is easy to handle and read. If illustrations are used, usually quite important, they should be realistic, with colors if necessary, to the point and very descriptive, in some instances more diagramatic. Ordinarily one would expect the cover to appeal to the user.

CRITERIA FOR NON-PRINT MATERIALS ON REFERENCE

Databases have been discussed in other articles sufficiently, so the only thing to mention here is that the more *user friendly* such materials are, the more used they will be by both librarians and patrons. From all appearances, it seems that database producers are aware of this and are trying to achieve the goal by making their work readily accessible to those who have a fair amount of computer literacy.

Audio-visual materials that are used primarily for description of reference materials, or helpful in any other way to aid others to use libraries well, are in existence. Some questions that should be asked about these are the following: Is the medium well chosen, appropriate? Is the scope broad enough to present a truthful, accurate and up-to-date picture of the subject? Is there adequate treatment of specific concepts? How effectively are the purposes of the film, filmstrip, slides, etc., accomplished? What are the educational advantages of this topic presented in this manner? Does it suggest follow-up material? Is the continuity logical and satisfactory? Does the vocabulary coincide with the interest level of the viewer? Are the colors, sound effects, narration and photography satisfactory? Are the facts recorded accurately? Is the material modern? Do the main facts stand out clearly in the midst of details and are they relevant? Does the picture include items or elements of known size so that the observer may secure an accurate idea of the unknown elements? Is there a manual or manuscript to follow a clearly defined sequence? Is the voice of the narrator pleasant, the diction good, the enunciation clear? Is there sufficient variation provided so that the listening span of the person is not taxed or comprehension hindered?

CONCLUSION

My hope is that this material will prove beneficial to authors, publishers, and reviewers. Much of the material has been developed over a period of many years, picking and choosing an idea from books, periodical articles, and whatever other sources might be available, including discussions with librarians on the job. At this stage, it would be impossible to credit each person with the germ of the idea that has been presented here. Should librarians or authors recognize their own ideas amid these, I hope they will take it as an endorsement of their fine ideas and not be perturbed that I was unable to cite properly the correct bibliographic information for their ideas. Hopefully, the material presented will allow many to consider seriously how and why they choose certain reference tools for specific purposes.

REFERENCES

1. *Reference Sources for Small and Medium Sized Libraries*, compiled by the Ad Hoc Committee for the 4th Edition, RASD, ALA, Jovian P.Lang, OFM, Deborah C. Masters, Co-Editors and Chairpersons. Chicago, American Library Association, 1984.

Reference Book Reviewing Tools: How Well Do They Do the Job?

James H. Sweetland

Although there is little evidence on exactly how reference/information librarians choose their tools, the consensus is that the reviewing sources are not very good. This view, well articulated by Kister,[1] states that the tools most used are not "professional" enough: "the reviews" do not offer clear, critical judgments; they do not offer comparative information on the sources covered; and that they are not very well written. While the question of writing quality is very subjective, the other claims are open to objective analysis. While such analysis has been performed on particular tools, there is a lack of a general comparison. Although Whitmore[2] made such a study in 1971, followed by Bone's in 1976[3] and McCleod's excellent comparison of *Choice* and *Library Journal* reviews appeared in 1981,[4] two recent studies did not deal with the subject in depth. Bunge's 1981 survey[5] emphasized the timing of the reviews, while Rettig's[6] involved the stated policies of the reviewing sources, rather than the impact of those policies. The time is ripe for a new study of the content and quality of the reference book reviews.

METHOD

Given the overall agreement on the most important sources, these were chosen as the objects of study. The tools chosen included: *American Reference Books Annual*, *Choice*, *Library Journal*, *RQ*, *Reference Books Bulletin* (title changed from *Reference and Subscription Books Bulletin* as of 1 September, 1983), and *Wilson Library Bulletin*. Since *Reference Services Review* did not have a regular review column during the time studied it was excluded.

Professor Sweetland is at the School of Library and Information Science, The University of Wisconsin-Milwaukee, P.O. Box 413, Milwaukee, WI 53201.

A sample of three hundred of the reviews in the reference sections of the journals noted above was selected from all reviews appearing in 1983. (Since *ARBA* claims to cover everything, it was not part of this portion of the study.) This year was chosen to permit appearance of reviews later than the original, but still to be recent enough that current policies and practices were in effect. As noted below, this guess is borne out—a rather large number of the sample was reviewed in the next year, or even later, by at least one source. After each review in each journal was numbered, a random number table was used to produce the list—with duplicates eliminated during the sampling until three hundred different titles were chosen. This sample appears to meet general requirements for representativeness—in other words, the conclusions drawn below should be correct for all reviews appearing in the sources noted.

Once the sample was taken, *Book Review Index* was searched beginning with the publication year of the title in question, through the December, 1985 issue (the most recent available at the time of the study). Where more than one review appeared for the same item in the same journal, the earlier review was chosen, leading in a few cases to use only of reviews appearing before 1983. Each review was then read, and, in addition, all citations in the *ARBA* reviews double checked against the *BRI* citations.

An interesting problem appears, based on this method—*Book Review Index*, at least as far as reference tools are concerned, is not 100% comprehensive. In fact, a total of forty-five reviews were not listed. Another apparent problem with BRI is a lack of consistency—sometimes a given item is entered under title, sometimes under author/editor/compiler; at least once, under both in the same annual. This situation is surprising enough that further research into the consistency and accuracy of *BRI* is warranted.

Each review, as read, was coded for content, including recommendation; comparisons within the review, and total number of items per review, as well as for date of appearance.

GENERAL COVERAGE

An overall look at the results shows coverage to be about what was expected: the most comprehensive tool is definitely *American Reference Books Annual*. The surprise is that it only reviewed 236 titles, or 79% of the total sample. The smallest coverage is with

RQ—reviewing only 60, or 20% of the total. Considering only the total coverage, after ARBA, the ranking is *Choice* (189, 63%), *Reference Books Bulletin* (168, 56%), *Library Journal* (134, 46%), and *Wilson Library Bulletin* (105, 35%).

The definition of "reference book" itself, of course is not totally clear. A small number of reviews appeared in the journals, but *not* in the reference sections. (These reviews are included in the tally above). These include four in *Choice*, one in *RQ*, and fully sixteen in *Library Journal*. The sum of all reviews is only 892, or just under three per title. Or, to look at it another way, since all titles, by definition, should have been found in both the original source (from the sample) and in *ARBA*, the overlap is much lower than expected. In fact, of the 300 titles, forty-four were reviewed only once. The majority of unique titles appear in *Choice* (17) and *Reference Books Bulletin* (14). *ARBA* has only one; *LJ* has five, and *WLB* seven. *RQ* reviewed no unique titles. While the overlap of coverage is much better than that noted by Glennan[7] for the period 1953-57, or Goggin and Seaberg for 1962,[8] these findings suggest that librarians must continue to rely upon more than one tool for comprehensive coverage.

CURRENCY OF COVERAGE

For this study, each review was coded for the month it appeared, but no more specific date was selected. Based on receipt of the journals, *RQ* was coded as though the Spring issue arrived in March, Summer in June, and so on; the July/August *Choice* was coded as July. Further detail was not needed, since past studies have done a good job of discussing currency.

As expected, the majority of reviews appeared in 1983—a total of 574 (out of the 1800 possible reviews). Most of the journal reviews for 1982 titles appeared in 1983, some even into 1984. However, the journals' record for 1983 publications is better—the majority of their reviews appearing during that year. In keeping with past findings, *LJ* remains the fastest—a natural considering its use of proofs rather than the finished volume. Overall, by the end of 1984, with one exception (a review in *RBB*), all the reviews which were going to appear, had appeared. This compares with *ARBA*, where about half of the '82 titles were covered in 1984, yet nearly all '83 titles were, in fact, covered the next year.

This apparent improvement in currency across most sources is curious. It is possible that a conscious attempt to improve performance, perhaps based on criticisms published in 1981, has had an effect. Once again, further research, over a longer time span, is indicated.

REVIEW CONTENT

The primary interest of this study, however, was not timeliness, but content. Are there problems with the contents of the review, or not?

After the initial attempt at coding the content of the reviews, an apparently simple procedure, we find there are actually several problems. Ignoring, for the moment, the discovery that the definite recommendation (e.g., buy, don't buy) may not agree with the general tone of the review, we find that many reviews are not positive or negative, but mixed in some fashion. The final coding, in fact, allowed for six possible types of content: positive; mostly positive (e.g., "this is a good book, but not definitive," or, "it is unfortunate that the binding is so poor in a title which will deservedly get heavy use"); mixed (an equal balance of positive and negative statements); mostly negative (e.g., "while seriously flawed, this is the best available title on the subject"); purely negative; and merely descriptive. While the categories were collapsed for the purposes of some analysis, the mere existence of the sixth indicates that the problems suggested by Kister and others remain—not all reviews in fact evaluate the item reviewed.

In addition, after attempting to code a number of reviews picked more or less at random, it became clear that it would be necessary to make a distinction between the review itself, and the recommendation. The comments following deal at this point only with the body of the review, other than a specific recommendation.

In the first place, the complaint that most reviews are too positive appears valid. Of the total reviews 42%, or 372 were wholly positive, while less than 4% (32) were wholly negative. The generally positive category includes another 218, for a total positive score of 590, or 66% positive. The mixed (where positive and negative remarks about the title were about evenly divided) represent 12% (110) of all reviews, and mere descriptions another 10% (89). Or, the odds of getting a positive review are about two in three.

The sources vary, of course, in the degree of criticism. Based on this sample, the most critical is clearly *RQ*, with 21% (13) of its reviews negative, and only 52% (31) positive. Compared to this, *Library Journal*'s 76% positive and 9% negative appears almost Pollyanna-ish, although *Wilson Library Bulletin* (74% good, 7% bad) is not far behind. *ARBA*, with its reputation for longer, more considered reviews, still finds 71% of its titles good, and only 7% bad.

Besides having a strong tendency to avoid condemnation, reviewers also avoid any clear evaluation at all about 10% of the time. Rather surprisingly, the worst "offender" in this regard is *RBB*, with 15% of its reviews failing to go beyond pure description. *Choice*, on the other hand, maintains its reputation, with the lowest figures in this category—only 5% of its reviews failing to review. The scores for the others: *ARBA*, 9%; *WLB* and *RQ*, 10%; *LJ*, 11%.

Before becoming alarmed at these numbers, one must remember two important facts. First, at this stage, we consider only the content of the review, *other than any definite recommendation*. And, while the critics have been quite hard on the reviewers, there is no objective evidence to suggest that two-thirds of all new reference books are not worthy of some consideration. On the other hand, there is no question that most reviews are quite favorable; few reference tools receive negative comments. On the other hand, leaving out the purely positive comments, and the mere descriptions, nearly half of all reviews do include at least some negative comments.

RECOMMENDATIONS BY REVIEWERS

It is not unreasonable to expect that reviews will lead to recommendations, either to buy or not to buy. For the most part, instructions to reviewers make this clear—with the exception of ARBA (which notes the review itself should be sufficient in content to indicate a recommendation).

Unfortunately, such recommendations are not as clear-cut as the instructions would imply. Certainly, in many cases, as expected, the review either ends with a clear statement, or contains such a statement in the text. When the text of the review is clear, this can be sufficient to provide guidance in selection. In fact, *ARBA* indicates to its reviewers that a specific recommendation is not needed. However, when combined with either a mixed review, or a mere description, the lack of recommendation makes the review rather pointless. Fortunately, this is a relatively minor problem, appearing only in *ARBA* (12 titles, or 5%) and *Reference Books Bulletin* (10 titles, 6%), and once in *Wilson Library Bulletin* (1%).

A much larger, and more serious problem, is failure of agreement between the review and the recommendation, such as a positive review followed by a negative recommendation. In fact, this disagreement is large enough to cast a pall on previous studies which merely code reviews as "positive" or "negative." How, in fact, is a selector supposed to deal with such mixed signals?

Statements such as "suitable for larger collections" or "buy where there is need," appear on their face to be recommendations. However, when they conclude a negative assessment, they might be called a failure in courage, or perhaps, a failure in editorial control.

None of the sources studies wholly avoid this problem. The worst offender is *RBB* with 22 (13%) such reviews, followed by *RQ* (7, or 12%), *Choice* (21, 11%), *LJ* (13, 10%), *ARBA* (16, 7%) and *WLB* (6, 6%). The overall record is 85 such reviews, for just under 10% of all reviews.

When added to the total lack of recommendations, this indicates a real problem with the reviews. It is one thing to have an honestly mixed review—dissonance between review tone and recommendation does not help the selector.

These findings also point up an interesting anomaly: *Choice*'s argument against signed reviews for many years was that anonymity permitted greater critical honesty. However, the semi-anonymous committee reviews of *Reference Books Bulletin* and the wholly anonymous ones of *Choice* are not particularly better than the other sources in this area.

OVERALL AGREEMENT AMONG REVIEWS

Accepting the intra-review problems as a given, one might at least hope for consistency among reviews—a consensus that given titles are good, or bad. Unfortunately, this is hardly the case. In short, while there tends to be a slight positive correlation among journals, this is very weak. Overall, there is only agreement among reviews for 136 of the 300 title sample: in keeping with the accepted wisdom, this is overwhelmingly positive, with 114 titles receiving only positive or mostly positive recommendations from all sources reviewing the title. Again in accord with accepted views, only four titles receive universal condemnation. Fourteen titles consistently cause problems, and the last four receive mixed recommendations. This particular finding was so surprising that a number of tests were run on the file created for this study, revising the coding a number of different ways (for example, "not reviewed" considered as "negative" on the basis that a failure to review at all is, in effect, negative). This recoding had very little effect. It would appear that there is little agreement as to which reference titles published in a given year are worthy of selection (and even less, by the way, on those which are clearly not worthy of such selection).

On the other hand, a somewhat different point of view results from including the plurality (e.g., two positives outweigh one negative and vice versa). With this point of view, we obtain generally positive reviews for 233 titles, and generally negative reviews for nine. Positives and negatives balance each other in six more cases. The other fifty-two titles include positives, negatives, mixed, and problems in various proportions.

NUMBER OF ITEMS IN A REVIEW

One possibly interesting element of a review is the number of items actually reviewed. This can be considered in two different ways—the titles formally covered and the titles which are compared with the reviewed item.

Certainly, the most typical review is the single, where only one title is to be reviewed. However, while nearly all the reviews in *ARBA*, *Choice* and *LJ* are for single titles, only 91% of those in *RBB* are such. The sources with the smallest number of reviews are also most likely to use the multiple approach—*RQ* covers one title only 65% of the time; *WLB* does so 83% of the time. Regardless of the number of items per review, there is no particular tendency to be more or less favorable.

On the other hand, comparisons within the review are supposed to be good. The emphasis on comparisons is found not only in critiques of reviews, but also in the editors' instructions to their reviewers. In particular, *Choice*'s good reputation is based on its comparative reviews.

In order to see how well all sources met this consensus criterion, this study coded each review not only for a specific number of comparisons, but also permitted a generalized statement, such as "outshines all other works in the field" to be considered. Surprisingly, total comparisons, even with this liberal definition, are rather few.

The tool least likely to compare a reviewed title with anything is *ARBA*, with only 113 (48%) compared. The most likely place for a comparison is *RQ*, with 44 or 73%. The biggest surprise, however, is *Choice*, which does what it claims to do, and is praised for doing, only two-thirds of the time (126 titles, or 67%). The scores for the other titles: *LJ*, 72 titles (54%); *RBB*, 89 (53%), *WLB*, 61 (58%). If comparing is good, then the sources have a long way to go. Interestingly, the longer reviews and longer time in which to review the item permitted by *ARBA* does not improve the odds of getting such a comparison.

CONCLUSION

The general feeling in the profession is that reviewing tools, overall, tend to be too positive, fail to be critical, and in general cannot be relied upon as much as one might wish.

This study confirms that the criticisms are well-founded: there is, in fact, a general lack of comparison within reviews; most reviews are generally favorable; there are few mixed reviews and even fewer wholly negative ones.

However, there seem to be other problems as well. First, there are a number of reviews in which there is no evaluation of any kind. Secondly, there are a number of reviews where the recommendation does not follow from whatever evaluation was presented. In effect, such "reviews" do not deserve to be called such.

Third, consensus is rather low. Of 300 titles, only 136 receive a consistent ranking across all sources which do such. These include 114 wholly positive reviews, 4 wholly negatives, 4 qualified, and 14 where all sources presented problems. In other words, the profession agrees on the value of a given reference tool less than half the time.

The performance of the several tools is rather interesting. In particular, the fairly high showing of *RQ* may be surprising, in view of the small number of titles covered (after all, it's only a quarterly), and a tendency of both publishers and librarians to fail to mention it as a first-choice tool. In fact, *RQ* is among the most likely to provide critical, comparative reviews.

By the same token, the relatively poor showing of *RBB* in a number of areas is surprising. It has a good reputation; it covers many titles; it is especially praised for its very lengthy, comparative "omnibus" reviews. However, possibly due to the collective nature of its more "typical" reviews, it tends to be surprisingly uncritical.

Choice also presents some surprises, especially in the lack of comparisons. While 2/3 is not bad compared to most of the other journals (except *RQ*), it is hardly the proportion that one would expect to find in the reviewing source most thought of as "comparative."

ARBA, certainly a well-received tool, also surprises, particularly for its coverage. While a given number of the titles in the sample will not be eligible (since it does not review annuals, continuations, and similar works every year), 79% coverage, with only one unique title, is far less than expected.

On another front, the very difficulties encountered in attempting to rate the sources in question are also surprising. From previous studies, a plus/minus rating ought to be fairly easy. In fact, the need to code both review and recommendation separately, and to have more than two exclusive categories was unexpected. At the same time, this more complicated rating system may lead to more error. There is an obvious need for a test of the reliability of the coding, preferably by more than one rater. Just as there is an apparent inter-reviewer reliability problem within the journals, there may be some such among the journal raters. While this should be studied, the issue is not hopeless. After all, both *Magazine Index* and *National Newspaper Index* provide rankings from A to F for each of the reviews they index.

The "problematic" category is another issue: Will different raters see the same problems; will they see the reviews in the same way? Since this study is the first to have indicated this particular problem with reference tool reviews, the approach should be further tested.

And, the apparently minor problem of indexing by BRI needs considerable care. Librarians have assumed that it was reliable, yet a rather simple test shows it is not always so. A further study of this particular problem is already underway, and should prove of interest to both publishers and librarians.

While not directly related to this study, the apparent lack of consensus can be considered a problem. This can be tested by, among other methods, comparing the various lists of "best reference books" produced by *Library Journal*, the American Library Association, *College and Research Libraries*, and *Choice*.

To summarize: at the present, the best advice for the working reference librarian needing to purchase new printed reference tools is still—read several reviews, and be careful. The best advice to the reviewers, and to their editors remains—try harder to do the job—truly critical reviews are difficult (we all like to be considered "good guys"), but the need for them is very great.

REFERENCES

1. Ken Kister, "Wanted: More Professionalism in Reference Book Reviewing," *RQ* 19 (Winter, 1979), 144–148.
2. Harry E. Whitmore, "Reference Book Reviewing," *RQ* 9 (Spring, 1970), 221–226.
3. Larry E. Bone, "Choosing the Best: A Review of the Aids for the Selection of Reference Books," *Reference Services Review* 4 (July, 1986), 81–83.
4. Beth McCleod, "*Library Journal* and *Choice*: A Review of Reviews," *Journal of Academic Librarianship* 7 (March, 1981), 23–28.
5. Charles A. Bunge, "Reviewing of Adult General Reference Material for General Libraries," *The Reference Librarian* Nos. 1/2 (Fall/Winter, 1981), 21–29.
6. James Rettig, "Reviewing the Reference Reviews," *Reference Services Review* 9 (October/December, 1981), 85–102.
7. Catherine N. Glennan, "Reference Books and Reviews," Unpublished master's project paper, School of Library Science, Western Reserve University, September, 1959; cited in Margaret K. Goggin and Lillian M. Seaberg, "The Publishing and Reviewing of Reference Books," *Library Trends* 12 (1964), 446, 451.
8. Goggin and Seaberg, 440–444.

Book Reviewing in Sociology

Sharon Quist

The value of book reviews in a discipline such as Sociology may range from merely useful to indispensable. They are consulted to enhance or reinforce one's impression of a work and they may be influential in determining the course of a career. Busy professionals rely upon the book review as a means of coping with the information explosion. In order to keep aware of current work in a discipline, the professor or scientist may depend upon the book review to provide a relatively brief initial contact with a new title or author. Because "titles can be ambiguous, misleading, or simply uninformative, we all need assistance in selecting from the continual flood of new books those few that will really serve our particular purposes."[1] The review may be as close as the reader ever gets to the actual work. In 1984, according to the *Bowker Annual*, 6,257 books were published in the fields of Sociology/Economics; of these, 5,293 were new works rather than reprints of earlier editions. Obviously, the need for qualified, unbiased reviewers with "a knowledge of scholarship as well as of text"[2] will not diminish in the near future.

Book reviews also serve as a source of feedback to the author. Critical review from one's peers may be painful but should also be instructive. Both positive and negative evaluation, offered fairly and without personal bias, are of value to the author. Unfortunately, all too often reviews are not totally objective. Norval Glenn wrote in a 1978 editorial in *Contemporary Sociology* his concern that "book reviews are widely used to help estimate the quality and importance of books published by academicians and thus to help make decisions about hiring, promotions, and salary increases."[3] He went on to warn that it is unrealistic to assume reviews have been written by qualified, conscientious, unbiased persons. Of course, journals which publish book reviews generally, by policy, seek to avoid reviewers with a known strong personal bias but the occasional

---

The author is Reference Librarian, Hamilton College, Clinton, NY.

© 1987 by The Haworth Press, Inc. All rights reserved.

mismatch occurs—as evidenced by the "Letters to the Editor" columns which often contain an author's lament that the reviewer should never have been allowed near his/her book. Glenn warns that a reviewer may be motivated by jealousy, feelings of obligation, and similar emotions which may cause them to either refrain from publishing their private negative evaluations or, conversely, to search for flaws and weaknesses in order to make themselves appear perceptive and insightful. Glenn urges that general ratings of an author should not be influential in promotion or hiring considerations but specific criticisms and points of praise of the work should be considered and compared with the original text for accuracy.

INFLUENTIAL FACTORS

Studies conducted by Snizek and Fuhrman (1979) have examined the possibility of certain factors influencing the evaluative content of book reviews in Sociology. They acknowledge the importance and influence of the book review and their studies of 150 reviews of 50 books published over a ten-year span reveal certain interesting conclusions. In comparing the reviews as found in three prominent Sociology journals: *Contemporary Sociology* (*CS*), *American Journal of Sociology* (*AJS*), and Social Forces (*SF*) they determined that "systematic differences in the degree of favorableness or unfavorableness of book reviews across the three journals studied proved to be statistically insignificant."[4] The reader can be assured, therefore, that one journal is not going to present consistently slanted (either more or less favorable) reviews. This does not mean, however, that bias does not exist nor manifest itself in any or all of the journals.

Studies of author and reviewer characteristics and their influence on the evaluative content of the reviews were enlightening. "Older, more professionally experienced authors were likely to receive more favorable reviews of their work than younger, less experienced authors."[5] In *CS* and *AJS*, the author's experience seems to weigh more heavily than age, while in *SF*, the opposite was true. In attempting to evaluate the reasons for this influence, Snizek and Fuhrman present several possibilities: older authors have built up a larger network of allegiances and credits than their younger, less experienced counterparts or perhaps are accorded almost automatic respect due to membership in a "generation unit" or because of the tendency in the field of sociology to hold age and experience in high esteem.

PRESTIGE

Whatever the explanation, the value of book reviews as a basis for personal and career evaluation of an author is questionable. Beyond the age—experience factor, the study also revealed that authors who reside at prestigious institutions receive comparatively more negative reviews than those received by authors from the less prestigious institutions. Two explanations are posited: envy may exist toward authors at the more prestigious institutions, or they may quite possibly draw more prestigious critics. An obvious conclusion from the findings of Snizek and Fuhrman, and the caution by Glenn and others is that book reviews should not be naïvely accepted as the final judgment on an author or work. Reviewer biases do exist and not every reviewer is conscientious or professional enough to keep these from affecting their review. The reader should be aware of the ramifications of the reviewing process as well as attuned to the marks of a well-written review. Wolfe states:

> A good book review consists of three things. First, a brief description of what the reviewer read. Second, an evaluation: a clear statement of whether the reviewer enjoyed or didn't enjoy the book and a close look at strengths and weaknesses—with examples. Third, an attempt to place the work in a larger perspective . . . how does it differ in tone or content from other books on the subject?[6]

If a review provides feedback to the author, there are also benefits for the reviewer. Certainly reviewing has not always been looked upon as significant work and reviewers have received their share of criticism. S.T. Coleridge wrote, "Reviewers are usually people who would have been poets, historians, biographers, if they could: they have tried their talents at one or the other, and have failed; therefore they turn critics."[7]

PUBLISH OR PERISH

Currently, in the academic world, a combination of factors has created a climate in which the competition to publish—even reviews—is strong. Colleges and universities apply pressure to faculty members to produce publications while, concurrently, scholarly and scientific book and journal publishers are becoming very selective with "fewer than one in every hundred submitted manuscripts"[8] reaching publication. Faced with administrative demands for resumés which reflect quantity scholarship, professors now recognize reviewing as "a forum from which both to be heard and to remain professionally active."[9] Unfortunately, this sort of motivation can result in more reviews written for the purpose of reflecting glory on the reviewer rather than objectively evaluating the book.

Interviews with members of the Sociology department at Hamilton College, Clinton, N.Y. reveal this skepticism with the entire reviewing process. Professors interviewed had indeed been recruited to review for two of the leading journals in the field, *Contemporary Sociology* and *Social Forces*. One spoke of the repercussions caused by a critical review he had written which was deemed honest and "on-target" and yet considered a bit more honest than acceptable—not quite "playing by the rules." Another referred to the sociological network from which friends tend to be selected to act as reviewers; sometimes even a protege from the ranks of graduate students may be given the opportunity to add a published review to the list of their credentials. Both mentioned examples of reviews which merely reflected the rivalry existing between adherents of opposing sociological theories or reviews used as weapons by competitors in the field.

Although the Snizek and Fuhrman (1981) study on the influence of theory group associations seems to suggest more instances of support than competition within a discipline, the suspicion remains. Because of their familiarity with the reviewing process, the Hamilton professors do not rely upon reviews to determine whether or not they read a new work. They turn to the reviews simply to find a colleague's perspective on the book; or they suggest to students that a review may clarify a work with which they're struggling.

LOCATION OF REVIEWS

Although book reviews are essential in aiding librarians with acquisitions decisions, generally the scholarly type of review found in a journal such as *American Journal of Sociology* is not consulted. More concise reviews written specifically for this purpose are found in journals such as *Choice* or *Library Journal*. The reference librarian will, however, need to be aware of sources of in-depth reviews when faced with a student seeking this information for one of two reasons: to augment their understanding of a book they have read or to find a summary of a book they should have, but failed to, read weeks ago and will face on an upcoming test. Fortunately, the librarian need not distinguish between the motives since the procedure for securing the reviews will be the same in either case. Sociology book reviews are accessible through the following indexes: *Book Review Digest*, *Book Review Index*, and *Social Sciences Index*. For retrospective searching, the following indexes are useful: *Current Book Review Citations* and *Book Review Index to Social Science Periodicals*. Possible on-line databases which would yield Sociology book reviews: *Book Review Digest* and *Social Sciences Index* are both available through *WilsonLine*; *Book Review Index* is provided by *Dialog*; *Sociological Abstracts* and *Social Science Citation Index* are offered by both *Dialog* and *BRS*.

A questionnaire completed by Sociology faculty members at Hamilton College indicated their preference for the following journals as a source for book reviews in the field:

Contemporary Sociology; a Journal of Reviews (1972–). This bi-monthly publication of the American Sociological Association is considered their reviewing "arm." Coverage includes symposium reviews, survey essays, review essays, and a "Publications Received" section. (Pre-1972 reviews published in *American Sociological Review*.)

American Journal of Sociology (1895–). This bi-monthly journal is often considered the standard in the field for sociology articles. Approximately 175–200 critical, signed book reviews are included each year.

Sociology: Reviews of New Books (1973–1983). Although this journal has ceased publication, it provided timely, brief, evaluative book reviews.

The following journals have also been identified as core literature in the field and they each include a number of book reviews:

Journal of Marriage and the Family (1964–). Published quarterly by the National Council on Family Relations and the approximately 10–12 books reviewed in each issue reflect this subject orientation.

Social Forces: An International Journal of Social Research (1922–). This quarterly journal includes between 40–50 reviews per issue on books dealing with theoretical and applied sociology.

Sociology and Social Research: An International Journal (1921–). University of Southern California publishes this quarterly periodical which reviews 15–25 books per issue.

SCHOLARLY VS. POPULAR SOCIAL SCIENCE

When seeking a review of a sociology book, one should be aware of the differences between a more scholarly work in the discipline and what can be termed a trade book in popular social science. Of course, there are books which almost seem to belong to both camps. A student will do well to remember that popular social science books are especially prone to intermingle myth and science and "post-publication reviewers, then, inherit the major responsibility of providing substantive criticism."[11] Unfortunately, reviewers in many literary and library magazines as well as journals of political and social commentary fail in this responsibility. Reviews found in these journals often reflect less subject knowledge and discernment than those in periodicals such as *Scientific American* which are specifically designed to channel scientific knowledge to the general public. Periodicals and newspapers whose sheer size and wealth enable them to maintain a staff of science reporters competent in a variety of fields are also more likely to do an adequate job of separating the myths from the science and provide a critical evaluation (examples would be *Newsweek* and the *New York Times*).

A study by Hixson (1981) of reviews of four popular works in social science revealed that "while reviewers in specialized periodicals did a competent job, those in daily newspapers, library journals, and literary and entertainment magazines failed to provide critical and informed opinions."[12] In seeking reviews of books in a discipline such as Sociology, students would do well to consult primarily the specialized periodicals in the field.

COMPARISON OF REVIEWING SOURCES

A random selection of thirty-two titles reviewed in either *American Journal of Sociology* (AJS) or *Contemporary Sociology* (CS) was studied to provide additional insight into this world of book reviewing. Publication dates of the books spanned an eight-year period and each title was traced through all pertinent volumes of

Book Review Index (BRI) and *Book Review Digest (BRD)*. Selective titles were also traced on-line.

Although thirty-two titles is admittedly a sample too small to yield definitive results, some observations can still be made. For the most part, the library reviewing journals, *Library Journal (LJ)* and *Choice* were the first to review a title. *Kirkus Reviews (KR)* are most timely—in many cases providing a review before the book is actually published—but this source covered only five of the thirty-two titles surveyed. Librarians relying solely upon *KR* for acquisitions decisions will find it difficult to adequately develop a subject area such as Sociology. Similarly, a librarian selecting only from *LJ*'s "Social Science" section may miss works valuable in the field; an example is Jessie Bernard's *The Female World* (1981) which received many positive reviews from major Sociology journals but was designated by *LJ* as part of "The Contemporary Scene" rather than "Social Science." Subject assigning of reviews in *LJ* seems almost to be done on the basis of title rather than book content as evidenced by *Forms of Talk*, categorized as "Language;" *Machine Politics in Transition*, assigned to "Political Science & International Affairs;" and *The TV Ritual* channeled into "Communications." Of course, these are books whose contents cross discipline boundaries but their subject matter certainly lies within the parameters of Social Science. Perhaps *LJ* would provide more of a service by eliminating the sometimes confusing and confining subject area designators for reviews.

The major library magazines, *Choice* and *LJ* reviewed the same title about one-third of the time and out of those evaluations they agreed only half the time (since this observation is based solely on this particular study, it might not hold true in surveying a larger sample). A comparison reading of reviews in these two journals reveal those in *Choice* to generally be of a more scholarly nature. As observed by Vivian Scott Hixson:

> In 1964, the generally dismal library review scene was illuminated by the appearance of *Choice*. Each issue of *Choice* was prepared with the help of a long list of academic consultants and the *Choice* reviews clearly reflected their expertise.[13]

Perhaps the fact that evaluations matched only in about one-third of the instances in which *Choice* reviewed a book which was also reviewed by one or more of the major Sociology journals bears further examination. Certainly one should "be aware of . . . wide divergence in assessment of scientific work even among eminent scientists"[14] but in this study, discipline journals rarely disagreed and the most discrepancies were found between reviews in library journals and those in the more scholarly publications.

INDEXING PRACTICES

Another area which seems to warrant further scrutiny is the indexing of *Contemporary Sociology*. Considering its reputation among sociologists and importance as the major book review journal in the field, the indexing of *CS* (as examined in this sample) seemed surprisingly sporadic.

The journal is not, at this time, indexed by the Wilson publication, *Social Sciences Index*. Perhaps the survey currently being conducted among Wilson subscribers will result in the addition of *CS* to the list of accessed journals. Although *Book Review Index* does indicate coverage of *CS*, of the reviews studied in this sample, those included in *CS* were sometimes completely omitted by *BRI* and others were not cited during the year they appeared in the journal but picked up a year later. A tangential study of reviews in the January, 1984 issue of *CS* revealed that none were included in the 1984 print *BRI* nor were they in the on-line database which is updated three times each year. An inquiry to *Book Review Index* offices resulted in the information that a subscription problem during the years 1983 and 1984 resulted in intermittent receipt of the issues of *Contemporary Sociology* for that time period. This would explain the delayed entries in both the print and on-line indexes during the years mentioned.

Although half the titles which appeared in *BRI* were also included in *Book Review Digest* (*BRD*), attempting to supplement a search of *BRI* with one in *BRD* will not necessarily be successful. Because *BRD* has allowed for much flexibility in the titles to be included, those found in *BRI* are definitely not assured a place in *BRD*. Since this index considers only those nonfiction titles which are published in Canada or the United States and receive at least two reviews within eighteen months of the book's publication, the coverage in *BRI* is significantly more comprehensive than that of *BRD*.

Searching *BRI*, however, can be tedious. Due to the time gap which exists between a book's publication date and the date it's picked up for review in a particular journal, references to a single title in BRI may appear over as extended a period as four years. Since the benchmark journal in the field of Sociology, *American Journal of Sociology* rarely reviews a book earlier than three years after publication, one must check many separate volumes of *BRI* to be certain of locating all the major reviews of a work. The alternative to searching numerous separate volumes of *BRI* is to search on-line; since this is not yet economically feasible for all libraries, it would be helpful if the Gale Research Company published five-year cumulations.

This entire problem of comprehensive and timely indexing of sociology journals may be alleviated by the publication of the fifteen-year cumulative index currently being prepared by the American Sociological Association. As reported by Bettina Huber, Deputy Executive Officer, the index is intended to include the journals sponsored by ASA as well as *American Sociological Review* and *Social Forces*. Individual book reviews as well as *Contemporary Sociology* review essays will be accessed. ASA's intent is to achieve publication by December 1986. Such an extensive cumulative index in the field of sociology will be very useful to librarians and other researchers.[15]

POPULAR SOCIAL SCIENCE

Although this study focused more on the discipline-related journals, several of the thirty-two titles studied seem to fall into the realm of popular social science and are, therefore, indexed by *Magazine Index* and *Readers' Guide*. Although the "grades" assigned by *Magazine Index* are interesting (for example, Alan P. Bell's *Sexual Preference* received a "D+" from the *New York Times Book Review* and an "A" from *Psychology Today*), neither of these indexes access the more scholarly journals. Students should probably not be encouraged to use these tools when searching for Sociology book reviews since a search, although yielding citations, would not provide the "meatier" sources.

CONCLUSION

Longfellow referred to reviewers as "sentinels in the grand army of letters, stationed at the corners of . . . reviews, to challenge every new author."[16] In today's world, reviewers play a vital role in making the information flood more manageable. Their responsibility is not so much to challenge as it is to summarize authors; and although the responsibility for honest reviews in a field such as Sociology lies heavily upon the reviewers and journal editors, the librarian also plays a part. In order to assure the most realistic representation of a book (or author), the librarian must be fully cognizant of these "sentinels," the workings of the reviewing process, and the tools through which one can access the widest spectrum of scholarly, informative reviews.

ENDNOTES

1. Richard B. Woodbury, "On Book Reviewing," *American Anthropologist*, 79, September 1977, p. 551.
2. R.S. Wolper, "'A Grass-Blade': On Academic Reviewing," *Scholarly Publishing*, 10, July 1979, p. 327.
3. Norval D. Glenn, "On the Misuse of Book Reviews," *Contemporary Sociology*, 7, May 1978, p. 254.
4. William E. Snizek and E.R. Fuhrman, "Some Factors Affecting the Evaluative Content of Book Reviews in Sociology," *The American Sociologist*, 14, May 1979, p. 111.
5. Snizek, p. 111.
6. M. Wolfe, "Reviewing the Reviewers," *Canadian Forum*, 59, November 1979, p. 6.
7. S.T. Coleridge, *Lectures: Shakespeare & Milton* in *The Home Book of Quotations*, edited by Burton Stevenson, 6th ed., revised (New York: Dodd, Mead & Co., 1952), p. 341.
8. Duncan Lindsey, *The Scientific Publication System in Social Science* (San Francisco: Jossey-Bass, 1978), p. 14.
9. Snizek, p. 108.
10. Much of information on indexes and journals is from: Bill Katz and Linda Sternberg Katz, *Magazines for Libraries*, 4th edition (New York: R.R. Bowker Co., 1982).
11. Vivian Scott Hixson, "Caveat Lector: Reviewing Popular Social Science," *Journal of Communication*, Spring 1981, p. 169.
12. Hixson, p. 168.
13. Hixson, pp. 176–77.
14. Lindsey, p. 14.
15. Letter from Bettina J. Huber, Deputy Executive Officer, The American Sociological Association, 29 January 1986.
16. Longfellow, *Kavanagh* in *The Home Book of Quotations*, p. 342.

BIBLIOGRAPHY

Baughman, James C. "A Structural Analysis of the Literature of Sociology." *Library Quarterly*, 44, October 1974, pp. 293–308.
Budd, J. "Book Reviewing Practices of Journals in the Humanities." *Scholarly Publishing*, 13, July 1982, pp. 363–71.
Carroll, Margaret, comp. *Book Reviews: A Guide to Locating Reviews of Books in the Social Sciences & Humanities*. ERIC ED 152664.

Glenn, Norval D. "On the Misuse of Book Reviews." *Contemporary Sociology*, 7, May 1978, pp. 254–5.

Hixson, Vivian Scott. "Caveat Lector: Reviewing Popular Social Science." *Journal of Communication*, Spring 1981, pp. 168–77.

Hoge, James O. and James L.W. West, III. "Academic Book Reviewing: Some Problems and Suggestions." Scholarly Publishing, 11, October 1979, pp. 35–41.

Huber, Bettina J. Deputy Executive Officer, the American Sociological Association. Letter written 29 January 1986.

Katz, Bill and Linda Sternberg Katz. *Magazines for Libraries*. 4th edition. New York: R.R. Bowker Company, 1982.

Lindsey, Duncan. *The Scientific Publication System in Social Science*. San Francisco: Jossey-Bass Publications, 1978.

Snizek, William E. et al. "The Effect of Theory Group Association on the Evaluative Content of Book Reviews in Sociology." *The American Sociologist*, 16, August 1981, pp. 185–95.

Snizek, William E. and E.R. Fuhrman. "Some Factors Affecting the Evaluative Content of Book Reviews in Sociology." *The American Sociologist*, 14, May 1979, pp. 108–114.

Stevenson, Burton. *The Home Book of Quotations*. 6th edition, revised. New York: Dodd, Mead & Company, 1952.

White, Carl M. et al. *Sources of Information in the Social Sciences*. 2nd edition. Chicago: American Library Association, 1973.

Wolfe, M. "Reviewing the Reviewers." *Canadian Forum*, 59, November 1979, pp. 5–7.

Wolper, R.S. "'A Grass-Blade': on Academic Reviewing." *Scholarly Publishing*, 10, July 1979, pp. 325–28.

Woodbury, Richard B. "On Book Reviewing." *American Anthropologist*, 79, September 1977, pp. 551–54.

REVIEWS AND EVALUATION: TWO PROPOSALS

Publication of Reference Tools for Special Collections

Daniel Traister

Rare book and manuscript libraries need reference tools for exactly the same reasons that other libraries require them. Readers and librarians both need to know what books or manuscripts on a subject or by an author exist and where they can be located. They require various kinds of information which reference books supply: the names, perhaps the biographies, of authors, publishers, illustrators, previous owners, binders, people mentioned in books; dates of birth, death, publication, activity; information about repositories of other rare books or manuscripts and their holdings; demographic, economic, scientific data.

If the reference requirements of special collections are peculiar at all, it is, first, in their need for somewhat more precise *bibliographical* information than some other library situations or users require. For a portion of the clientele of a rare book library, it may not be sufficient to know that one repository or another owns a text. It may be essential to know the version and provenance of the text which libraries report. The *National Union Catalog, Pre-1956 Imprints* cites several locations for Joel Barlow's *Columbiad* (Philadelphia, 1807); but what *state* of the 1807 edition does each location represent? How may a reader interested in the bookbindings of John Roulstone, Jr., which may be found on many different books or on various copies of the same book, locate examples of his work? How many—and, more important, which—books from the Sidney family

---

For their very helpful (not to say picky) readings of this essay, I want to thank Professor Terry Belanger (School of Library Service, Columbia University) and Dr. Kathleen Reed (Special Collections, Van Pelt Library, University of Pennsylvania). My colleague Emily Fayen (Van Pelt Library) provided critical assistance at a particularly vexing moment. The help of James N. Green (The Library Company of Philadelphia) calls for special thanks. It is a pleasure to be able to call upon the expertise of such people at will.

The author is Curator of Special Collections, Van Pelt Library, University of Pennsylvania, Philadelphia, PA 19104.

© 1987 by The Haworth Press, Inc. All rights reserved.

library at Penshurst Place (a seventeenth-century catalogue of which has recently been found; see Germaine Warkentin in the *TLS* [December 6, 1985], pp. 1394–5) are now located in North American libraries, and are they annotated in any way?

Second, non-encyclopedic discursive studies—that is, the sort of scholarly works which academic libraries normally collect for their general, publicly-accessible collections—may occasionally also function as *de facto* reference tools for the staff and readership of rare book collections. Such books are not commonly located in the reference departments of general libraries. Dorothy A. Harrop's *History of the Gregynog Press* (Pinner, Middlesex, 1980) and B. E. Bellamy's *Private Presses and Publishing in England Since 1945* (New York, 1980) include those lists we normally think of as bibliographies. But the significance of such works for collections of private press books lies in their texts at least as much as in their lists. A book with no lists at all (for instance, James J. Barnes and Patience P. Barnes, *Hitler's Mein Kampf in Britain and America: A Publishing History 1930–1939* [Cambridge, 1980]) can be useful to staff and readers in a collection with a focus on modern Anglo-American publishing in much the same manner as Lotte Hellinga's *Caxton in Focus* (London, 1982) and Elizabeth L. Eisenstein's *The Printing Press as an Agent of Change* (Cambridge, 1979) are for collections of early English imprints, incunabula, and sixteenth- and seventeenth-century imprints.

From many points of view, the resources available to assist readers and librarians who study and work with rare books and manuscripts are rich, variegated, and growing. Author bibliographies particularly appear with regularity from both university and independent trade or library publishers. Other sorts of reference tools are also abundant. Some appear in new formats: microfiche; online databases. Activity in the field is great.

But it is also haphazard. One result of this situation is that a thousand flowers may bloom. But so do lots of weeds. For reasons I hope are obvious, central planning does not seem a reasonable approach to satisfying the needs of special collections and their users. But better understanding of those needs and of the possibilities of the market may be useful to producers and authors alike. I want to begin with a very few examples indicative of the current situation. One is a carelessly flawed reference work which is nonetheless of real importance. Another is simply inadequate, its contents not self-evidently useful to any conceivable audience. The third "example" does not exist: its lack suggests a failure of imagination in thinking about the need for reference tools for rare book collections and their users.

I

Example 1

One positive result of the Anglo-American bibliographical tradition is that, between Evans, Bristol, Shipton-Mooney, Shaw-Shoemaker, and their successors and supplements, on the one hand, and Pollard and Redgrave's *Short-Title Catalogue*, Wing, and the Eighteenth Century Short Title Catalogue (ESTC), on the other, both British and American imprints through 1800 are controlled (or about to be controlled) more completely than seems to be true of any other major national literatures. As of this writing, the American Antiquarian Society plans late in 1986 to load online bibliographical records for its own eighteenth-century American imprints into ESTC, a database available through RLIN. They presently intend to enrich their contributions through the addition to the database late in 1988 of records for North American imprints from other repositories (North American Imprints Program). A rudimentary nineteenth-century short-title catalogue (NSTC), drawn from the records of The British Library, the Bodleian, Cambridge University Library, the National Library of Scotland, the Library of Trinity College, Dublin, and the University Library, Newcastle, has been begun by Avero (distributed in this country by Chadwyck-Healey); its first series runs from 1801 through 1815.

It is thus a bit disconcerting to realize how little is actually known about early American publishing history and early American books. One can point quickly to a few standard works: e.g., Lawrence C. Wroth's *The Colonial Printer* (2nd ed., Portland, ME, 1938; rpt. Charlottesville, VA, 1964); various of Rollo G. Silver's publications (*The American Printer, 1787–1825* [Charlottesville, 1967]; *Typefounding in America, 1787–1825* [Charlottesville, 1965]); some specialized studies such as Richard F. Hixson's *Isaac Collins* (New Brunswick, NJ, 1968) or older works such as Shipton's *Isaiah Thomas* (Rochester, NY, 1948). Yet no one can embark on a serious effort to learn the fundamentals of the early American book trade without recourse to Thomas's own history, first published in 1810 (and still available in various modern editions). Thomas's enduring vitality is a tribute to his labors. His continuing necessity is no tribute to anyone else. Studies of early American publishing and its products are of importance to those who work with or care for older American imprints. Thus, when William Clarkin's *Mathew Carey: A Bibliography of his Publications, 1785–1824* appeared (New York, 1984), the work was received with warm expectations. It offered, first, improved control of the publications of an extremely prolific and important American publisher. (Carey's Philadelphia firm, founded in 1785, is still in existence as Lea and Febiger, specialists in medical publishing and the oldest continuously active American publishing firm.) Second, its apparatus might have provided basic documentation of an American publisher and his operations, broadening our understanding of the book trade in the early national period.

It did neither satisfactorily. Carelessly proofread, with indications of equally careless editing, the book fails to be complete even within the limits of what had already been known about Carey's publications, does not guide its users through suppressed reprintings and distinct issues, and makes little effort to place Carey in the context of American publishing in his period. Although it certainly contributes to our knowledge, it is by no means as useful as it ought to have been, and the nature of its flaws suggests some more general difficulties in the publication processes that affect reference books of this sort. It is not my intention to review Clarkin's *Carey* here (see, however, James N. Green's review in *American Book Collector*, n.s. 6:3 [May–June 1985], 43–45). But I cite a few representative difficulties.

Clarkin's item 105 (p. 17) describes John O'Keeffe, *The farmer: a comic opera* . . . (Philadelphia, 1792). Clarkin's title-page transcription reads: "By John O''Keefe [sic], Esq." Readers may suppose that the "sic" refers to the double inverted commas in "O''Keefe"; they would be wrong. However, even readers with a copy of the book in hand may not understand their error. Readers who see "O'Keefe" on the title-page may suspect instead an issue of the book (with single inverted comma) unrecorded by Clarkin. But the double inverted commas are merely Clarkin's typo. So far as I know, they appear on no copies of the book's title-page. The "sic" refers to the one "f" (instead of two) in O'Keeffe's surname.

The last line in Clarkin's title-page transcription reads: "Dec.

14,—D.DCC.XCII". The year should read, of course, "M.DC-C.XCII." And so it does, on the original title-page.

One further typo disfigures the entry, a reference to the Boston Public Library copy of *The farmer* which "has at the tend two pages of Carey advertisements." The type is not all that is wrong here. Does Clarkin mean readers to believe that, in the Boston copy, these pages are integral with the book? Surely not. But what is his purpose in remarking this point in terms that allow the possibility of an unintended ambiguity of description?

Similarly, Clarkin remarks that, "while the EAI [Early American Imprints] microcard" of *The farmer* "used the NN [NYPL] copy (which . . . [I] also used)," the EAI microcard contains no date on the title-page ("Dec. 14," etc.). Does Clarkin mean that the *NYPL copy* lacks the date on its title-page, and that he is therefore reporting a separate issue of the book? Or does he mean that the *EAI microcard* omits information found on the book it purportedly reproduces? (He means the latter. I am grateful to Mr. John Rathé of NYPL's Rare Book and Manuscript Division for checking NYPL's copy of O'Keeffe for me.) Since, as Clarkin mentions, he has examined NYPL's copy, he might have answered this question himself, instead of leaving it unanswered and providing again a possibly ambiguous bibliographical description. In short, at least four difficulties mar this one entry alone.

Item 122 (pp. 19–20), Epictetus's *Enchiridion* (1793), has two preliminary unnumbered pages, followed by pages 3–22 (the Greek text) and [1]–12 (the Latin translation). Clarkin does not notice another 1793 Epictetus (it is at The Library Company of Philadelphia) which collates—in his style—(ii), 3–22, [1]–23, [1]; nor does he remark the resemblance between the 1793 copy which he does list and an earlier 1792 edition which he also lists (item 98, p. 16). A bibliographer might have wanted to speculate about, and might even have been able to demonstrate, a relation between these various 1792 and 1793 Epictetuses, perhaps showing that Clarkin's item 122 (1793) is really a reissue of 1792 with a new title-page and old sheets while the unmentioned 1793 edition found at The Library Company represents a new setting, perhaps of the whole, perhaps only of the Latin translation. (I have *not* made such a demonstration. I am only suggesting one possible explanation for what I have seen.) But on this matter, a basic desideratum for a descriptive bibliography, Clarkin is silent. (Mr. Green, Curator of Printed Books at The Library Company of Philadelphia, provided me not only with this example but also with extensive guidance through the thicket of Carey bibliography. He permitted me to consult both his annotated copy of Clarkin and several of The Library Company's numerous Carey holdings. See, in addition to his review of Clarkin, Green's *Mathew Carey: Publisher and Patriot* [Philadelphia, 1985], which places Carey in his context as a pioneer American publisher.)

Some other problems might be more briefly mentioned. Clarkin omits Evans 34146, Jedidiah Morse's *Geography made easy*, 6th ed. (Boston, 1798), a Thomas and Andrews imprint "sold by . . . M. Carey, Philadelphia," as its title-page informs us. (It belongs on p. 55, between items 321 and 322.) Carey did not print this book. But Clarkin lists other books not printed but only sold by Carey, including Thomas and Andrews's 1813, 1814, and 1816 editions of Morse (items 755, 802, and 920). Why omit 1798? Carey frequently acted as a retail bookseller for others; Green shows that, during his career, Carey grew increasingly to function like a publisher in the modern sense of that word. Books such as Morse thus illuminate an important aspect of his activities.

Clarkin mentions a ghost (item 9, p. 2), "An epistle to Mr. Eleqzer [sic] Oswald" (Evans 19539), identified "from an advertisement." The advertisement's location might have interested a reader. Did Clarkin feel that, since Evans cites its location, he had no need to repeat it?

It is unnecessary to go on. Clarkin's book must be approached with considerable caution. But it is the only extant guide to Carey's publications through 1824, and it serves a real need.

Example 2

Special collections need not concern themselves solely with the antiquarian. They may, and frequently do, attempt to gather modern publications; their interest in modern manuscripts is well known. Most often, we may suppose, the modern imprints they collect are privately-printed or artists' books. But some rare book collections attempt to speculate in contemporary authors or groups of authors (e.g., Philip Roth; Latin-American novelists; women poets). Others may choose a current field to concentrate on while its literature is still growing (e.g., the experience of Americans of Oriental extraction; the local effects of urban renewal programs; space exploration). One current field that has attracted relatively widespread interest is the literature—both historical and imaginative—of the Vietnam War.

In 1973, Michael Wolfe published *Man On a String* (New York). A mystery, Wolfe's book concerns an American correspondent caught up in the war. It qualifies as a Vietnam novel, but goes unmentioned by John Newman, *Vietnam War Literature: An annotated bibliography of imaginative works about Americans fighting in Vietnam* (Metuchen, NJ, 1982). Another novel by Wolfe, *The Two-Star Pigeon*, published two years after *Man On a String*, is mentioned. Both novels were published by a major trade publisher.

Newman's item 42 is Joe W. Haldeman's *War Year* (New York, 1972; Newman also mentions a 1978 Pocket Books reprint). Newman's annotation offers a succinct summary of Haldeman's plot:

> John Farmer, a nineteen-year old draftee, is sent to the central highlands . . . as a combat engineer. . . . He makes friends, engages in battle, and is wounded. After recovering from his wounds, Farmer is assigned as a supply clerk in a rear area, but he fails to salute the jeep of a brigadier general and is sent back to the field as punishment. He is killed in an ambush while trying to clear a landing zone for a helicopter. . . . (p. 23)

Only with great difficulty can one conceive a purpose for this annotation, a sort of *Cliff's Notes* version of Haldeman's plot apparently suited only to someone anxious to avoid reading his book. But even putting aside the question of its utility, this particular example is, if not exactly wrong, then certainly incomplete.

In Haldeman's 1972 novel, John Farmer does *not* get "killed in an ambush." After having ended his 365-day tour "pushing papers in the supply room" (p. 120), Farmer is back "in the world," at home in the States, receiving a letter from the parents of a friend who was killed. I guess that, instead of the 1972 Holt first edition, Newman read the 1978 Pocket Book paperback to which his entry also refers. I have not myself located a copy of that "reprint." But I have seen a 1984 Avon mass-market paperback edition in which Farmer's first-person narration stops quite suddenly on page 107, while page 108 describes the delivery of a telegram to Mrs. Beatrice Farmer in a small Oklahoma town. In 1984, John Farmer *is* dead, as he was not in 1972. Without having seen the 1978 edition, I can only hypothesize that Haldeman revised his 1972 Holt novel for its 1978 Pocket Book appearance which the 1984 Avon reprint was later to follow; and I further guess that Newman read 1978 without suspecting that it represented a revision of 1972. But users of bibliographies normally think it the job of a bibliographer to supply them with information about revisions, especially if the bibliographer cites various editions of a work and thus implies that he or she has seen all of them.

I have already quoted one sample of Newman's plot summaries and suggested some doubt about their purpose. Let me simply assert that, when Newman rises from summary to "literary criticism," his annotations do not rise with him.

Newman's book may aid students, readers, or librarians with an interest in the imaginative literature of the Vietnam War. But it requires at least as much caution as Clarkin's *Mathew Carey* and I, at least, fail to be convinced that it will prove as useful.

Example 3

In the spring of 1985, a historian of bindings visited the University of Pennsylvania Library seeking examples of Italian Renaissance bookbindings. The Special Collections Department at Penn has no guide to its bindings. Two members of the staff therefore accompanied the historian into the normally closed Special Collections stacks to assist his work as best they could while also overseeing the security of the collections. I was one of them. During the afternoon I showed the historian a sumptuous Italian Renaissance binding on a Venice 1481 imprint, an apparently unique copy of a vernacular romance on Charlemagne.

To my embarrassment, the binding was not Italian. It was Spanish. (I am relieved that it at least came from the right period.) As the afternoon wore on, the historian found numerous examples of Spanish Renaissance bindings on our books, more, he said (perhaps politely) than he had ever seen in one place before, outside Spain. Neither our predecessors nor my colleagues and I knew we had them; and I, as is obvious, would not have recognized them as such in the first place.

My Department collects books and manuscripts. But we do not buy books for their bindings. That is the province of such repositories as The Pierpont Morgan Library or the Spencer Collection (NYPL) in New York. Our readers seem to be quite as happy with a book in an ordinary binding as with one in a sumptuous binding. Since fine bindings are neither a specialty nor a requirement the additional expense of sumptuous bindings is one we choose not to bear.

But we have bindings of remarkable quality and interest anyway. Most collections of older books do. They are cared for, if that is the word, by curators many of whom are (like me) vastly ignorant about this decorative art, even though, in the course of preparing for work in special collections librarianship, we may have spent a few weeks studying the history of bookbinding. If a librarian wants to learn more about the history of bookbinding, in order to identify, access, and care for the significant bindings in the collections for which he or she is responsible, how does that librarian proceed?

Short of spending a great deal of time in a variety of scattered printed sources on various national schools and individual binders, as well as examining as many bindings as possible, that librarian doesn't. There is no adequate single history of binding to consult.

There are monographs, as well as articles and notes. *The Book Collector* regularly prints a very short essay on a binding, one in each issue, by people such as the late Howard Nixon and, now, Mirjam Foot and others. E. Ph. Goldschmidt published a two-volume work on *Gothic and Renaissance Bookbindings* in 1928. Paul Needham's *Twelve Centuries of Bookbindings 400–1600* appeared from the Morgan Library some years ago (New York, 1979). Dorothy Miner's great Walters catalogue, *The History of Bookbinding 525–1950 A.D.*, appeared in 1957 (Baltimore). The Bodleian's catalogue of *Fine Bindings 1500–1700 from Oxford Libraries* appeared in 1968 (Oxford). Bernard C. Middleton has written *A History of English Craft Bookbinding Technique* (New York, 1963, with later reprints). Nixon's studies of Grolier's bindings (London, 1965), *English Restoration Bookbindings* (London, 1974), and *Five Centuries of English Bookbinding* (London, 1978) may be consulted. There are several enormously expensive, and generally out-of-print, studies of fine binders by Nixon, A. R. A. Hobson, and others, to say nothing of European studies at least equally difficult to locate.

The literature of fine and important bookbinding is fugitive or prohibitively costly. In addition, as Philip Gaskell remarks, "there is no general work on trade binding in the hand-press period" (*A New Introduction to Bibliography*, Oxford, 1974, p. 308). Despite the work of scholars such as Ruari McLean and Sue Allen, the situation for the machine-press period is little better.

The student of American binding faces similar troubles. Hellmut Lehmann-Haupt edited a collection of essays on the subject in 1967. The Morgan published a catalogue of Michael Papantonio's collection of early American bindings now at the American Antiquarian Society (New York, 1972; a second edition has been announced [Charlottesville, 1985] but I have not yet seen it). *Bookbinding in America 1680–1910*, based on the collection of Frederick E. Maser, was published by the Bryn Mawr College Library in 1983. As this essay was being written, the American Antiquarian Society published seven essays by Hannah D. French, *Bookbinding in Early America*, containing Willman Spawn's catalogue of bookbinding tools (Worcester, 1986). One historian of whom I am aware is at work on a monograph concerning early American bookbinding, but the subject's difficulties are indicated by the fact that his files presently contain more than 18,000 rubbings. Some 6,000 represent early work, before the historian was able certainly to distinguish between American and British bindings. The field is tricky.

This subject cries out for synthesis, even granting that much of the monographic spadework on which a truly useful synthesis must be based has yet to appear. Works on bindings, however, are expensive propositions for a publisher to undertake—they *must* be extensively illustrated in order to be useful—and their market appears to be, at best, specialized and therefore severely limited. The publisher willing to attempt an introductory survey has yet to be found. The best one can point to is the altogether inadequate survey by Edith Diehl in *Bookbinding*, originally published in 1946 and now available in paperback (New York, 1980). Much of Diehl is devoted to techniques, not history. As history, Diehl is in any case rather out of date.

For special collections, as already suggested, reference works need not only be places in which one looks things up. They may also be discursive studies of subjects—bookbinding; the history of a collection now largely dispersed, such as the Bibliotheca Lindesiana; the impact of the introduction of printing in the Renaissance—which help to make sense of the selection and arrangement of materials in closed-stack collections. Such works therefore assist the librarian or user in promoting or gaining a new kind of access to these resources. Imaginative publishers might well perceive a history of the development of bookbinding as possessing potential appeal to an art history as well as a bibliographical audience. Numerous libraries might find it possible to use such a work as the basis for improved study of this aspect of their own holdings, making them accessible from a new point of view to a new user community. So far, at any rate, no publisher has. The necessary reference tool remains to be written.

II

Present funding levels at many libraries affect the publication of reference works, particularly of special collections-oriented reference works which occasionally require more expensive means of production than those intended for other library uses. When Nicolas Barker's recent study of early Greek typography appeared for $500 (*Aldus Manutius and the Development of Greek Script & Type in the Fifteenth Century* [Sandy Hook, CT, 1985]), many librarians must have paused before leaping to their acquisitions terminals. Such pauses are increasingly common as the prices of reference books continue to mount.

In 1980, the Libraries of the Claremont Colleges published five hundred copies of a fine catalogue of *The Herbert Clark Hoover Collection of Mining and Metallurgy* (Claremont, CA) for the noteworthy price of $125. In the same year, Hans Schmoller's edition of Giovanni Mardersteig's *The Officina Bodoni: An Account of the Work of a Hand Press 1923-1977* appeared for $95 (Verona). The next year, two volumes of Stanley Morison's *Selected Essays* appeared from Cambridge for $275.

These prices were not cheap then. They remain worth mentioning. I have written about such prices in a somewhat different connection elsewhere ("Books about Books," in *Rare Books 1983-84: Trends, Collections, Sources*, ed. Alice D. Schreyer, New York, 1984, pp. 81-2). Even if they represent the high end of the scale, such prices nonetheless indicate that libraries must be quite cautious about the value of the reference works for which they spend their money, no matter how much they need such works. Limited acquisitions funds for reference materials would mandate such caution in any event. But special collections need to budget not only for current but also for retrospective reference books, some very much more expensive than their modern counterparts—and no less important. Moreover, for the larger libraries of which rare book departments are only a part, reference books may have to be purchased in duplicate: one copy for general reference (or the stacks), a second for the rare book department's reference collection (where its accessibility will most frequently be strictly curtailed). Such duplication of already expensive materials can become *very* expensive very quickly.

If the three different sorts of negative examples I have provided can be accepted as representative, then libraries are not at present consistently receiving value commensurate with the money they are spending. Needed reference tools too frequently prove either flawed (Clarkin) or inadequate (Newman) upon close examination—or they are not being produced at all (bookbinding history). Several factors help to account for this state of affairs. These include the shift in the locus of much reference publication away from the university press to the specialist publishers who aim their wares at the library market; the shrinkage of acquisitions funds; the inability of most libraries to fund reference publications based on their own holdings; and the difficulty of doing highly specialized bibliographical research. Bibliographers whose memories we now venerate seem, alive, to have been peculiar folk; and they had an unhappy habit of dying before their projects came to completion. Finding their successors is not always easy: the precedents are, from some points of view, not the most engaging of role models.

With some exceptions—the Pittsburgh Series in Bibliography (of American authors) edited by Matthew J. Bruccoli and the Soho bibliographies now issued by Oxford come quickly to mind as examples—much bibliographical publication no longer originates in the university presses but rather in the library press. Houses like Garland, Greenwood, G. K. Hall, Scarecrow, and their like perform a real and a valuable service in publishing the reference books they do. Pressures on all publishers make it increasingly difficult even to complain about the physical appearance of many library press products, frequently offset from reduced typescript, although such complaints used to be common. This form of publication is no longer restricted to one end of the publishing world (see, e.g., Oxford University Press's 1984 edition of *The Works of Thomas Vaughan*, edited by Alan Rudrum and Jennifer Drake-Brockman).

Nonetheless, even if some of the differences between them are slowly disappearing, library presses are not like university presses and do not behave as though they were. Most obviously, library presses tend to have a contract with an author in advance of the delivery of his or her manuscript. They also have a certain amount of product to get into the marketplace in order to justify their overhead. Thus they face real pressures to regard peer review very differently from academic presses, with their own and their institutional reputations to maintain and academics to whom their managers report. As this essay was being written, I spoke with a person under contract to one library publisher. That firm's in-house editor had recently told him that it was company policy to read only the first of several introductions to works intended for inclusion in a bibliographical series. No substantive critical or scholarly reading of later introductions would follow, if the first proved acceptable.

Much of what is troublesome about Clarkin's *Carey* could have been caught by a qualified reviewer and careful editing long before publication. The need for his work would have been clear. The merits of much of what he had chosen to include would also have been clear. He might have been advised to avoid such excrescences as the inclusion of ghosts in his main series (they ought to have been relegated to an appendix) or the citation of notoriously incomplete location reports from Evans and *NUC*. A good deal more work distinguishing between variant issues and states might have been suggested to him, while proper editorial assistance might also have turned up some of the Evans entries for Carey publications which he missed (see Green's review) or other inconsistencies in his work. (Just to have unburdened his text of its typos would have improved it.) Such efforts might have added considerably to the time it took Clarkin to finish his work. University presses are frequently willing to demand that their authors take the time necessary to improve a manuscript in which they are interested. One hears from too many sources to discount the rumor as merely anecdotal that the library press does not always demonstrate similar patience. In this case, improvement of the finished product would have been worth the additional time. However, vigorous review and editorial attention add to any press's production costs. They would thus add too to the prices which publishers have to charge for their product (already high). Higher prices would cut into their market (already thin). More careful review and editing may not, therefore, seem easily justified to library publishers. Their absence, unfortunately, seems to permit the appearance not only of flawed works, such as Clarkin's, but also of works very nearly useless, such as Newman's. Even more unfortunately, a poor product attracts other poor products while scaring off the creators of good ones.

This is not merely a theoretical problem. One bibliographer of my acquaintance has turned down a contract with a library publisher precisely in order to seek the expert services of the readers which an academic publisher routinely provides. This bibliographer is willing to take additional time on the project, now several years in the making, in order to accommodate the suggestions for improvements or alterations which such readers may make. The eventual utility of the publication, this bibliographer feels, will more than compensate for whatever additional work is eventually required. By contrast, although specialist readers are also retained by library presses, their suggestions and criticisms seem to carry far less weight than those offered by their readers to academic presses. Both from authors and from reviewers for library presses, one hears of suggestions and criticisms brushed aside in the rush to see the product into print. Such comments are also anecdotal, to be sure. They are, however, remorselessly consistent. Less editorial assistance is apparently provided library press authors than that which academic houses normally supply their authors, and the library press also apparently curtails the effect of scholarly readers's reports. The library press product suffers as a result.

Nonetheless, whatever the deficiencies of the products which library presses put forth, academic presses are not rushing to fill a vacuum of quality in the bibliographical or reference book field. They have their reasons. One university press officer, considering a second edition of the bibliography of a living author active in many fields and with a large public following, recently reported to me that the publisher of the first edition of the bibliography in question (a major New York trade publisher) had sold some seven hundred copies since the volume appeared in the very early 1970s. This is not a field for big bucks. The library press manages to squeak by not because of economies of scale attained through large sales volume but rather because costs are calculated very sharply and relatively tiny press runs priced so as to turn a profit (they hope) on closely-figured anticipated sales. (Clarkin, for example, is priced at $60. The number of libraries which require a copy of the book is not high; the number of individuals is very small.)

Some university presses have good luck with bibliographical publications. Cornell, for instance, published the catalogue of the Morgan Library's exhibition, drawn from Gordon N. Ray's collection, of *The Art of the French Illustrated Book 1700 to 1914* (1982). At $185, the two volumes were clearly not a casual purchase; in addition, they competed against a two-volume paperback edition distributed by the Morgan itself for less than a third of the hardbound price. Even so, a Cornell University Press representative informed me that the edition was just about exhausted within a year of its appearance, and the catalogue has begun to appear among the offerings of booksellers specializing in antiquarian bibliography for considerably more than its published price. Of course, between them, Ray and his cataloguer (Thomas V. Lange, then of the Morgan Library) produced what one reviewer called "the most comprehensive history of French book illustration for the period it covers" (Marie E. Korey, in *PBSA*, 79:4 [1985], 547). For research libraries, the book was a prize. But one rather suspects that, viewed from university press offices, its success was something of a surprise and not a harbinger of resurgent demand in the bibliographical marketplace.

From a librarian's point of view, the current high prices, and anticipated limitations on the quality, of many reference books require a gingerly approach to their purchase. From publishers' perspectives, the limited funds at libraries' disposal make reference publications even riskier ventures than they have been in the past. Few sales at best are all they can anticipate. (This factor affects other forms of publication than reference books alone. The author of an important study of a major English author, published by a university press of considerable stature, told me—some four years after his book's appearance, by which time its literally revolutionary stature was widely recognized within his well-populated subspecialty—that slightly more than nine hundred copies of his book had been sold. That is not a figure markedly superior to the seven hundred-copy sales figure achieved by the author bibliography mentioned earlier. I might add that the book was published for less than $15; its price could have represented a stumbling-block to very few of its potential purchasers.)

The library press, which specializes in supplying what it perceives as the needs of the library community, is better able to calculate its market than the university press, which lacks this specialized orientation. Publishing for historical, scientific, literary, and, occasionally, the trade communities, as well as for libraries, university presses cannot anticipate sales of bibliographical publications as closely as the specialists. But they have every reason to be as aware of the restraints on library acquisitions funds as any other publisher. That they publish relatively few bibliographical works is thus hardly astonishing.

Those bibliographies that they do publish may be enumerative. The Pittsburgh and Oxford series mentioned above exemplify the best of such publications. So too does such a non-series bibliography as Thomas R. Adams's study of British pamphlets about the American rebellion, 1764–1783, *The American Controversy* (Providence, 1980).

Much university press bibliographical publication, however, tends to be discursive: books which special collections libraries may require even though they are not traditional "reference" books. (They are instead the sort of book which a history of bookbinding would be.) Examples, in addition to the books on British fine printing by Harrop and Bellamy or on early printing by Hellinga and Eisenstein already mentioned, include such studies as Miriam Usher Chrisman's *Lay Culture, Learned Culture: Books and Social Change in Strasbourg, 1480–1599* (New Haven, 1982), or Robert Darnton's *The Business of Enlightenment: A Publishing History of the Encyclopédie 1775–1800* (Cambridge, MA, 1979). These studies may be accompanied by a more traditionally enumerative reference book: see, e.g., the companion volume to Chrisman's *Lay Culture*, her *Bibliography of Strasbourg Imprints, 1480–1599* (New Haven, 1982). But one wonders if this volume would have seen daylight over Yale's imprint unaccompanied by the discursive book published simultaneously with it.

The mere fact of university press auspices for such publications, whether enumerative or discursive, is no guarantee of a work's quality, of course. I have published critical reviews of both Eisenstein and Chrisman (see *Printing History*, 4 [1982], 71–73, for Eisenstein, and 6 [1984], 28–30, for Chrisman), and I have not (to my knowledge) been noticeably idiosyncratic in my views of these studies. University press-published enumerative bibliographies are perhaps more generally successful than discursive bibliographical studies—if one may hazard such a generalization at all—and it sometimes appears to me that one reason for this state of affairs is that the discursive publications in this field are often produced by scholars who, like Eisenstein and Chrisman, may possess fine historical skills but no similar qualifications in bibliography itself. Such scholars are naturally inclined to publish through university presses, and their readers are likely to come from their historical fields, not out of bibliography. I do not want to push this notion too hard, however; and one must bear in mind that a percentage of the scholarship in any field at all, whatever its auspices, will eventually be found to have limited utility. Moreover, their limitations to the contrary notwithstanding, such publications are both valuable in themselves and welcome prods to the investigation of bibliographical subjects by other scholars; and the importance of a work even with the flaws of Eisenstein's is beyond question.

Libraries themselves offer an alternative to publication of reference tools by either university or library publishers. Several books mentioned above are library publications. These include the Bodleian catalogue of *Fine Bindings* and the British Library catalogues of the bindings of Jean Grolier and English Restoration bookbindings. More recent examples include the American Antiquarian Society's 1986 publication, also mentioned above, of Hannah D. French and Willman Spawn on *Bookbinding in Early America* or The British Library's 1984 publication of Marianne Tidcombe's *The Bookbindings of T. J. Cobden-Sanderson*. These are more or less elaborate publications. Most library-produced publications are exhibition catalogues, normally distinguished by considerable modesty of presentation. (Marie E. Korey has surveyed some recent library exhibition catalogues in *The Papers of the Bibliographical Society of America*, 79:4 [1985], 543–66).

Many such publications are collection-specific, informative about the resources of the issuing institution. Exemplary of the best in this kind is Roger S. Wieck's *Late Medieval and Renaissance Illuminated Manuscripts 1350–1525 in The Houghton Library* (Cambridge, MA, 1983). Some libraries are able to issue more general studies or references. Tidcombe's study of Cobden-Sanderson's bookbindings is not limited to British Library holdings alone. John Plummer's *The Last Flowering* (New York, 1983), a catalogue of French illuminated manuscripts, 1420–1530, is not limited to the Pierpont Morgan Library's Collections. The Library of Congress's 1983 collection of essays on *The Early Illustrated Book*, though rooted in the Lessing J. Rosenwald Collection, is not limited to the contents of that donation.

The funding available to most libraries is, however, severely restricted. Active library publication programs are as a consequence relatively few in number. For similar reasons, the vast majority of library publications are ephemeral in nature, typically the exhibition catalogue, paperbound and cheaply printed or offset from typescript. Such a publication may be superb. But it can all too easily sink without a trace. Such a fate seems to have fallen on Margaret A. Howell and Charles F. Mullett's *English Dissent: Catalogue to an Exhibition of Eighteenth Century Pamphlets* (Columbia, MO, 1979), which deserved far wider publicity and circulation than it received.

Clearly, the most exciting prospects for special collections reference work are presented by the online databases. This form is not one which we normally think of as "publication" (although the controversy which arose a while ago over OCLC's copyright of its records indicates that some people have been faster thinkers than others about these matters.)

From my point of view, the availability of, for instance, the ESTC records online through RLIN constitutes publication, and a far more useful form of publication than their presentation in print might have provided. The development of a format for archives and manuscripts control (AMC), a database also available through RLIN, is similar in effect. Like ESTC, which, when it is completed, will change the ways in which English and American eighteenth-century imprints are accessed, AMC will change in altogether fundamental ways the reference environment of manuscript collections and their users. As this essay is being written, libraries and other repositories have entered some 50,000 records into the RLIN AMC database. Anecdotal evidence is already beginning to accumulate about the impact of this superb reference tool on researchers. Anyone who works in a manuscript collection or archive knows the acute limitations of the other available manuscript reference tools. *NUCMC* and *American Literary Manuscripts*, to mention only two of the large number of such tools, have many virtues along with some faults; but whatever their virtues, they represent only the tip of the archival iceberg in a fixed, non-manipulable, and at best awkwardly cumulative form. These limits, at least, an online database overleaps at a bound. AMC's 50,000 records may represent American manuscript resources somewhat less impressively than a single grain of sand alleged to stand for Rehobeth Beach. But these records are growing at an ever-increasing pace, and they can be searched jointly, as well as rapidly, making it possible to search many repositories simultaneously for as complete a sense of available records as can be hoped for.

The great OCLC and RLIN databases themselves, while in the main containing records only of recent acquisitions and thus of recent imprints, are constantly enriched by the addition of records from retrospective conversion projects and the slow but ongoing original cataloguing of older materials. These databases too offer at least a distant prospect of online records for author, title, and subject searches useful in ways not now possible to those whose work engages them with the records of the past.

III

I have been critical of library press reference publications. I do not wish to seem to have tarred them all with the same brush; they produce good and useful books along with flawed and imperfect ones. I have been only a bit less critical of reference publications spawned by university presses. Libraries themselves have made important, if sometimes ill-produced and poorly distributed, contributions in the service of their own reference needs, despite generally underfinanced publication programs.

In the online databases which library networks have cooperated in creating and maintaining, however, and in the special files which these databases are beginning to contain, much of the future of special as well as of general collections reference publication seems to lie. Discursive reference tools—the histories of bookbinding and their friends—will not emerge from the databases, to be sure. These need to be encouraged and patiently nurtured. It will surely prove as difficult for libraries to fund bibliographical research by bibliographers and librarians as it is for them to fund library publications. But the publicly-accessible and easily-manipulable records of library holdings which the databases carry, indifferent to whether they represent old, new, printed, or handwritten holdings, offer good news for the reference needs of the rare book and manuscript community.

In this electronic environment our reference tools will increasingly be built, almost the incidental byproduct of the creation of national databases intended first and foremost to serve the needs of users of current materials. Despite the segregation of certain classes of materials into specialized ghetto databases such as AMC and ESTC, records of older materials will coexist in the online databases alongside records of the new, printed alongside the handwritten. Thus we may become increasingly aware of the essential indivisibility of library resources now segregated by format or age. Reference—and research—should both benefit as a result.

New Reference Sources on Women: An Analysis and Proposal

Helen B. Josephine
Deborah K. Blouin

Women's studies as a field has continued to grow from 16 courses offered in 1969 to over 20,000 courses in 1982.[1] An undergraduate major in women's studies is offered in 54 out of 11,131 two-year colleges.[2]

Keeping pace with this increase in courses has been the publishing of reference works in women's studies. The Office of Women's Studies at the University of Wisconsin compiles an annual list of reference works related to women—in 1983, thirty-two works were included; in both 1984 and 1985, thirty-seven were listed.[3]

The continual interest in "women" as a subject of research is also collaborated by the growth of the collections of the Arthur and Elizabeth Schlesinger Library on the History of Women. In 1973 the manuscript inventories and catalogs of the Schlesinger Library were published by G. K. Hall in three volumes; the 1984 edition is in ten volumes and is "testimony to the growth of scholarly interest in social history, in the history of women, and in the broader interdisciplinary area of women's studies."[4]

In this essay the authors will discuss publishing of reference works in women's studies, by analyzing current reference sources in women's studies and by suggesting areas where new works are needed. Of the 74 reference sources in women's studies published in 1984 and 1985, ten were chosen for analysis because they are representative of the wide variety of reference books published in women's studies.

Helen Josephine is a Reference Librarian, and Deborah Blouin is the Women Studies Specialist and Reference Librarian at the Hayden Library Arizona State University, Tempe, AZ 85287.

© 1987 by The Haworth Press, Inc. All rights reserved.

CRITERIA

The criteria outlined by Katz in *Introduction to Reference Work*, third ed., were used to analyze these works.[5] Five areas must be considered—purpose, authority, scope, proposed audience, and format. The purpose of the work is usually stated in the preface or can be deduced from the table of contents or other introductory material. The author's qualifications and sources used to compile the work constitute authority. Scope and timeliness of the work are also usually stated in the preface or promotional material. The audience is the field of scholars who will find the work useful and of course, the general public. The format of the work can be the most critical. Poor arrangement, lack of indexes and appendixes will make even the most scholarly or fact-filled work totally useless.

The overall purpose of the ten reference sources chosen for analysis is to help researchers in the field of women's studies. After passing this first test, they were examined more closely. Seven of the ten were found to be outstanding examples of reference works, three were found to be lacking in one or more critical areas.

OUTSTANDING SOURCES

Each of the seven sources filled a specific need in the literature of women's studies, whether because it filled a void, as in the *Women's Poetry Index*; *The Women's Annual: The Year in Review*; and the *Women of the World* series; because a new edition was needed, as in *The New Our Bodies, Ourselves* and *Films for, by and about Women*; or because a new approach was appropriate for the topic, as in the *Dictionary of Women Artists* and *Women's Legal Rights in the United States*.

Librarians are numerous among the contributors to the *Women's Poetry Index*, *The Women's Annual*, the *Dictionary of Women Artists*, and *Women's Legal Rights*. The background and expertise of librarians is appropriate for the compilation of these works. The reliability of the *Women of the World* series and *The New Our Bodies, Ourselves* is affirmed by the stature of the groups which compiled and published the sources: the U.S. Department of Commerce, Bureau of the Census and the U.S. Agency for International Development, Office of Women in Development, along with the national statistical offices of the countries themselves for the *Women of the World* series and the Boston Women's Health Book Collective for *The New Our Bodies, Ourselves*.

The scope of the seven works is clear and reasonable. In the case where the title of the book appears to be attempting the impossible, as in *Dictionary of Women Artists*, *Women of the World*, and *Films for, by and about Women*, the author explains the parameters of the work. The *Dictionary of Women Artists* contains information about 21,000 painters, sculptors, printmakers and illustrators who were born before 1900. The introductions of *Women of the World* state that the information in the series is about women in developing countries. There is a separate book for most regions of the world and the chartbook brings all the material together for an overview. A sincere attempt has been made to include comparable information which has been collected by the national statistical office of each country. The author of *Films for, by and about Women* states in the foreword that her book lists "current productions, exceptional in content and in technical and artistic quality."[6] She also explains that she wants to list women filmmakers and their works.

The format of the seven reference works is excellent. Indexes appear in the sources where they are needed, and in several sources indexes provide access to information which enhances the value of the work. In the *Women's Poetry Index* the main entry for each poem appears in the "Poet Index" and not in the first line section. This arrangement allows the user to see at a glance how many places a poet's work has been published. Biographical information about the poets in the anthologies is indicated by an asterisk. In addition, the *Women's Poetry Index* includes the ISBN and Library of Congress card numbers for the anthologies indexed. The subject index of *Films for, by and about Women* includes entries for types of films (experimental, feature, documentary, and short). Each *Women's Annual* has an index, allowing access by subject, name, organization, and book title to each of the essays in the volume, greatly enhancing the usefulness of the work.

The bibliographies in these seven reference sources provide lists of the sources which were consulted in creating the work, as in the *Women's Poetry Index* and the *Dictionary of Women Artists*; or a list of sources consulted, notes of explanation, and sources of further reading as in *The New Our Bodies, Ourselves*. In the *Women of the World* series, notes are provided which explain the data, and bibliographic citations lead the user to studies and sources with more information. *The Women's Annual* contains several types of bibliographic information. All articles contain a list of references and a bibliography, some of these are annotated and some of the articles themselves are bibliographic essays on the scholarship in a field.

INADEQUATE SOURCES

Three sources were found to be weak or inadequate: *The Europa Biographical Dictionary of British Women*; *A Dictionary of Sexist Quotations*; and *The Woman's Encyclopedia of Myths and Secrets*.

The Europa Biographical Dictionary of British Women does fulfill its intention to include British women "whose place in history is recognized" or "whose work has had some sort of public impact."[7] However, the work would have been far more useful if the publishers had included indexes by subject, occupation, and time period as well as a standardized list of sources cited.

A Dictionary of Sexist Quotations and *The Woman's Encyclopedia of Myths and Secrets* suffer from a more fatal flaw—lack of scholarship. The only credential listed for the compiler of *Sexist Quotations* is "lecturer in economics." The introduction gives no clues about the purpose or scope of the work. The compiler offers no definition of sexism, or what unifying theme was used to choose quotations. As a result the work has no focus—entries are uneven, some pro-women and women's rights, some anti-women and women's rights. In all, the work is a classic example of a publisher jumping on the women's studies "bandwagon."

The Woman's Encyclopedia of Myths and Secrets has some of the same problems. No credentials are listed at all for the author, and no preface or introductory material is included. While the work is impressive in size and fascinating to browse, some of the secondary sources are out of date, information has been taken out of context, and the author has chosen to support the "sensationalist or minority view."[8] What could have been a standard source in women's studies for the areas of religion, folklore, and mythology is reduced to a coffee table book.

Are the publishers of these last three books unaware of the high calibre of scholarship and research in women's studies? Don't they realize that reference works that excel in the criteria listed above are in demand? Cost-cutting in book design means fewer indexes and appendixes—frequently the major difference between a useful reference tool and one that sits on the shelf. All too often publishers grasp at any opportunity to get a "women's book" in their catalog without checking the credentials or authority of the author.

NEW REFERENCE SOURCES IN WOMEN'S STUDIES

Beaubien, Hogan, and George in their book, *Learning the Library* discuss the development of a discipline and its corresponding reference tools. As a discipline matures from the pioneering stage to being accepted as an established field, the reference tools also evolve. In the pioneering stage, researchers must use standard indexes, bibliographies, and subject headings which may or may not be appropriate for the search. Once a field becomes established, guidebooks, histories, biographical sources, subject bibliographies, dissertation bibliographies, subject encyclopedias, and subject-specific indexing and abstracting sources become available.[9] Women's studies is a field which has become established—degrees are awarded in women's studies; research centers on women have been funded; specialized conferences of scholars convene annually; federal research grants are available. In some areas, however, the reference sources in women's studies have not evolved.

Gates, in *Guide to the Use of Books and Libraries*, outlines the characteristics of subject-specific reference materials:

1. They supplement general reference books by giving more specific information and by including specialized information omitted from the general reference sources.
2. They provide specialized definitions and explanations for the words and phrases in a given field which are not found in general word dictionaries.
3. They trace the growth of important ideas in a subject area.
4. They provide an introduction to the development of the literature of the subject.
5. They give authoritative information on major questions and issues in a specialized area.
6. They explain and clarify concepts.
7. They locate, describe, and evaluate the literature of the field.
8. They provide facts which indicate trends, and they summarize the events of a given year in a given subject field.[10]

After analyzing the current reference sources in women's studies as an established field and comparing them to this outline, four areas were found where new works are needed: statistical sources, encyclopedias, yearbooks, and abstracting and indexing sources including databases. This is certainly not an exhaustive list of sources that need to be published in women's studies. However, the lack of adequate sources in these four areas has hampered research and frustrated librarians for years.

STATISTICS

There is a need for a reference work which will bring together in one source social, demographic, economic, political, and military statistics on women in the United States and all the other nations of the world. The data should provide well-balanced and comparable information on women which is fully documented and presented in an integrated and logical format.

The sources of statistics on women which already exist have many limitations. Several works are out of date, the *Handbook of International Data on Women* by Boulding, *Women in Public Office* compiled by the Center for the American Woman and Politics, and *A Statistical Report of Women in the United States: 1978* published by the U.S. Department of Commerce, Bureau of the Census. In addition, the *Handbook of International Data on Women* is fragmented and difficult to use. The *Women of the World* series, while excellent for the countries it does cover, does not include the United States, Canada, the Soviet Union, Western Europe or some small Soviet-dominated nations.

In a book of statistics on women, demographic data should include population growth and distribution, including migration; longevity, fertility, and mortality; and marital status and living arrangements. The social statistics should provide data about the education of girls and women, about minority women, the health of women including mental health, birth control, and abortion, and women and girls as criminal offenders and as victims of crime.

Economic data should provide information about employment and occupations, volunteerism and self-employment, income, poverty and welfare, credit and women as consumers. Political statistics should include women as candidates and officeholders as well as voters. Military statistics, providing information on a worldwide basis from the standpoint of employment as well as defense, would also be useful.

The statistical material in each section should be introduced by a narrative statement which gives an overview of the material and then explains the general trends as well as the unique aspects or significant problems in the data. Each chart, table, figure, and map should have a title and a citation for the source of information which is presented. Footnotes which explain missing or inconsistently-reported data would also be useful.

A bibliography of sources which were consulted for compilation of the statistics and resources for further research should be provided and arranged by compiler—United Nations, U.S. Government, foreign governments, other agencies and publishers.

Appendixes which discuss the sources of data, tables which represent the data in different or more detailed ways than the main body of the book, lists of abbreviations, definitions of terms, and sample questionnaires are often included in superior statistical works.

Indexing for country, region, ethnic group, age group, occupation, and for subjects is an imperative feature of this hypothetical statistical source if it is to be used to its greatest potential.

ENCYCLOPEDIAS

A subject encyclopedia, an integrated account of the entire scope of women's studies in one reference work, is long overdue. This source should be composed of lengthy signed articles with bibliographies. The body of knowledge in women's studies is extensive enough today to produce a multi-volume encyclopedia, encompassing women's studies as a research field, feminist theory, and general topics of interest to women. Indexes for subjects, names and organizations are a necessity, and a glossary may be an appropriate feature.

The editorial board and the contributors should be experts in their fields. Care should be taken to avoid a social science emphasis; topics in the humanities and performing arts, law, the sciences and medicine should also be included.

The development of the areas of research in the field of women's studies from the historical perspective up through current research interests of contemporary scholars should be covered so that the final product provides comprehensive historical and current coverage.

Topics which need to be covered in this encyclopedia are the history of women and important issues such as the Equal Rights Amendment and the women's movement in the United States and the world. A chronology which lists the dates and descriptions of events and issues which document the progress of women worldwide is needed. Traditional biographical articles should be included and the achievements of important individuals and groups should be given, for example, the year women were granted the vote in each nation; the awards to women of prizes from scientific, medical, literary and other societies; the major contributions of women in war, peace and politics. Women's participation in sports, in geographical and space exploration, as well as their success in business should be documented.

A social history of women should be included, documenting the changes women have made in their lives which in turn have changed the course of women's experience as a group. Participants in this process are those women who have pioneered new fields, those who have made changes or are in traditionally women-dominated fields and those women who chose the primary role of caregiver/homemaker. Current issues and trends facing women need to be identified and their implications assessed.

This encyclopedia is the source where one should find information about women's organizations, social and volunteer, political, labor and professional. The fight for equal pay, pay equity and other issues in the workplace needs documentation. Sexual harassment, new-parent leave for men, E.E.O.C. suits, the Dalkon Shield, DES and Thalidomide are topics which should be discussed.

Information on the status of women in foreign countries is not available in one source. Collecting this information would not be easy, but there is a need for material about women in different countries around the world. The introductory material in Robin Morgan's *Sisterhood Is Global* provides the reader with consistent information on the demography, economy, government, "gynography" (marriage, contraception, prostitution) and the herstory for each country which can easily be used to compare the situation in one country to another.[11] Comparable information of this kind is particularly difficult to find, but it is frequently requested.

In the last eight years several encyclopedias have been published in rather narrow fields: the *Encyclopedia of Crime and Justice*, 4 volumes, 1983, the *Encyclopedia of Bioethics*, 4 volumes, 1978; and the *Encyclopedia of Social Work*, begun in 1929, is now in its seventeenth edition. Each of these fulfills many of the requirements of a good subject encyclopedia. In *Guide to the Use of Books and Libraries* Gates describes a subject encyclopedia as a source which gives " 'summary treatment' of the different phases and aspects of a subject, explains historical backgrounds, trends and influence of events outside the subject area . . . and traces the development of ideas in a subject field."[12] A subject encyclopedia for women's studies, fulfilling the criteria outlined by Gates and including the topics listed above, would be a substantial contribution to the field.

YEARBOOKS

A yearbook or a volume that presents the year in review for women's studies would be particularly useful. Because of the interdisciplinary nature of women's studies, scholars in one field often find that they must quickly assess research or need to identify scholars in related fields. Students look for review essays and trends in research. Information about women's caucuses within professional organizations are often hard to find. All of these topics could be addressed in a yearbook for women's studies.

Ideally a yearbook would contain feature articles and special reports as well as timely information on organizations, people, institutions, research and research in progress, awards, grants, politics, and legal trends. It would also need to cover the status of the 452 women's studies programs across the country, the status of the 40 research centers on women, and the status of women in professional organizations. Adequate indexes by name, organization, and subject would also be required. A commitment by the publisher to continue issuing the yearbook on an annual basis is also necessary.

DATABASES

Librarians and women's studies researchers are all awaiting the long-hoped-for announcement of an international, interdisciplinary database on women and women's studies. The problems encountered in searching indexes, abstracts and online databases for women's studies topics has been documented by Wheeler, Falk, Hildenbrand and others.[13] The interdisciplinary nature of the field is its most unique characteristic and also its most frustrating. Sex-biased language and index terms also present problems in using traditional abstracts and indexes. Wheeler lists seventy-five periodical indexes and abstracting services, citation indexes, and online databases that are relevant to research in women's studies.[14] Some researchers are looking for articles in one part of women's history—European Women in the Renaissance; others are looking for articles on current feminist issues—Pornography and Violence Against Women; while others are looking for articles on topics of general interest to women—Corporate-Sponsored Day Care. One single online bibliographic source where all of these topics can be searched is not available.

Catalyst, a non-profit organization founded to help women entering the workforce for the first time or re-entering after an extended absence, has produced an online bibliographic database to its collections of books, pamphlets, annuals, journals and newspaper articles. The file has been available through BRS since 1983 and its coverage is limited to 3,000+ citations on work-related topics—two-career families, affirmative action, day care, employee benefits, career planning, working mothers. Although work-related topics are only a small part of women's studies research, this online source fills a long-standing information void.[15]

Two other indexes specifically created for research on women—*Women Studies Abstracts* (*WSA*) and *Studies on Women Abstracts* (*SWA*)—are not available online. *Women Studies Abstracts* has been published since 1972, and, until 1983 when *Studies on Women Abstracts* began, *WSA* was the only index to the field. *SWA* covers 313 journals and is constantly adding new titles. *WSA* covers 278 journals; however, there is only an overlap of 88 journals in the two services and both are international in coverage. Both rely heavily on journal abstracts prepared by the author, although both list outside abstractors when they are used. *WSA* is primarily an index—of the 576 citations in volume fourteen, number two (Summer 1985), only 95 are abstracts. All of the citations in volume three, number six (1985) of *SWA* are abstracts—125 to journal articles, 23 to books. *WSA* also includes book reviews. The lack of cumulative indexes for some years makes searching *WSA* difficult at times.

Indexes and abstracts in other fields relevant to women's studies are also not available online (*Abstracts in Anthropology, Art Index*), while other fields—Psychology, Sociology, Education, Medicine—have excellent online sources. In the preliminary report of a study on end-user satisfaction with bibliographic searches in women's studies, Hildenbrand reports that of the 58 searches performed, 23 used four databases and the number of descriptors ranged from one to seven with the median being five.[16] Clearly searching the indexes, abstracts and online sources relevant to women's studies requires sophistication and persistence.

Librarians who work closely with researchers and students in women's studies have been addressing the issue of an online bibliographic database for some time. The Summer 1983 issue of *Feminist Collections* reports on the work of an ad hoc Data Base Task Force comprised of librarians working on a thesaurus of "clear and authoritative terms and phrases for concepts relating specifically to women."[17] Guidelines for evaluating databases in women's studies are reported by Pritchard based on criteria developed for other disciplines.[18] These guidelines were used by the Data Base Task Force to evaluate the currently available online databases likely to be used in women's studies research. The criteria included coverage (scope, completeness, timeliness); content of records; vocabulary and indexing; database structure; availability; and user effort. The evaluators found that

> taken as a whole, the major drawbacks in existing databases are the lack of coverage by both primary and secondary sources of the relevant subjects, the very problematic language barriers, and the inconsistencies in citation formats and search strategies.[19]

Using Pritchard's work as a foundation, the following areas should be addressed by a bibliographic database in women's studies:

1. It should encompass the whole of women's studies—art, literature, religion, philosophy, education, psychology, sociology, history, political science, criminology.
2. It should cover both concepts and people.
3. It should cover feminist theories and issues.
4. It should represent the experience, interests and concerns of all women—lesbians, poor, working-class, women of color, physically or mentally handicapped.

5. It should be international in coverage.
6. It should be current and retrospective.
7. It should be priced so that searches can be afforded by everyone.

CONCLUSION

The study of women has brought about changes in traditional curriculum at all levels of education. Van Dyne and Schuster report that "by 1984, over fifty colleges and universities had developed curricular plans to restore quality and responsibility at the core of the liberal arts by integrating recent scholarship on women and nonwhite cultural groups rather than by ignoring it.[20] Called "curriculum transformation," these changes include an interdisciplinary perspective; gender as a category analysis, with race, class and cultural differences as sub-sets; and the study of subjects in their own terms, a true pluralism.[21]

This analysis of reference sources on women has shown that in some areas the sources have evolved to meet the needs of researchers and the general public, but some work remains. Taken as a whole, there are far too many bibliographies, anthologies, and self-help books. Reference sources in the four areas discussed above—statistical sources, yearbooks, encyclopedias, and indexing and abstracting services—are in critical demand. Obviously, these sources are expensive to produce and would require a commitment of continuation from the publisher. Women's studies demands nothing less.

REFERENCES

1. Catherine R. Stimpson, "Our Search and Research: The Study of Women since 1969," *Comment on Conferences and Research about Wo/men*, 14 (May 1983), p. 1.
2. "Statistical Portrait of Schools Offering Women's Studies Courses," *On Campus with Women*, 15 (Fall 1985), p. 9.
3. Susan Searing, *New Reference Works in Women's Studies*, 1982/83 and 1983/84, and Susan Searing, "New Reference Works in Women's Studies," *Feminist Collections*, Vol. 6, Nos. 2 and 3 (1985) and Vol. 7, Nos. 1 and 2 (1985, 1986).
4. Patricia Miller King, "Forward," *Arthur and Elizabeth Schlesinger Library on the History of Women in America: The Manuscript Inventories and the Catalogs of Manuscripts, Books, and Periodicals*, 2d rev. ed. 10 vols. (Boston: G. K. Hall, 1984), I, p. iii.
5. William Katz, *Basic Information Sources*, Vol. I of *Introduction to Reference Work*, 3d ed. (New York: McGraw-Hill, 1978), pp. 20–26.

6. Kaye Sullivan, *Films for, by and about Women*, Series II (Metuchen, NJ: Scarecrow Press, 1985), p. v.
7. Anne Crawford et al., eds., *The Europa Biographical Dictionary of British Women* (London: Europa Publications, 1983), p. v.
8. Rev. of *The Woman's Encyclopedia of Myths and Secrets*, by Barbara G. Walker, Choice, 21 (March 1984), p. 960.
9. Anne K. Beaubien, Sharon A. Hogan, and Mary W. George, *Learning the Library* (New York: R. R. Bowker, 1982), pp. 100–105.
10. Jean Key Gates, *Guide to the Use of Books and Libraries*, 3d ed. (New York: McGraw-Hill, 1974), pp. 163–164.
11. Robin Morgan, *Sisterhood Is Global; The International Women's Movement Anthology* (Garden City, NY: Anchor Press/Doubleday, 1984).
12. Gates, p. 165.
13. Helen Rippier Wheeler, "A Feminist Researcher's Guide to Periodical Indexes, Abstracting Services, Citation Indexes and Online Databases," *Collection Building*, 5 (Fall 1983), pp. 3–24. Joyce Duncan Falk, "The New Technology for Research in European Women's History: 'Online' Bibliographies," *Signs*, 9 (Autumn 1983), pp. 120–133. Suzanne Hildenbrand, "Researching Women's History on Bibliographic Data Bases," in *Data Bases in the Humanities and Social Sciences*, ed. by Robert F. Allen (Osprey, FL: Paradigm Press, 1985), pp. 218–224. Ellen Gay Detlefsen, "Issues of Access to Information About Women," *Special Collections* 3 (Spring 1984).
14. Wheeler, p. 6.
15. For an in-depth discussion and description of the Catalyst database see: Susan Barribeau, "Resources for Women: The Catalyst Database," *Special Libraries* 76 (Fall 1985), pp. 290–294, Cheryl A. Sloan, "Catalyst Resources for Women (CRFW)," *RQ* 23 (Spring 1984) pp. 351–352, and Eva M. Dadlez, "Catalyst Resources for Women on BRS," *Database* 6 (December 1983), pp. 32–43.
16. Suzanne Hildenbrand, "End User Satisfaction with Computerized Bibliographic Searches in Women's Studies: Preliminary Report of an Investigation," in *National Online Meeting: Proceedings* 6 (1985) comp. by Martha E. Williams and Thomas H. Hogan (Medford, NJ: Learned Information, 1985), pp. 215–219.
17. "From the Editors," *Feminist Collections* 4 (Summer 1983), pp. 3–5.
18. Sarah M. Pritchard, "Developing Criteria for Database Evaluation: The Example of Women's Studies," *The Reference Librarian*, No. 11 (Fall/Winter 1984), pp. 247–261.
19. Pritchard, p. 259.
20. Susan Van Dyne and Marilyn Schuster, "Education; Transforming the Liberal Arts," in *The Women's Annual* 5 (1984–85), ed. by Mary Drake McFeely (Boston: G. K. Hall), p. 8.
21. Van Dyne and Schuster, p. 13.

BIBLIOGRAPHY

Abstracts in Anthropology. Farmingdale, NY: Baywood Publishing, 1970 to present.
Ariel, Joan, Ellen Broidy and Susan Searing. *Women's Legal Rights in the United States*. Chicago: American Library Association, 1985.
Art Index. New York: H. W. Wilson, 1929/32 to present.
The Boston Women's Health Book Collective. *The New Our Bodies, Ourselves*. New York: Simon and Schuster, 1984.
Boulding, Elise, et al. *Handbook of International Data on Women*. New York: Wiley, 1976.
Center for the American Woman and Politics, comp. *Women in Public Office: A Biographical Directory and Statistical Analysis*. Metuchen, NJ: Scarecrow Press, 1978.

Crawford, Anne, et al., eds. *The Europa Biographical Dictionary of British Women*. London: Europa Publications, 1983.
Guy, Patricia A. *Women's Poetry Index*. Phoenix, AZ: Oryx Press, 1985.
James, Simon, comp. *A Dictionary of Sexist Quotations*. Totowa, NJ: Barnes and Noble, 1984.
Morgan, Robin. *Sisterhood Is Global; The International Women's Movement Anthology*. Garden City, NY: Anchor Press/Doubleday, 1984.
Petteys, Chris. *Dictionary of Women Artists; An International Dictionary of Women Artists Born before 1900*. Boston: G. K. Hall, 1985.
Studies on Women Abstracts. Oxfordshire, England: Carfax, 1983 to present.
Sullivan, Kaye. *Films for, by and about Women*. Metuchen, NJ: Scarecrow Press, 1985.
U.S. Bureau of the Census. *A Statistical Portrait of Women in the United States: 1978*. U.S. Department of Commerce, Current Population Reports, Special Studies: Series P-23, No. 100. Washington: U.S. Government Printing Office, 1980.
Vetter, Betty M. and Eleanor L. Babco. *Professional Women and Minorities; A Manpower Data Resource Service*. Washington: Scientific Manpower Commission, 1975 to present.

Women of the World series

Chamie, Mary. *Women of the World: Near East and North Africa*. Washington: U.S. Department of Commerce, Bureau of the Census; Government Printing Office, 1985.
Chaney, Elsa M. *Women of the World: Latin America and the Caribbean*. Washington: U.S. Department of Commerce, Bureau of the Census; Government Printing Office, 1984.
Jamieson, Ellen. *Women of the World: A Chartbook for Developing Regions*. Washington: U.S. Department of Commerce, Bureau of the Census; Government Printing Office, 1985.
Newman, Jeanne S. *Women of the World: Sub-Saharan Africa*. Washington: U.S. Department of Commerce, Bureau of the Census; Government Printing Office, 1984.
Shah, Nasra M. *Women of the World: Asia and the Pacific*. Washington: U.S. Department of Commerce, Bureau of the Census; Government Printing Office, 1985.
Walker, Barbara G. *The Woman's Encyclopedia of Myths and Secrets*. San Francisco: Harper and Row, 1983.
Women Studies Abstracts. Rush, NY: Rush Publishing, 1972 to present.
The Women's Annual: The Year in Review. various editors. Boston: G. K. Hall, 1981 to present.

REFERENCE PUBLISHING

Communication Between Publishers and Librarians: Cooperation or Conflict?

Martin Grayson
Carol Stuckhardt

Oil and water don't mix, right? Wrong, sometimes. Add an egg to emulsify, stir well, and you can get a stable, apparently homogeneous composition. It is called mayonnaise. Can publishers and librarians ever make mayonnaise? They certainly should have a very significant interest in common: serving the needs of the library user, that mythical creature, part businessperson, part professional specialist, looking for information in a book, journal or data base. However, the perception seems to be one of antagonism, not collaboration. The endless flap over copyright is one case in point: publishers and librarians appeared, as usual, to be in opposite camps.

What are some of the other conflicts? *Librarian*: Prices are too high. Books ordered do not arrive, assuming they are occasionally published when promised. Quality is sacrificed to expedient production. Fulfillment services are not provided by publishers to the degree offered by suppliers or jobbers. We are flooded with promotional literature, often uninformative, sometimes misleading. Reviews appear long after the book is out. *Publisher*: Clients are not informed of what is current and of interest. Funds are misallocated to overpriced, little-used journals or dated serials instead of new materials. Budgets are unrealistic. The publishing process is not understood. Property rights are ignored.

And so it goes. Is there anything to all this? Can one emulsify these plainly incompatible materials? We think so. Otherwise we

---

Dr. Martin Grayson is Publisher, Encyclopedia Department, John Wiley and Sons, Inc., 605 Third Ave., New York, NY 10158. Ms. Stuckhardt is Marketing Manager for the same publisher.

© 1987 by The Haworth Press, Inc. All rights reserved.

wouldn't have been able to select new subjects for Wiley encyclopedias and we certainly would not be writing this article. It seems to us that there are many areas of compatibility between publishers and librarians. One of the main ingredients in achieving this compatibility, maybe the emulsifier, is the process of communication between the publisher and the librarian. If this is well done, if we as publishers can find out what is needed, provide it quickly, efficiently, and in high quality, *and* tell the librarian what we have to offer in a clear, concise fashion, then we get mayonnaise.

How does this communication take place? Are there good models for it and how does the librarian participate in the process? These are the questions we want to address here. We should like to share with you ways that we at Wiley communicate with the library community, through market research and otherwise, and what we have learned about how other publishers do this as well.

THE LIBRARIAN IS THE KEY

A recent study concludes that it is the librarian who makes the bulk of all purchase decisions for the library.[1] This came as something of a surprise to some publishers, not to us. At Wiley, our Library Sales Department, among its many promotional activities, publishes a monthly called *The Librarian's Newsletter*. The survey cited above by the Center for Book Research, conducted for the Professional and Scholarly Publishing Division of the AAP, notes that librarians get a great deal of book information from such newsletters and promotional mailing pieces.

Perhaps on a par with the expert recommendation and reviews as sources for purchase decisions. In fact, in 1983 and again in 1985, Wiley conducted research on the format, integrity and utility of this catalog among its librarian users. Our Marketing Research Department sampled the mailing list at random and conducted a telephone survey among corporate, educational and public librarians. As a result, the Newsletter was saved from possible extinction as a cost-cutting measure when its value was confirmed and it was reformatted to accommodate user preferences for ease of access, utility and readability. So, despite the flood of promotional pieces alluded to by our fictional Librarian above, this is an important avenue of communication that Librarians welcome, unlike sales calls and telephone solicitations. As incontrovertible confirmation of this, one of us cites his personal library adviser who runs a corporate headquarters special business and technical library, his wife.

Perhaps there is not all that much antagonism between librarians and publishers. The Dessauer report[1] also cites data on the librarian's evaluation of professional and scholarly publishers and concludes:

> Most libraries(*sic*) believe that publishers serve their patrons well, that the editorial and production quality of their output is good or satisfactory, and that—except in the case of journals and newsletters, where they detect a surfeit—the number published is adequate.

When rated for editorial and production quality, librarians gave encyclopedias the highest marks; higher than books, journals, software and other reference materials.

That the library market is important to professional and scholarly publishers and requires special consideration for success has been discussed often enough, recently by Sexton[2] who points out that library sales of this kind are in the two-gigadollars-per-year range and the type of communication adopted for the trade-book area doesn't impress librarians. This overworked and underpaid profession shuns hype and prefers straightforward information. The status of the author and reputation of the publisher are clearly pertinent in the library decision-making process.

That librarians are helpful to publishers seeking information has been amply demonstrated by the response rate achieved by surveys aimed at the library market. The Dessauer report, for example, was based on a sample of 1,000 libraries and had a 31% response rate. A survey we conducted in May, 1983, of 1,000 libraries[3] had a similar response rate of 29% overall, including a remarkable 59% from the special librarians—special indeed! In addition to the fact that librarians are helpful, careful people, we learned a great deal else from this survey, which was designed to help develop the Wiley Encyclopedia Department in a program of diversification beyond its well known *Kirk-Othmer Encyclopedia of Chemical Technology*. This is the kind of two-way communication between publishers and librarians that really works. The proof ultimately being the sales response to our new products, which have begun appearing in the past two years, developed, in part, based on these survey results.

Incidentally, we were extremely gratified to find that 36% of the respondents had Kirk-Othmer in their collection and: "On a four-point scale, the *Kirk-Othmer Encyclopedia of Chemical Technology* was accorded the highest rating; used more frequently overall than any other encyclopedia mentioned in the survey." The rating was 3.33, where 4 = extensive use, 3 = moderate use, 2 = little use and 1 = never used; a statistic you can be sure we cited in our promotional literature.

HOW DO WE COMMUNICATE WITH LIBRARIANS?

How else do publishers find out what librarians want? The formal survey cited above was expensive and that sort of contact is limited to occasions when justified by the need for a large investment in a new area where our publishing experience is limited, users needs are unknown, pricing is uncertain, etc. For statistically less reliable, but still useful, information where cost restraints are paramount, we resort to limited samplings, sometimes by telephone, to round-table discussions with selected groups or to that ultimate standby, the use of a few reliable advisers.

In every case, the librarian is at the center of our attention. Wiley, and no doubt other Scitech publishers, have traditionally recognized librarians' significant role as information users, buyers and providers. Because of their unique function, librarians often possess keen insights into where to find answers and what topics are in greatest need of research. They are adept at sizing up information sources, evaluating reliability, content, format, etc., especially for the kind of reference works, such as encyclopedias, handbooks and dictionaries, that we publish.

We have alluded above to our survey of 1,000 librarians to measure utility of existing and proposed encyclopedias. This addressed the librarian's role as *user* of information, only one of three main aspects of this profession. We also noted the study of our catalog which covered the second role as a *buyer* of information. A third and extremely vital role is as a *provider* of information. As an example of communication with the librarian/information provider, in 1978 we carried out an extensive study of the perceived need for an encyclopedia in the statistical sciences among librarians and statisticians. As a result, we have to date published six volumes of the projected nine-volume Kotz-Johnson Encyclopedia of the Statistical Sciences which has received critical acclaim.

At the 1985 Annual Conference of the American Library Association, the Reference and Adult Services Division sponsored a panel discussion on the question of publisher-librarian relationships, including the competitive aspects as information providers through photocopying and electronic dissemination.[4] Participants from both communities came to the following conclusions:

— Librarians are (potentially) a rich source of market information for publishers. Unlike booksellers, who are interested in *movement*, librarians are *content* oriented.
— Each group should take pains to learn more about the other: publishers should seek out librarians more frequently for mutual education.
— Librarians need to know more about publishers' financial constraints and the costs of the information business.
— Librarians must assert their views independently. It is incumbent upon them to make their voices heard among publishers. When publishers do ask for input, librarians must answer fully—being sure to add comments and details, not simply provide superficial responses.

WHERE DO WE GO FROM HERE?

Our perception is that the publishing group that markets to the library has just begun this process of dialogue. It has produced excellent results for those of us that communicate with librarians on a structured basis, especially through market-research functions. As word of this gets around, it will no doubt be taken up by others. The trend toward market-centered organizations within publishing houses will accelerate and can only lead to further use of the kind of communication we have discussed here.

To be truly market oriented, the entrepreneur must have detailed information and first-hand knowledge of the market. In the past, this was often simply based on experience, anecdotal evidence and other "seat-of-the-pants" activities. Publishers like other business professionals are beginning to recognize that research is often the beginning of wisdom. The need to define the problem accurately and gather quantitative, statistically useful data can not be underemphasized. However, librarians should never forget that we are listening and we want to hear from you.

REFERENCES

1. *Library Acquisition Survey*, Center For Book Research, University of Scranton, John P. Dessauer, Director, 1985.
2. Mark Sexton, *Selling to the Librarian*, Scholarly Publishing, October, 1985, p. 73.
3. *Encyclopedia Survey, Report of Findings*, Marketing Research Department, John Wiley & Sons, 1983. Unpublished, proprietary report.
4. *Dancing in the Dark—Or Must Every Book be a Blind Date?* American Library Association Conference, Chicago, IL, July 6, 1985. No published proceedings; from notes by one of us (CS).

The Buzz Industry and the Book Industry

Fred Ruffner

Those of us in reference-book and similar types of publishing are said to be part of a wide universe called the "information industry." We produce the research tools that the student, the professional, and sometimes just the curious citizen use to fill in gaps in their knowledge. Our purpose is to inform—accurately, comprehensively, and in a timely manner.

And what tools we now have at our disposal to do that job! The printed word between two covers has long since been augmented by microforms and online databases and CD-ROMs. What wonders computer technology will next bring us to manipulate and disseminate information can scarcely be imagined. We use hardware and feed it software. We input, throughput, output. Screens glow, keyboards click, tapes spin. There has been an information explosion in the middle years of this century, and it is only through the wonders of electronic technology that we even begin to manage it.

RECOGNIZING OUR ROOTS

I have some problems, however, with how our role is sometimes perceived and with some of the buzzwords that the technologists impose on us in attempting to define or describe what we do.

I am concerned that people are losing track of what's behind this buzzword "information industry." We are all caught up in the exciting new world that the wizardry of technology promises—the bells and whistles, the sleek and gleaming machinery that whirrs

---

The author is President, Gale Research Co., Book Tower, Detroit, MI, 48266. The article is an expanded version of his address to the Association of American Publishers, March, 1985. Here he received the coveted AAP's Curtis G. Benjamin Award for "exceptional innovation and creativity" in publishing.

© 1987 by The Haworth Press, Inc. All rights reserved.

and stirs what we feed into it and gives us back data in a stunning array of presentations and uses.

But let's not lose sight of the *basis* of all this—the information itself. That is the foundation of our work and our industry. What seems to be increasingly forgotten and what is really the key process is the *gathering* of information. That must come first. That is the pick-and-shovel "mining" that long precedes the dissemination of the nuggets of information.

And it is that aspect of our work that we in the information industry, the reference-book publishing industry, love best. At Gale we dig skillfully and tenaciously for the elusive fact; we use the mails, the telephone, and above all the libraries. We mark and tear our newspapers and newsmagazines. We've held up traffic searching for a pencil to jot down a vital bit of information heard on a car radio; we've discovered new organizations on the marquees of convention centers; we've encountered an author on a hiking vacation in the Smokies and gathered information for his entry in *Contemporary Authors*. We gather, collect, *amass* information, using all the ingenuity and creativity that is unique to the human mind.

COMPUTER MIRACLES

I do not mean to denigrate or minimize the role of the computer in late 20th-century publishing. Certainly Gale Research Company, and probably all of our colleagues in this industry, would be totally different today, smaller and far less efficient, without the computer and its miracles. It has an important part in all aspects of our work—financial, personnel, production, editorial. It allows us to search our store of information with infinitely greater speed and precision than was possible a few years ago.

We can come up almost instantaneously with facts that would have taken days or weeks for an individual to find "by hand." The computer has greatly enhanced our ability to update our information. In the late 60s and early 70s, it took us two years to produce a 600-page *Encyclopedia of Associations*. Today, it takes less than half that time to produce a 3000-page, three-book set, a companion international volume, and a printed "update" service.

A number of our editors can remember, without a shred of nostalgia, that a few short years ago it took up to two months to alphabetize (the buzzword now is "to sort") the individual cards on which were typed our entries for a dictionary such as *Acronyms, Initialisms, and Abbreviations Dictionary*. Paper cuts were a hazard of the profession. Today, three or four times that number of entries are sorted overnight while our editors sleep (with unbandaged hands). The computer allows us to make our collected information available in a variety of useful arrangements and to track and quickly respond to our customers' reference needs.

Clearly, the use of the computer throughout the reference-book industry has been directly responsible for the increasing availability of very up-to-date information and very finely focused information. It is an absolutely vital tool—but it *is* only a tool.

COMPUTER TECHNOLOGY—A MEANS, NOT AN END

I am as amazed as anyone at what this tool can do: Search—Manipulate—Sort—"Massage," to use a particularly popular buzzword. But we speak of a "database" as though it is some recent invention of computer technology. Yet, the 4×6 cards that we used to "shingle" and mount on layout boards to produce earlier reference books were "databases" too. For a database is simply a collection of related facts stored together with a minimum of repetition.

The computer is a marvelous machine; but the machine, for all the attention it gets, is not the end in itself—it is simply a *means* to present information.

The "machine" is only as good as what is put into it, and that is why the *information* is key and why the people *behind* the database—the information gatherers and information interpreters, the wielders of pick and shovel who "mine" the libraries, organizations, individuals, and other sources of information—are so absolutely vital to our industry and always will be.

It is the editors, often in consultation with librarians representing their patrons' needs, who identify where an information gap exists, who track down the bits and pieces that can be molded into a perfect fit to fill that gap. A reference book, any body of information in any form, is not conceived and developed by computers, but by people. It takes on marvelous new forms with the help of technology, it is greatly enhanced, but it doesn't *start* there.

It starts with people—those who ask the questions and then those who gather the information that will answer the questions. These people have any number of tools that they use to accomplish this job, and the computer is one of these tools (certainly the most useful and versatile to come along in some time). The reference book and the computer do not compete; they complement each other. The new technology allows us to manipulate, arrange, and rearrange data. If the information available to library patrons today is more up to date than ever, if it is available in more forms and arrangements, we have computer technology to thank—after we thank the miners of information who researched, compiled, and refined the raw data before the computer began to work its wonders with it.

BOOKS—AN ENDANGERED SPECIES?

People in our field are frequently asked "Don't you feel threatened by on-line services, on-demand publishing? Is the book becoming obsolete?" These kinds of questions illustrate what most concerns me: that too many people have lost sight of what is really the lifeblood of our industry—information and information gathering. How that information is presented and disseminated is vital, of course, and has made quantum leaps through the miracles of technology. But we must always be able to look beyond and behind the machinery. We mustn't fall into the trap of defining the universe and future of the printed word only by its most currently popular presentations.

Let me present a familiar prophecy: The future of books is endangered and unpromising. The library of a rapidly approaching tomorrow will be filled with microforms and tapes and other compact means of storing data, and computers and audiovisual instruments will instantaneously find and project information to the user.

This vision is not from a paper presented at one of last year's high-tech conventions. It was a view widely held at a conference considering the future of the book—in 1954. That also happens to be the year I formed Gale Research Company, to publish that supposedly "endangered species," *books*. Both Gale and the book continue a healthy existence, not by competing with or fighting the new technology, but by *using* it: to enhance, to supplement, to reinforce, to improve.

This century has seen any number of premature announcements

of the demise of the book: bicycling and automobiling would spell the end to reading, the movies would do it, the radio would deliver the *coup de grace*, television would be the killer. Yet technological advance has served only to complement and enhance publishing, not to destroy it.

ON CO-EXISTENCE

The Librarian of Congress, Daniel Boorstin, in a recent eloquent report to Congress on *Books in Our Future*, quoted a printer as saying that "books and technology have been generating and regenerating each other since the beginning." People did indeed once think that radio, the movies, and television would kill the book—but none has. *What* we say is important, not the means by which we say it.

Dan Lacy, then senior vice-president of McGraw-Hill, wrote about "The Changing Face of Publishing" in the second edition of Chandler B. Grannis's *What Happens in Book Publishing* (New York: Columbia University Press, 1967). He pointed out that

> . . . when several thousand people want the same text, or access to the same information by the same approach, . . . the book is inherently more efficient than the computer, whose advantage lies rather in its ability to manipulate or rearrange data.
>
> [The computer provides] organizations of and access to the oceans of data that underlie books. . . . When a computer has organized masses of raw data into a form and arrangement in which it will be useful to hundreds or thousands of users, the most efficient way of fixing and disseminating the data in that form will be to publish it as a book, rather than to leave it in the computer to be repetitively and expensively recalled for one such user at a time.

There are, of course, very recent developments in electronic technology that *do* make the computer a prime provider of certain types of information. The online search, the CD-ROM, and other methods of information retrieval serve useful purposes in a number of applications, but none obviates another and each has its drawbacks. An online search can cost in excess of $80 per hour; one must, of course, have easy access to a terminal; and a fairly sophisticated level of searching skill is needed—a thorough knowledge of specialized commands and procedures. An article in the November, 1985 issue of *Monitor* describes some "ground rules" for the success of CD-ROMs: that the information be reasonably static, that it needs to be consulted very frequently. The article further warns that CD-ROM is not an online replacement. There are also very serious economic obstacles to electronic memory banks ever displacing the printed word entirely—prohibitive start up and operational costs, for instance.

For a one-time purchase price, a reference such as Gale's *Encyclopedia of Associations* (*EA*) is used thousands of times per year. If usable only online, the cost would be 20 or 30 times what it is otherwise. In addition, a library patron can use a source such as *EA* without being "computer literate" or having technical skills, except perhaps the ability to use an index. (And even if *that* skill is lacking, any librarian can quickly come to the rescue.)

Perhaps the point is that *none* of these systems is a pure replacement for another, and the book has a vital place in the scheme. One may browse through a book (and through any number of related titles), for instance, picking up "things I learned on the way to looking up something else," to paraphrase columnist Sydney Harris. One does *not* "browse" online, at least not without a thick bankroll to back up that luxury.

But the online search has its niche, as do CD-ROMs, on-demand publishing, and the efficient, economical, portable, easily maintained *book*. There is no reason why these various packages of information should not co-exist and prosper side by side. But behind them is one common element on which they are all absolutely dependent for their ultimate quality and value—*the information itself*, whether it's on paper, tape, or shiny silver disk. Dan Lacy, again in "The Changing Face of Publishing":

> Publishing will no doubt always be judged by *what* it disseminates even more than by how widely or efficiently it achieves that dissemination. And the central concern of the successful publishing executive must remain the fostering of those acts of creation to which publishing can give only a means of expression.

FROM BEECH TREES TO BOOKS

It's interesting, I think, that the word "book" comes from the Germanic root "boka," which means beech tree. It evolved because the ancient Germanic peoples carved "runes," the letters of their alphabet, on the trunks of these trees. That beech is primitively analogous to the printing press and the computer. They have all been *tools* through the centuries to advance and enhance the communicating of information.

Beech tree, printing press, computer—their basic premise is the same, differing only in their level of sophistication. What makes the difference is the human creativity behind these tools, the creative juices that flow in the people *behind* the "databases."

We're not threatened by technology; we're thankful for it. It's another useful tool for us.

And the book will endure. The "portable, compact, prerecorded, replayable" book, as Samuel Vaughan described it in Elizabeth Geiser's *The Business of Book Publishing* (Boulder: Westview Press, 1985).

It is, after all, the most "user-friendly" medium I know.

On the Writing of Reference Books: Real and Ideal; In Which the Author Discourses on Motivation, Process, Publication, Reviews and Rewards

Marda Woodbury

"While novelists and popular nonfiction catch the public eye . . . new reference books—like Marda Woodbury's *Childhood Information Resources*—arrive with little fanfare. Pioneers rarely hear fanfares, and this is an ambitious pioneering effort. . . . " Linda Perkins, for the *San Francisco Chronicle*.

"Some concern remains with the reviewers. . . . Will the right people find out about this publication and read it?" Mary Stuart Mason and Christina J. Dunn, in a review of my *Selecting Materials for Libraries: Issues and Policies* in *School Media Quarterly*, Summer 1980.

Unless you thought up the *Book of Lists*, writing reference books seems better suited for professional prestige or as a tax dodge than as a means of making money. It's a career I'm about to put behind me. I have some regrets, since I'm a long-time reference books buff as well as a reference librarian. Still—though I'm grateful for the thought—I've decided against my daughter's suggestion that I try my hand compiling tomes on sports or sex. Sports, certainly, is not my thing, and over the years I have put in more time than I care to remember researching and writing eight reference titles, two in multiple editions, for four publishers. Like any retiree, I'm prepared

---

The author is the Director of Research Ventures, 3050 College Ave., Berkeley, CA 94705 and the Library Director of Life Chiropractic College-West in San Lorenzo, CA. She is also the author of reference works.

© 1987 by The Haworth Press, Inc. All rights reserved.

to be a mentor to those starting out and will try to help others approach the task more realistically than I did.

My gripe is that reference books are part of a commercial enterprise for publishers and, as such, should provide a reasonable source of revenue for their authors. Although I do like the products (especially my latest book!), research and writing is a long, lonely process of deferred gratification. Payment to the author comes in the form of rather small royalties based on sales. And of course the eventual sales depend not only on a book's value but on a large proportion of potential users becoming aware of the existence and scope of the book. This requires publishers' getting the book reviewed in appropriate publications. It also demands an individualized targeted marketing strategy that seems to be beyond the means or capabilities of most reference book publishers.

The rewards are hard to define: perhaps the satisfaction of a job well done and the knowledge that certain important information is finally conveniently assembled for use. Since librarianship is such a process occupation, a final tangible, three-dimensional book is an accomplishment in itself. (Regrettably, it starts going out of date in the very course of publication.) There's the occasional right-on, perceptive review and the occasional statement by librarian or other user that "I just love your book!" I have definite prejudices about style, readability, format, practicality, and indexing, and writing a reference book myself allows me to do it right. I try to write the reference book I'd like to use.

DRIFTING INTO WRITING

It's hard to separate the motives that eventually led me to writing reference books from those that led me to become a reference librarian: a combination of voyeurism and bookishness, a need to know, a desire to be of service to a public that also needs to know, a certain gift for language, and, perhaps, a tendency to drift rather than plan. It was not a huge step, since I love reference works and have always issued newsletters, displays, and a formidable number of minibibliographies. In concept, my books supply a portable librarian. I particularly like to compile, for a wide audience, multidisciplinary guides that integrate scattered sources and materials and, in the process, teach research techniques to users. In essence, I prepare the book I wish I'd had at hand.

Reference Publishing   *141*

I drifted into writing my first published book, *A Guide to Educational Resources*, back in 1971 when I was research librarian for the Far West Laboratory for Educational Research and Development. At that time, Far West held a well-funded federal contract for training EICs (educational information consultants), and I eventually succeeded in convincing the project director that it might be wise to provide these consultants—whoever they were—with a handy compilation of information sources. It took a bit of my worktime and 37 hours of overtime (the indexers took longer) to produce the very first guide that combined ERIC's references with sources used in public and education libraries. Since it was prepared for the federal government, my only reward (aside from 37 hours' pay) was my name on the title page. Eventually—around the fifth edition when the publication had been given over to Stanford University—my name was taken off this page after I suggested that it might be courteous for Stanford to consult me on changes and additions. Still in print the last time I looked, this *Guide* is basically the same book with the same format I designed.

Two years later a severe funding cut at Far West turned me and 37 other luckless employees loose on the world. It happened that I was laid off the same week my mother died and I just couldn't seem to find a new job. Tired of always coming in second or third in a field of fifty, I decided to write *A Guide to Sources of Educational Information* to occupy my time while looking for work. Revenge, I think, was another motive: I wanted to show how much I knew about educational information. The book was easy enough to sell. First, I wrote a query letter and set up an appointment with a nice editor at the University of California Press; I brought the shorter guide to the interview. He considered my proposal for a few days, decided that it wasn't quite right for U.C. Press, but suggested I contact some reference publisher whose books I liked. I then queried Information Resources Press—mainly because I liked the format and appearance of their books—and was offered a contract for a book to be finished in six months. I did not notice that the contract did not require the publisher to produce the book within any specified time.

The mechanics of writing this pre-computer book were simple enough. To save money, I had moved out of my Oakland apartment to a house I had bought in the country near Mendocino, California. Once there, I used the intended greenhouse/storage room as an office. (Some sort of private office is essential!) It contained a card table, an old office chair, a second-hand IBM Selectric, and a long counter-height shelf designed for plants, as well as a battered couch I could lie on to invite the muse. (It also had an ocean view.) I put my reference works (dictionaries, etc.) and my chapters (in double-pocketed folders stored in Princeton files) along the counter. For some now obscure reason, I had at hand a large supply of half sheets of green typing paper that I used for my annotated citations, which I typed and retyped. Each chapter had its own folder; in these, I arranged completed citations in alphabetical order in the right-hand pocket, incomplete references in the left, and the ones I was working on in the middle. Without job interviews and job applications, I had plenty of time to write and polish and was able to follow a routine dedicated to writing. Each morning at nine, I went to the post office for mail and did my shopping. Then I wrote until lunch, perhaps took an hour off, then back to work until five, with an afternoon break to say hello to my children. Mendocino was a small town almost completely without library resources. I had to go to the local bookstore to use *Books in Print* and to make a 35 cent call to the county library in Ukiah for other verification. Working away from libraries, I had to approach services and organizations directly for information and to scrounge review copies from publishers. This, I think, gave my book a freshness and kept it more current than if I had relied exclusively on reference books. When I did make a library run to the city, I worked intensively. Although the book kept growing beyond the length I expected, I did manage to finish it within range of the contract date, and was able to find a good typist—a young mother—in the next town. We submitted a beautiful clean manuscript.

This intensive writing experience stood me in good stead when I applied for—and landed—the only possible job in town, as newspaper correspondent. Two months later, a long-distance phone call urged me to apply for a position that was half education librarian/half editor. Since I had promised my ex-husband that I would move our kids back to the San Francisco Bay Area if work came up, I went down for the interview and eventually accepted the position, another challenging federally funded project that folded completely in a year and a half. At that time, my book was not yet published. It had been put aside (twice) for other manuscripts that seemed more timely to the publisher. Over that period, I had been sending in additions and updates; relations with my publisher and editor were tense, to put it mildly. When the book—a beautiful-looking, well-edited book—finally came out, the interest in education had already peaked. By that time, I was embarked on free-lance library consulting and research.

THE GRANT STORY

With this book published and well reviewed, I started applying for grants for a project dear to my heart—a reference book to integrate all the facets of childhood scattered throughout many disciplines. At that point, I learned that grants originally intended for independent writers tend to get diverted to academicians and that multidisciplinary projects are less likely to get funded than proposals that fit neatly in an existing niche. I should have realized then that books that cross disciplinary boundaries are similarly less likely to get reviewed.

Eventually, after my last child left home, I wrote this book without a grant while supporting myself as a part-time librarian. (In the meantime, I had prepared a three volume multifaceted guide—now out of print—on *Selecting Materials for Instruction*, and had prepared a second edition of *A Guide to Sources of Educational Information*.) To avoid hiring typists yet another time, I purchased an early Kaypro II computer to use in preparing this guide. My computer approach satisfies me, although it might seem primitive to computer buffs. The Kaypro II came with Select word processing software, which is not a good editing system for a writer who rewrites as much as I do; however, it is an excellent system for correspondence and quasi-form letters. Since I can understand and manipulate Select, I use it for writing letters and for printing and dividing files. I bought Perfect Writer software for editing, although it's so complex that I do not use all its capabilities; still, I'm about to use it to index my current book, *Youth Information Resources* (Greenwood Press). (Although I use Wordstar for my library work, I don't like it: it doesn't have either the almost foolproof simplicity of Select or the editing capabilities of Perfect Writer.)

I put each chapter (sometimes two) on a disk and break chapters up when I have to. At today's prices, one could buy a hard disk machine for longer works, but I get along without it. I don't bother with data base or bibliographic software but arrange annotations in order within chapters and can change order or search with word-processing software. I edit both onscreen and on runoff copies. It's much easier to see the whole on paper; mistakes stand out much more on a fresh, new paper copy. Although I lost one 36-page chapter in Perfect Writer (always prepare backups!), I'd never go back to writing without a computer. Still, it wasn't much harder to prepare my first book on a typewriter, except that I can't type well enough for a manuscript copy.

The presence of computers brings its own problems, however, with raised expectations for writers. Ideally, publishers should take authors' disks or typed manuscript copies, convert these to their own computer systems, and edit from there, submitting edited copy to authors to check. This would bring the benefits of the computer age to the authors and result in a speedy, inexpensive, edited book. My last publisher insisted on retyping the book in-house—thus raising the time and cost of the book. At the moment, I'm struggling with a contract that does not require the publisher to edit, but requires me to prepare camera-ready copy, complete with page numbering and running heads. Preparing one chapter of camera-ready copy might be a learning experience but doing more than one is a time-consuming chore, particularly with my computer setup and my skills (which do not include typesetting or pasteup).

Writing reference books has affected my perceptions of both reference books and their reviews. I am definitely more likely to question authority, since I've found factual errors in so many titles. I have also lost my faith in book review sources in general, although I admire *American Reference Books Annual* and *Reference Services Review*. I no longer believe that book reviews will help me locate and evaluate a large proportion of the titles I need for a particular library or research project. I even discovered (horrors!) that the book review entries in *Library Literature* and *Education Index* do not catch all the reviews in the periodicals they index; *Book Review Index*, though slow, reveals more. It's discouraging to see reviewers bypass valuable works (not only my own). It is also discouraging to see subject specialists or reviewers accept superseded books as authoritative. Few reviews are truly thoughtful or thorough; many fail to comment on such basics as style, scope, and arrangement or to compare the book with others. Far too many repeat publishers' brochures or other reviews or contain inaccuracies that make it appear that the reviewers have not opened the covers.

And, as an author, I'm amazed at how difficult it is to get a book reviewed at all. Reference book publishers, I fear, contribute to this situation by mentally consigning reference works to library use only. Their promotions are limited almost exclusively to library audiences even when there are obvious large potential audiences among practitioners and/or the general public. The promotion departments of small publishers tend to be small or understaffed, depending on your interpretation, and are not willing to invest funds in individualized campaigns. Yet, trade publishers may offer even lower royalties and may not promote your works either, although they might achieve more reviews and/or greater sales.

ADVICE TO AUTHORS

GO SLOW! Examine your motives for writing, and be aware of the investment of time and effort it will take (six months to five years) compared with the rewards involved. Everything—your research and your writing—will have to be checked and checked again. You will be responsible for writing for permissions to reprint excerpts from other works and for preparing the index. Your monetary rewards are apt to dribble in slowly.

If you do decide to prepare a reference book, consider yourself a professional author as well as a professional librarian; then negotiate with publishers from that stance. Don't be so thrilled at being offered a book contract that you fail to read the fine print. Two writers' groups, the Authors' Guild (234 W. 45th St., New York, NY 10036) and the National Writers Union (13 Astor Place, Seventh Floor, New York, NY 10003), have prepared standard authors' contracts and suggestions for authors. I have culled these—and my own experience—to suggest some areas to consider before signing any contract.

1. Be realistic about the time it will take you to complete this book.
2. Be sure to get a clause stating that your book will come out within a specified time (six months or a year at the most) after the manuscript is received.
3. Get some written guarantee that your book will not become an orphan if your editor leaves.
4. Insist that the publisher commit to some form of editorial assistance—at least copy editing and proofreading. It is almost impossible to capture all the errors or stylistic idiosyn-

crasies in your own writing. Do not accept a charge for editing.
5. Keep the copyright for yourself if possible. If not, make arrangements for it to revert to you if the book goes out of print or if copies are about to be remaindered.
6. Try to get the publisher to assume the time-consuming task of writing for permissions; at the least, the publisher should assume the fees for permissions.
7. If the design and artwork on your book are important to you, ask in your contract for the right of consultation.
8. Similarly, get a clause giving you close consultation on marketing strategy *before* publication. Determine the size of the advertising and promotional budget before publication and use this as a guide to choosing a publisher.
9. Get as many free copies as possible, since you will wind up doing your own promotion to some extent. Beyond these, get the right to buy copies at a 50% discount.
10. Look for an arbitration clause in case of disputes.
11. Get some escape clause for yourself if the book is not being published or promoted in a timely way.

And if you do decide to proceed, plan for space and privacy, get a good typewriter or computer, and secure the cooperation of your colleagues and loved ones. It will be a challenge!

Reference Books From a Scholarly Publisher

Marilyn Brownstein
Nora Kisch
Mary R. Sive

Many reference works, from the *World Almanac* to the various Oxford Companions, to *Chemical Abstracts*, originate with publishers, who arrange to have them compiled and then produce and market them. Except for some highly specialized bibliographies, it is the rare reference book that comes to an editor's attention as an unsolicited manuscript or proposal. Though librarians know reference books best and use them to advantage, few have the time during their busy days to note and suggest needed titles. When they do, they are likely to be good ideas, though sometimes challenging to execute. What is recognized to be needed and useful does not always correspond neatly with scholarly expertise. On the other hand, what scholars wish to publish is often too narrowly focused to be viable. A good reference book must successfully address a need shared by more than a few specialists.

Developing a reference book often is a vast undertaking, involving many people, research in wide areas, and considerable expenditure. The rewards are uncertain for both author and publisher. Authors or volume editors are not usually serving their professions in a scholarly sense: they are providing useful tools for researchers by disseminating information in an accessible format, a more pragmatic goal than that served by more theoretical scholarly work. Nevertheless, a well conceived and executed reference book can become a perennial, a notable tool indispensable to research in the field, not just another scholarly exercise or personal statement. Such exposure and durability is gratifying of itself and should result in

---

All of the authors are with Greenwood Press, 88 Post Road West, Box 5007, Westport, CT 06881. Ms. Brownstein is Editor, Humanities; Ms. Kisch is Sales Manager; and Ms. Sive is Editor, Social Sciences and Library-Information Science.

© 1987 by The Haworth Press, Inc. All rights reserved.

reasonable financial compensation. A publisher also will find profitability in a widely accepted reference book and may enjoy an enhanced reputation based on it.

DEVELOPING REFERENCE BOOKS

A successful reference book may well beget others. Charting the success—or failure for that matter—of a book often will yield evidence of related needs and suggest possible approaches. Generally, from reading in the field, review feedback, sales records, and other sources, editors will develop ideas for future reference books. Reviews in library periodicals frequently are instructive as indicators both as to what kind of reference book is needed and how it should be executed. At Greenwood Press, a staff editor may then suggest an idea for a reference book to a potential author or volume editor. Ideas are refined in editorial meetings and with the project editor. For quality control, Greenwood Press editors also utilize standards set by the library profession, such as the guidelines of the RASD Bibliography Committee, which we routinely send to our authors. Attending meetings of the Reference Tools Advisory Committee at ALA Midwinter conferences as an observer has also been helpful in providing us with a better understanding of what our market looks for in reference books.

Thus, staff expertise, bolstered by information from outside sources and a measure of intuition, comes into full play. Even when not in an actual series, books from certain publishers tend to have a unique style that is not solely the result of book design and manufacturing; rather it is a reflection of the experience of the editorial staff. This is not to denigrate the overreaching role of the volume author or editor and contributors, for it is their expertise that gives the book its value. The point here is that an initiating role very often is taken by a staff editor, who then continues to guide the project to a successful conclusion.

Potential reference book authors are actively sought by publishers. Often they come to the attention of staff editors through their own prior publications, particularly in professional and academic journals, and through papers delivered at conferences. A busy staff editor working in a broad subject area may find it difficult to keep abreast of current research and publications, and publishers usually find it advantageous to conclude advisory arrangements with outside scholars to augment inhouse research. Greenwood Press has a large number of "repeat" authors, and, reference books being a major thrust of our publishing program, authors of relevant monographs or contributors to reference books often are encouraged to take on editorial responsibility for projects that have the potential to become major reference books. Frequently also, an author's own proposal of a monograph or collection of essays may spark an idea for a broader reference book.

GREENWOOD'S REFERENCE PROGRAM

In a sense, all Greenwood Press publications are reference books. All of our monographs are required to have appropriate indexing so as to yield their information readily. Nevertheless, reference books per se—encyclopedias, dictionaries, handbooks, bibliographies, indexes, and the like—are an important and growing part of our publishing program, representing nearly half of our annual production of some 350 original titles. As a scholarly publisher, Greenwood Press attempts to ensure that all its titles are significant to university-level collections. Thus, even a reference book on a "popular" topic, such as a bio-bibliography of a film star or a discography of rock music, must have sufficient weight to yield information useful to a college level audience and to people undertaking serious research in the field (though the book will be marketed to and must be useful to public and specialized libraries and to individuals interested in the subject matter as well). Greenwood Press publishes almost every type of reference book in the social sciences and humanities, both those intended to answer a user's questions and those devised to lead the user to the proper sources. However, we specialize in historically focused reference works and are less involved in directories and serial reference publications. (A notable exception to the latter is our quarterly *Index of Current Urban Documents.*) We have identified needs for comparative international surveys in virtually all disciplines and fields, and we also find a strong reference need for institutional histories and biographical information of all kinds. Subject areas emphasized in both our monograph and reference programs include women's studies, Black and ethnic studies, military studies, political science, American history, gerontology, and information sciences.

Many of our major reference books are published in series, notable among them the *Greenwood Encyclopedia of American Institutions*, the *Greenwood Encyclopedia of Black Music*, *Historical Guides to the World's Periodicals and Newspapers*, and the *Handbook of American Popular Culture*, and related *Popular Culture Reference Guides*. More specialized bibliographies, indexes, discographies, and bio-bibliographies are published in some thirty series defined by subject area as well as outside of series. We also publish certain reference books under our Quorum imprint, which specializes in business, legal, and other professional books and subscription publications.

Certain features are hallmarks of Greenwood Press reference books, and we ask that authors provide them. We will not publish a reference book that is not adequately indexed and that does not contain internal cross-references if relevant. Users are entitled to those aids, which enable them to make fullest use of these tools. Our major reference works—encyclopedias, historical and biographical dictionaries, international handbooks—always include bibliographies and usually include one or more appendixes that supply additional data or offer alternative retrieval approaches to the volume's contents.

EDITORIAL PROCEDURES

Greenwood Press editors work in broad subject areas: history, humanities, political science, legal studies, social and behavioral sciences, and library science. Interdisciplinary fields, such as women's studies, are generally shared by the subject editor as relevant. Recent emphases on reference tools within the broad areas have included composer bio-bibliographies, discographies, literary companions, theatre production histories, historical dictionaries of eras and events, historiography and historical writings, religious biography and denominational histories, comparative military statistics, world political parties, ethnography, and institutions and documents relating to public policy and public issues.

The editors have a two-fold function: acquisition and fulfillment. Their responsibilities extend to all kinds of publications, but reference books are primary and occupy perhaps seventy percent of editorial staff time. Reference books are actively sought by staff and developed by outside editors with considerable staff input. Staff editors provide direction at the inauguration of a project and aid throughout the process, from conceptual and organizational matters, to advice on soliciting collaborators and contributors, through assistance on details of format and style.

An editorial administrative support staff tackles an enormous recordkeeping job. As we publish hundreds of books a year and many, particularly our major reference books, may be several years in the manuscript development stages, we find ourselves dealing with well over a thousand works in progress at any one time, while also investigating new possibilities for the future. Additionally, many of our reference books each involve dozens, sometimes hundreds, of contributors, all of whom must be carefully tracked. This large volume of activity may sometimes result in delay in replying to correspondence, and an author who telephones may not immediately be recognized or put together mentally with his or her project; but the editorial staff finds this regrettable and strives mightily to offer the personal services of a small publisher from one that has recently become one of the largest publishers of scholarly works in the United States. (On January 1, 1986, Greenwood Press acquired the Praeger Publishers division of CBS Inc.) Our commitment to provide continued editorial support is greatly appreciated by authors, one of whom commented in the preface of his reference book: "I have received the kind of help and sustenance from Greenwood Press that most authors only dream about."

PRODUCTION PROCEDURES

The attention of our editorial staff is duplicated by that of our production editors, designers, and compositors. Manuscripts that go through our typesetting process are carefully copyedited and proofread under the direction of skillful and conscientious production editors, who are in close communication with authors once the manuscripts are transmitted from the editorial to the production department. Greenwood's production methods were called "innovative" and "remarkable" by *Publishers Weekly*. They employ state-of-the-art technology, including some automated typesetting through the use of an optical scanner. We are able to accept some computer disks and tapes from our authors, who often are eager to provide these; and we are working to overcome problems caused by hardware incompatibility, to increase our capacity to offer electronic transmission, and generally, to stay in the forefront of the technological revolution as regards book production.

Reference books pose particular problems for production, being long and complex on the one hand, and often not as clean, polished, and uniformly edited as a monograph on the other hand. More time and care must be taken in copyediting, typesetting, and proofreading. Further, many reference manuscripts are composite works prepared in batches on different typewriters or computers, thus requiring special attention of skilled compositors and defying the ministrations of our more "advanced" technology.

Our manufacturing standards have always called for adherence to library specifications for binding and paper, and the results are appreciated by librarians and library users particularly with respect to the more heavily used reference books. Although a detailed explanation of our production procedures is beyond the scope of this article (and not the special expertise of these writers), we should like to point out that it is through the combined efforts of our editorial and production staffs—not to mention the authors!—that Greenwood books have an enviable record of being named "best of the year" by various professional selection groups and of winning other awards.

PROMOTION AND MARKETING PROCEDURES

Bringing our books to the attention of such selection groups, as well as to reviewers, libraries, wholesalers, dealers, and ultimately to readers, is a function of our marketing department. Most Greenwood Press books are sold by direct mail. Our marketing department conceives, produces, and mails more than 100 different catalogs, subject brochures and single title brochures every year. Most such efforts are mailed to 10,000–35,000 individuals and institutions. Included are reference and subject librarians at all levels, department heads and professors at colleges and universities, subscribers to appropriate academic journals, and previous buyers in the respective subject area.

Our major reference books are featured in special subject brochures which include other titles in the same or similar areas as the featured work. A minimum of a full page and more often two or three pages are devoted to the featured book. We provide a full description of the work as well as biographical information on the author or editor. In addition, we include sample pages, appendixes, a table of contents, full bibliographical data and cataloging information. A typical brochure is 4 to 8 pages long and subject catalogs are 16 to 48 pages in length.

In spite of all our direct mail efforts, we are aware that many librarians base their book buying decisions on reviews in various library and professional media. Review copies of all reference books are sent to appropriate journals. While many of our books are reviewed from galleys or page proofs, most reviewers prefer to see a finished reference book to judge its usefulness. Therefore our reference books are generally distributed for review after publication. Greenwood Press reference books are most often reviewed in *Choice*, *Library Journal*, *Reference Books Bulletin*, *Wilson Library Bulletin*, and *American Reference Books Annual*, as well as various specialized professional journals.

Of particular importance in selling reference books is a strong presence in the foreign market. Greenwood's reference books are developed with these markets in mind as well as domestic markets. Exclusive distributors abroad sell Greenwood books, producing promotion and advertising in their own languages. As a consequence, you are as likely to encounter a Greenwood reference work on the library shelves of the University of Tokyo as you are at the New York Public Library.

Though we began by saying that most reference books—in general and specifically at Greenwood—are conceptualized by staff, we should like to end by encouraging readers to submit ideas or outlines for reference books. Librarians no longer are passive "keepers of the books," but increasingly see themselves as active agents in the efficient transfer of information. Surely a part of that function must be participation in the creation and design of needed information products. Here at Greenwood we consider no one better qualified to help determine the shape of our reference books than the reference librarians who are at the frontline fielding questions from students and the general public.

Unsolicited reference book proposals always receive attention, and we commonly issue contracts for reference books on the basis of a prospectus and sample materials, usually after some staff-author interaction and amplification. Some of our most successful authors are librarians.

From Book Idea to Contract: Writing Reference and Professional Books

Pat Schuman

Librarians and libraries have a symbolic relationship with reference and professional publishers—they are often not only the major market (buyers) for these books, but they are also often the creators. Numerous reference books I have either edited or published began with a "card file:" a specific library compiled for its own use.

A full picture of how reference books are produced and published is not complete without an understanding of the role of author, editor, and publisher in the process. Having been in all three positions during my career, I can personally speak to the fact that each of us has his or her own personal stake and specific role in the publishing process. Each player is important to the process, as is the trust and communication between them. But, for this trust and communication to take place, each step in the process must be fully understood.

Writing, publishing, and selling any book is time-consuming, complicated, and often frustrating. This is particularly true in professional and reference book publishing for the library field. Ours is a specialized and limited area of the book industry. It is one in which neither author nor publisher can expect to reap vast financial gain.

Library science and reference book publishing is geared towards an institutional market—libraries. While it is difficult to generalize, an average sale for a monograph or reference book geared toward the library market will probably range from 1,500 to 2,500 copies. A good sale would be from 2,000 to 3,000. A fantastic sale would be from 5,000 to 10,000 copies.

The author is founder and President of Neal-Schuman Publishers, Inc., 23 Cornelia St., New York, NY 10014.

Despite the fact that the library market is relatively small, there are about 40 publishers who specialize in this area. Many of these companies have been founded by librarians or employ librarians as editors. Their authors are most often librarians writing for librarians.

Library science and reference publishing differs from normal "trade" publishing in many aspects. But the basic similarity between all publishing is the general division of responsibility between author and publisher. Although these responsibilities often overlap, they are distinct phases of the process.

The author's major responsibility is to develop the idea, to write the manuscript, and to deliver it to the publisher in an acceptable and readable form. The author is normally responsible for all elements of the manuscript—this includes the written text, all illustrations, and the indexes. Any costs associated with these elements are considered "author" costs. If a publisher, for example, hires an indexer to produce the index, or pays permissions fees, this is normally charged as an advance against royalties. Naturally, at each step along the way, the author should expect help and guidance from the publisher.

The publisher's role—and financial responsibility—usually involves finding or developing the right author or manuscript, evaluating the project and its potential revenues, producing the book—from initial design through dealing with the printers, planning, marketing, and selling the project—to reach the right audience, and selling the book, receiving orders, filling orders, insuring delivery, collecting money. Publishers often delegate many steps in the process, e.g., printing and filling orders, to persons or firms outside the house. What makes a "publisher" is the integration, control, and success of these processes.

Authors are most closely involved with the publisher during the writing and editing processes. There are many elements involved in this stage. The first part of the process is acquisitions: to put it simply, the process of finding and/or developing a manuscript. The crucial issue in acquisitions is to select the right manuscript—or the right person to write a manuscript; often an acquisitions editor will approach an author with an idea. Once a proposal is developed by an author and accepted by a publisher, a contract is negotiated. When the contract is signed, the process of writing the manuscript, and sometimes rewriting it, begins. At this stage, authors often deal with one or more editors and editorial processes.

Sponsoring editors handle the development of the manuscript

with authors. Managing editors coordinate all editorial functions by keeping track of schedules, managing traffic, and ensuring that publication plans are carried out. Copy editors, often referred to as "line editors," check for accuracy, syntax, style, grammar, and consistency. In small companies, these various functions are often performed by one person. Your manuscript will go through all of these editorial processes—if not people—at one time or another. Once these are complete, your manuscript will enter a stage called "production"—the typesetting, printing, and binding of the book.

Do not expect to see your name in lights, much less *The New York Times*, if you write a library science monograph. Because costs are high and the market is small, the amount of time and money feasible to devote to one book is limited. Yet, it is crucial that the publisher market your book and ensure that it is sold to its full potential. Professional and reference books are sold to the library field basically through direct mail. Some space advertising and the exhibition of books at various conferences is also a more limited part of this process. It is the publisher's job, with your help, to make sure that books are reviewed in appropriate journals. Many authors bring promotional material to speeches and workshops they are giving. Most publishers will be happy to have your suggestions. As author you are intimately involved in the field, and so know it best. If you think about it, you are probably thoroughly familiar with the network of people who are your potential audience.

Hand in hand with decisions on how to sell a book is the pricing decision. How do publishers decide on a price? Formulas for pricing vary in different publishing houses. But it's important to realize that the size of the book and its potential market are only two factors in pricing.

The cost of selling to the library market, because it is relatively small, can be high. Just filling an order (and many sales are for a single copy)—can be as high as $2.00 to $3.00 per book. This includes postage, warehousing, packing, etc. Libraries take anywhere from 90 to 120 days to pay a publisher—or a wholesaler. Partially as a result of others' slow payment, wholesalers sometimes take at least that amount of time to pay publishers. The high cost of money today, and the expected late payments, can add another several dollars to the cost of the book. The number of pages in a book, the number of copies printed, and the design and typography of the book are also important cost factors. The type of binding used is a cost factor, but really not that significant. For example, a publisher might save $1.00 to $1.50 per copy of a 300-page, 6" × 9" book by binding it in paperback.

Publishers use a formula for pricing their books. Below is a typical scheme based on the list price of a book.

20% for design, typesetting, and printing costs
10% for damaged books and returns
10% for royalties
10–15% for marketing
10% for fulfillment
25–30% for overhead

Overhead includes office space, heat, light, and salaries. If you add this up, you get somewhere between 80 and 90 percent of the list price of the book. There's a reasonable profit if the publisher has guessed right on the print run—but not a tremendous one.

Once a manuscript is complete and acceptable, the production process can take anywhere from six months to a year. That time line holds for most publishers if manuscripts are delivered on time and with complete materials. Do not expect a publisher to drop everything the moment your manuscript arrives if it is not expected or incomplete. Most publishing houses plan their schedules at least a year in advance.

DEVELOPING A BOOK

Every book starts with an idea. Sometimes the original idea begins with the publisher and the publisher seeks the right author. More often, the original idea is the author's. Usually, a final idea is developed by negotiation and communication between author and editor. Some publishers will send your proposal to outside reviewers, often professionals who are potential buyers, for their input. Some also will send completed manuscripts to reviewers for critical comment. If you think you have a book idea, here are some questions you should ask yourself and your colleagues—and also be prepared to discuss with a publisher: Is there a need for the work you are proposing? Does your idea fill this need? How big is the need? Who will actually buy the book? Are there already similar books in the field? Will (and how will) your book differ significantly from other works?

Don't hesitate to talk to a publisher or publishers informally. Call, write, or even stop by their booths at ALA and other conferences. Letters of inquiry and detailed proposals can and should be sent, but do let a publisher know if you are talking with other publishers as well. If you don't know exactly who to write to, check *Literary Market Place* for the correct editor to submit materials to. It is amazing the number of letters we receive at Neal-Schuman addressed to "To Whom It May Concern." A short query might serve to elicit initial interest, but an in-depth book proposal is what you need to convince a publisher.

It's important to remember that book publication represents a substantial investment of time, effort, and money by both publisher and author. Developing an idea for a book, thinking it out thoroughly, planning your work, and selling both the project and yourself can be almost as much work as actually preparing the manuscript. It's a long way from even a good idea to a usable book.

Here's a sample of the book proposal checklist Neal-Schuman sends to authors.

BOOK PROPOSAL CHECKLIST

1. A general description of the purpose of the book: background information, including why such a book is needed, how it will be compiled or written, the audience or market to which the book is directed, possible secondary audiences and markets, and comparison with other similar books.
2. A Table of Contents, even if this is tentative, including some estimate of the length or number of entries (or pages) for each chapter or section, as well as the length of the total manuscript. Please specify types and approximate size of indexes.
3. A tentative outline describing in detail the main topics to be dealt with.
4. Any chapter or sample entries available in draft form, which are representative of the elements of the book, including tabular material, illustrations, etc.
5. The tentative date for completion of the manuscript.
6. A brief personal resume, including other publications, related activities, etc.

Most publishers will want to see from one to three sample

chapters or substantial numbers of entries to get an idea of your writing style and your approach to the particular subject. It's better if you can send these with the proposal, but if you want to try out your idea first, send at least the description and outline, a resume explaining your qualifications for writing this particular book, and any available samples of your published writing. Send an original and one copy with a stamped, self-addressed envelope.

Receipt of your proposal will be acknowledged almost immediately, but—depending on the publisher—it may take from four weeks to four months to hear any further word. What happens while you're waiting? Your proposal will be evaluated from both an editorial and a marketing standpoint. From the editorial point of view, the publisher will try to determine if the proposed book is viable, needed, workable, and appropriate for their particular list. If the answer is yes, then the questions become: How many copies will a book sell and is it financially feasible? The publisher will estimate how much it will cost to edit, typeset, print, bind, and promote. It can be a lengthy process, so be prepared.

If you think you have a viable book project, do not be discouraged by rejection from one publisher. Rejections are based on various factors, for example, what books the publisher is already committed to. (Every publisher has a skeleton in the closet of the bestseller he or she turned down.) What is viable for one publisher may not be feasible for another, due to overhead, design, and other financial factors. Some library publishers can afford a print run of less than 700 for a $20 book, while others cannot even consider a run double this size.

Be prepared to estimate your own costs carefully. Advances against royalties are hard to come by. You may have an excellent plan for a directory, but your compilation costs could be high. If a project is based on mailings, carefully estimate clerical and postal expenses. Publisher's policies differ, but substantial royalty advances are unusual because of the limited market. If you are planning to use illustrations or to reprint materials, this is an additional cost usually borne by the author.

CHOOSING A PUBLISHER

What do you need to know about choosing a publisher? On what basis should you choose one? Ask yourself what matters most to you. Pricing? Marketing? Design? The amount and type of editorial direction available?

Shop for a publisher. Check out the "look" of various publishers' books, as well as their advertising and promotional brochures. Visit their exhibits at conferences. Talk to other authors who have written for them. Read their catalogs to see what similar titles they may have published. Publishers want as few disgruntled authors as possible, and most will be very straightforward if you ask the right questions. What potential markets do they foresee? What are their promotional plans and preliminary sales estimates? What type of composition and design do they plan? What kind of editorial guidance can you expect? How long will it take to publish your book after receipt of your final manuscript? Who will have the final say as to whether your manuscript is acceptable; outside reviewers, an editorial committee, an editor, an accountant, or any number of combinations of these is possible. How many copies of similar titles has the publisher sold? If possible, meet the editor you will work with. Some will offer detailed guidance, others none. Be sure you are on the same "wave length."

You, as an author, must gauge the difference between various publishers—and they do differ. First, you must realistically try to assess the potential for your work and the type of publisher it will need. The number of copies *any* publisher can sell of a highly specialized library science bibliography or a dissertation is very limited. On the other hand, the potential of a textbook or basic reference book is high (at least in library publishing terms), and the combination of factors—price, timing, look, and promotion—can be crucial.

In most cases, you cannot expect to support yourself in the style to which you are accustomed by writing for the library field. You can make some supplemental income and you should not ignore monetary considerations. How much you can expect to earn on a book varies both with the individual book and the individual publisher. Authors usually earn income based on a percentage of sales—a royalty. Although a few publishers do not pay royalties until a certain amount of copies are sold in order to recover initial publishing costs, royalties usually begin somewhere between 10 and 15 percent, with built-in escalations after various quantities are sold.

Check royalty arrangements carefully; analyze them in relationship to the type of production, the kind of editorial guidance, the pricing policies, and the amount of promotion a publisher offers.

Obviously a ten percent royalty on a 1,500 copy sale of a $25 book will earn you more than 15 percent on 750 copies of a $25 book. You will have to wait for your money. An average length of time from book idea to publication is between eighteen months and two years. This allows time for your proposal, the publisher's evaluation, your writing, rewriting, editing, design, production, printing, and binding. Only then will the book start to sell. Often larger sales come in after reviews appear.

THE BOOK CONTRACT

The author-publisher relationship is based on trust—but neither participant has to be blind. Publishers rarely are when it comes to contracts, but authors—particularly those anxious to be published—often are. Contracts are one of the most crucial points in the publishing process, since all facets of the author-publisher relation are formalized in it.

Most publishers have printed contracts that are lengthy and written in "legalese." They contain both very specific and very vague clauses. Publisher's contracts tend to be fairly standard, with key elements in common. But, it is important to know that a few simple words can change both author and publisher rights.

Some contract wording and clauses are negotiable, others are not. The degree of negotiability varies with who the publisher is, who the author is, and just how important a book may be to the publisher.

The first element in any contract is usually the manuscript clause. It covers the date the manuscript is due, its form, its size, the number of copies to be delivered to the publisher, and whether the author is responsible for illustrations and indexing. Most contracts state that the author is responsible for all illustrations, to be delivered in "camera-ready" form. This can be expensive. Most publishers also make the author responsible for the index. If you cannot do the index yourself, find out if the publisher will find an indexer and bill you for the cost, or if you must pay out-of-pocket expenses.

Make sure that the delivery date of the manuscript is a reasonable one for you. If you are going to be late, keep your publisher informed. Most manuscript clauses also specify that the manuscript be "acceptable" or satisfactory to the publisher in content and form, that the publisher can reject the manuscript outright and request that any advance be refunded, and that if the *form* of the manuscript is not acceptable, a publisher can have the manuscript retyped at the author's expense.

Just what is an "acceptable" manuscript? Few legal contracts can define a term that implies judgment. But, both publisher and author have a stake in making the manuscript acceptable. Constant communication as to both the author's and publisher's expectations is the important element here. A detailed proposal is the first step. Your publisher should also provide style guidelines and review your early chapters. Any major changes in your manuscript you decide to make *after* submitting your outline or sample chapters should be communicated to your editor. If the vagueness of the term "acceptable" bothers you, you can try to make it more specific by asking that your original proposal and/or sample material be made a part of the contract.

The grant clause of a publishing contract defines what rights you are assigning to the publisher. Normally, for the full term of copyright, the publisher is assigned exclusive right to publish and sell the book throughout the world. This clause usually includes all subsidiary rights—often, to quote from one contract—"now known or hereinafter invented." It also spells out who owns the copyright.

In reference and professional book publishing, copyright is often taken out in the name of the publisher. Does this make a difference? Rarely. It is just easier for the publisher. Most contracts have the author assign all rights to the publisher in any case. On balance, though, it is probably better protection for the author to hold the copyright.

Some publishers are adding another provision to this clause that can drastically affect authors' rights. This is a paragraph including the term "work made for hire." The 1976 copyright law says (italics are mine):

> Where a work is specifically ordered or commissioned for use as a contribution to a collective work, motion picture, translation, atlas, instructional text, test, compilation, supplement to any work, answer to a test, then as to those uses, *if the parties expressly agree in a written instrument that it is a work for hire, then it will be deemed a work-for-hire.*

This means in effect that you have been hired to write the work and that *all* rights are vested with the publisher. You are no longer an author, but merely someone who was hired. You lose *all* control. Sometimes this clause is justified. For example, some publishers have a specific project for which they hire an author or editor. But, beware of signing your rights away.

The permissions clause spells out your obligation to obtain permission for the use of previously copyrighted materials or new material. The author is responsible for paying any fees for these permissions; sometimes a publisher will be willing to pay these fees as an advance against royalties.

The warranty clause assures the publisher that you are the author of the book, own all rights, and have full power to enter into this agreement; that the book is original and not in the public domain; that it does not violate or infringe any copyright; that it contains nothing libelous or illegal. In addition to these declarations, as author you will be asked to "indemnify and hold harmless" the publisher from any and all loss, damage, liability or expense, including reasonable attorney's fees, arising out of any breach or "alleged" breach of these warranties. What does this mean? It means that should there be a suit, you may have some financial liability. This clause rarely comes into play within professional and reference book publishing.

The royalties clause is usually the one authors are most interested in since it specifies how much you will get paid and when. Although this clause varies from publisher to publisher, there are some basics. Standard royalties in our type of publishing usually begin at 10 percent of the "net cash receipts." Net cash receipts is an important term—it means *actual* money the publisher has collected. This is very different from 10 percent of the list price, which is what many trade book authors receive. However, library/reference books are seldom discounted more than five to 12 percent to wholesalers, so the difference is not that great. In other words, if your book lists for $25.00, and the publisher sells it to Baker & Taylor at a 10 percent discount for a price of $22.50, your 10 percent royalty will be $2.25 not $2.50.

Royalties are usually paid out on a sliding scale, but even this can vary from publisher to publisher. For example, one publisher offers 15 percent after the first 1,000 copies; another offers 10 percent on the first 5,000 copies, 12-1/2 percent on the next 5,000, and 15 percent thereafter; and a third offers a royalty only after 750 copies are sold. Rarely do percentages exceed 15 percent.

Again, you cannot judge the amount of money you will make by percentages alone. There are several key questions to ask, including: How often does the publisher pay royalties? (Most publishers pay twice a year; some only once.) How many copies will the publisher sell? How much will the book sell for?

Another component of the royalty clause deals with subsidiary rights. Normally this is a fifty-fifty split between publisher and author of net cash receipts. These rights cover such items as translation, foreign rights, microfilm, serial rights, and computer rights. Rarely do these come into play in library science publishing. An author's royalty is usually reduced in half for remainders, paperbacks published by the publisher, sales of overstock, and the like.

The third component of the royalty clause is usually a specification of when royalty statements and payments are due. Most publishers pay royalties twice a year. Most contracts will specify a cut-off date for sales and payments. For example, a publisher will pay for sales as of August 30 on November 30. The normal time is usually 90 days from the end of the sales period.

It's important to realize that you are only paid royalties on copies that are *sold* and *paid* for. Publishers provide review copies to journals and sometimes to faculty—you won't receive royalties on these.

The royalties clause also covers any advance against royalties. In library science publishing, advances are very rare, though sometimes a publisher will advance money to cover out-of-pocket expenses, such as postage or typing. Remember, most advances are returnable if you do not deliver an acceptable manuscript.

The publishing clause sets forth the publisher's obligations to publish the work. Most contracts say the publisher will publish the work within a "reasonable" time, or something like "at such time as it determines conditions are suitable," at the publisher's own expense, and in such style and at such price as it in its "sole judgment" shall consider most "appropriate" to promote its sale.

You may want to ask for a time limit, instead of "reasonable time," for example, one year or 18 months, in which to publish or return the manuscript. In terms of marketing, few publishers will be willing to set out specifics. This is because market conditions—and the way to reach the market—can change. This does *not* mean you should not ask detailed questions about how the publisher intends to market your book.

If the design and format—typesetting and binding—is of concern to you, your best protection is to discuss this with the publisher. Few will give an author design approval, but most will freely discuss their plans.

Many contracts contain a clause about a publisher's right to make changes. The wording of this can either give the publisher carte blanche to change anything, to make changes with your approval, or to limit changes to style, punctuation, etc. This is another subject you should discuss with your publisher.

The author corrections clause states that the author will read and correct proof and that the author alterations—those corrections which are not typographical errors, but actual author changes—which exceed 10 percent of the cost of typesetting will be charged to the author's royalties. While it is rarely spelled out in the contract, it is important to know whether your publisher also hires professional proofreaders rather than relying solely on you to proofread your manuscript. If you are not a good proofreader, you will want to know this.

Most reference and professional book publishers retain rights to revised editions. For example, here's a fairly standard clause (italics are mine):

> The Author agrees to revise the said Work when the Publisher, after consultation with the Author, shall decide, *in its sole judgment* that a revision is desirable. Should the Author be unable or unwilling to undertake such revision, or be deceased, the Publisher may arrange for the preparation of a revised manuscript, and in such event the royalty percentage and/or fee provided for in the contract between the Reviser or Revisers and the Publisher shall be charged against the account of the Author and deducted from the royalty percentage and/or income accruing to said Author on sale of such revised edition. The Publisher *in all events* shall have the right *in its sole judgment* to use the name of the Author and/or Reviser or Revisers on any revisions of the Work.

Questions you need to think through about this wording are: Will a revision be important? Is there a good reason for the publisher to have this right? Can this be a mutual decision? Do you want your name to be used when the publisher "in its sole judgment" decides?

Most publishing contracts have some sort of clause that deals with what happens when a book goes out of print. This clause varies widely from publisher to publisher. The first question to ask is: Will the publisher tell *you* the book is out of print? Most contracts state—believe it or not—that "the author shall inform the publisher" when the book is out of print. And do the rights get returned to you? When? Most publishers will give you the right to buy the plates or film from which the book was printed. But, not all publishers return the rights to you automatically. You may want to make this clause more specific.

How is "out of print" defined? Some contracts state that as long as *any* edition is in print, including foreign editions, the work is still in print. You might want to add wording that substitutes the term out of print for "discontinuance of manufacture or sale." In other words, if the publisher is no longer *selling* your book, if it does not appear in current catalogs, all rights should be returned to you.

Other standard clauses found in contracts include binding agreements and applicable assignments. Usually a contract states that you cannot "assign" any part of the agreement to anyone else without the publisher's permission—except your right to receive money. Usually, though, publishers do have the right to assign the agreement in case of licensing, foreign sales, sale of the company, paperback editions, and other similar situations. The contract also states that this is a "binding agreement" and constitutes the full understanding of both parties—that both its obligations and benefits shall be binding on your heirs, the publisher, and any successor or assignees of the publisher. The applicable law clause covers which state laws apply to the contract. Usually it is the state in which the publisher is located.

What happens if you cannot complete your work? Here's an example of standard wording (italics mine):

> Should the Author be unable for any reason to complete his commitment as per Paragraph I herein, the Author or his estate *shall relinquish* all claims and rights including but not limited to royalty income, *except* that if a considerable body of material has been produced and delivered to the Publisher which the Publisher may choose to use as part of a work for publication, the Author or his estate shall receive from the Publisher a royalty as determined by the Publisher substantially equal to the portion the Author's published work bears to the entire Work when published. In the event of revision, the

Publisher will pay to the Author or his estate such royalty as the Publisher determines is substantially equal to the portion of the revised Work that the Author's contribution bears to the total.

This clause is appearing more and more frequently, particularly in reference book contracts where revised editions are a distinct possibility. Again, it very much depends on particular cases. Did the idea originate with the publisher or the author, for example? All of us in the field are familiar with the various incarnations of *Guide to Reference Books* in various editions by Mudge, Winchell, and Sheehy.

Most publisher's contracts contain a clause which prohibits the author from publishing a "competing" work. Again, this is often a vaguely worded clause covering, for example, "any work that is liable to compete or interfere with or injure the sale of the work." If you plan on writing another book on the same topic, you may want to limit this clause further. However, it is to no one's advantage for you to compete with your own work.

Some publisher's contracts contain an option clause, giving the publisher the "option" to publish your next book. Try to have this clause stricken if possible. There's no reason for you to be tied down to one publisher.

Author copies is the clause that spells out how many free copies of your book you will receive and at what discount you can buy others. Six copies is the normal free allotment. Additional copies for personal use (*not* for resale) are usually sold to authors at discounts of from 25 to 50 percent.

There are numerous additional clauses that can be added to publishing contracts, depending upon specific situations. Most "survival" guides for authors deal with trade book publishing; however, you might want to read one, such as Carol Meyer's *The Writer's Survival Manual* (Bantam, 1984). If you consult a lawyer, make sure he or she has a specific knowledge of publishing contracts.

In the final analysis, good faith, not a contract, will determine your relationship with a publisher. Most are honest and want to be fair. They want to keep you as an author—and to publish your colleagues as well. Knowing your rights, understanding the process, and communicating with your publisher are the keys not only to a successful relationship, but to a successful publication.

Who Are the Whos:
The Uses of Biographical Reference Sources for Social Demography

Adele Hast

Standard biographical source books, found on the reference shelves of most libraries, are designed to provide information on contemporary individuals. Alphabetic organization by name allows quick access to biographical data on persons known to the searcher. However, beyond the obvious information available to readers, biographical reference volumes have been used in other ways in basic research studies. The books have proved to be important sources in sociological studies of elite groups in American society. An analysis of the demographic uses of such books is valuable to the reference librarian in revealing the full value of these volumes as research tools.

This bibliographic review will define and discuss the elite groups studied by researchers in demography, and show the relative importance of specific variables of information found in the biographical sketches. Analysis will also reveal both the limitations and the strengths of biographical reference books as sociological sources; in this connection, discussion will include methodologies adopted by researchers to fit the topics covered.

OVERVIEW OF ELITE STUDIES

During the twentieth century, sociologists have given considerable attention to studies of elite groups in American society, as part of a larger analysis of sources of power.[1] As one researcher has summarized, "Elites and the power they exercise in society are

---

The author is Editor-in-Chief, Who's Who in America, 200 East Ohio St., Chicago, IL 60611.

among the central concerns of sociologists. Indeed, the study of elites is often considered to be coterminous with the study of power: elites are individuals who exercise power."[2] In addition to full-length books, these analyses include several dozen articles dealing with elite groups in a number of areas, such as business, government, academics, and religion. Specialized studies deal with women leaders and with geographic sources of leadership.

This review will discuss a sampling of articles, chosen to show an accurate pattern of the types of elite groups analyzed by researchers. Biographical reference books have been used in different ways to extract information on elites. *Who's Who in America* is the most frequently used title, sometimes as the prime source, but often in conjunction with other books. Definition of elites ranges from individuals with specific occupations, for example, college presidents, to persons whose inclusion in a biographical reference book is taken as proof of eminence. Approaches include both analysis of an elite group at one period and historic studies comparing two or more time periods.

BUSINESS ELITES[3]

Consistent with the sociological interest in elites as persons with power, more studies have been done of corporate elite groups than of any other leadership cadre. The studies analyze the characteristics of chief executive officers, presidents, and directors of major corporations. What are the questions asked about these business leaders? In assessing the power of business elites, the studies look at membership on two or more corporate boards of directors, participation of corporate elites in top posts in the nonprofit and governmental sectors, education of corporate chief executive officers, and overlap between the elite class of high achievers and the upper class of *Social Register* listees. The studies of Freitag and Dye analyze the interchange of elites between governmental and corporate institutions. Similarly, Hong examines post-retirement employment of high-ranking military officers to assess their power in business and other sectors of the economy.

How are the biographical reference books used? In most business studies, the investigators define the positions they are seeking, and find the names of the incumbents in a variety of directories, such as *Standard & Poor's Register of Corporations, Directors, and*

Executives, Dun & Bradstreet's *Million Dollar Directory* and *Reference Book of Corporate Managements*, and the *Directory of Directors in the City of New York*.[4] The biographical reference books then supply data for each individual on specific demographic characteristics under study. In addition to *Who's Who in America*, a number of other reference sources provide biographical details. For business elites, the Who's Who books for *Finance and Industry, East, Midwest, South,* and *West* were also consulted. Other titles included the *Dictionary of American Biography, Current Biography, New York Times* obituaries, and similar sources.

The prevailing method of defining elites by positions, locating their names in directories of corporate officers, and then seeking biographical information in other publications, sheds light on both the strengths and limitations of biographical reference books as research sources. The most critical requirement of biographical sources for sociological research is completeness in two respects: comprehensive listings to include enough of the elites to make the studies possible, and sufficient data within the sketches on the variables under analysis. For librarians, the question of completeness of information is critical, for it indicates the value of each title for reference work.

How do the sources stand up against the measures of complete information? Obviously, the biographical sketches yielded sufficient data to produce the studies under question. Yet, while meeting sampling requirements, the studies showed a broad range of degree of inclusiveness. In most studies, a significant proportion of the names sought was listed in *Who's Who in America*. Priest, "Education," analyzing education and career in three time periods, found 87 percent of the names for 1940, 96 percent for 1955, and 97 percent for 1970. Similarly, Priest's "Note," covering two time periods, with three volumes of *Who's Who in America* used for each period, showed a range from 84 percent of the names in a single volume to 98 percent in three consecutive volumes. At the low end of the sampling spectrum, Dye located only half the individuals in the biographical volume and Useem found 58 percent. While sufficient for sampling, these data yielded less rich results than the more complete selections. These ranges reveal one of the limitations of biographical reference books as sources. Since the data come from the listees, with publisher-researched sketches of non-responders limited to the most important individuals, those who decline to answer will not be found in the volumes.

Similarly, a few variables of data yield meager information. Little analysis can be done on political or religious affiliation of elites, because fewer than half of the *America* listees include that information in their biographical sketches.[5] Most listees, however, provide information on the critical variables, such as career, education, directorships, club memberships, and other characteristics analyzed in studies of power.

In the majority of studies of business elites, the researchers concentrate on single time periods. However, about one-third of the studies are historical, comparing two or more time periods. Thus, Priest, "Education," studies three evenly spaced dates between 1940 and 1970, while Allen and Priest, "Note," each covers two periods. Freitag's study is a comprehensive analysis of cabinet members from 1897 to 1973.

WOMEN ELITES[6]

Like business elites, women leaders have received a great deal of attention in demographic studies. Throughout the twentieth century, sociologists have used the information in biographical reference books to analyze the characteristics of such women. Again, *Who's Who in America* is the prime source of information, with some use of *Who's Who of American Women* by Tidball (1973) and data from volumes of *Who Was Who* in Farley's study.

However, the methodology differs from that used in the studies of business elites. All of the studies of notable women define elites as those who are listed in the "Who's Who" books. Methodologically, the researchers use the universe of women found within the books as the elites under study, allowing for use of the total number or of a sample designed to suit the study. The samples may range from 100 for each of two years studied, as in Chafetz, through half the women in the source in Oates, to analysis of virtually all of the women in the book, as done by Kiser and Visher. The methodology of defining elite women as those listed in a specific reference book is basically different from that used in the business studies. While the latter begin with their own definition of elites and seek such persons in biographical sources, the studies of women accept the definitions of elite set forth by the publishers of the books used, by virtue of inclusion in the volumes.

For the most part, studies of women leaders focus on single time periods. Only one article in the series cited, Chafetz, compares elite women in two periods, 1925 and 1965, in assessing changes in social status.

OTHER ELITE STUDIES

While business leaders and women elites have been the most frequently studied groups, other elite cohorts have also been analyzed through the use of data in biographical reference books. Edward C. McDonagh et al. have examined the academic credentials of presidents of universities.[7] The study sets forth comparative data on presidents of 101 universities for academically-related characteristics, such as education, career patterns, age at entering presidency, and specialized field.

Media directors have been analyzed in Edward G. Weston's study of social characteristics and recruitment.[8] Weston examined the education, age, and gender of 145 presidents and board members of the largest print and broadcast media.

A number of studies concentrated on characteristics of all elites, rather than leadership groups within specific professions. These studies are based methodologically on listees found in *Who's Who in America*, as the automatic determinant of elite status. Scott Nearing reviewed the birthplaces of 10,000 biographees in *Who's Who in America* for 1912–13 to compare the geographic areas of the United States as sources of distinguished persons. A few studies have analyzed the religious listings in *Who's Who in America* and correlated religion with other characteristics, drawing their samples from the minority of biographees who provide data on religion.[9]

VARIABLES ANALYZED

For the librarian assessing the reference value of biographical sources, it is useful to know the variables in which researchers have an interest and the extent to which the sources can provide the data. As has been pointed out, since fewer than half of the biographees give information on religion or political affiliation, analysis of these characteristics is severely limited, and few researchers select information on these characteristics.

Several variables are considered critical and are analyzed in all groups of elite studies, whether business leaders, women, educators, or others. One key trait is occupation, covering both the profession of the individual and the position attained. Education is almost universally analyzed, with different emphases, depending on the group. Studies of women compare graduates of coeducational and women's colleges, while analyses of business leaders review the nature of the colleges attended: ivy league versus state institutions, northeastern locations compared to universities in other parts of the country.

Place of birth and age or birthdate are also of interest in a wide variety of studies. Other traits are specific to one group of elites. In women's studies, marriage is analyzed in great detail and specificity: age at marriage, number of children, name used after marriage. Only in the analysis of women elites was there inquiry into the status of the spouse, that is, whether the husband was also listed in a "Who's Who" book. For women who did not include marital data, there was no way to know whether they were unmarried or had chosen not to provide the information. Membership in social clubs and in business policy associations, as well as on corporate boards of directors, emerged for analysis in research on business elites.

Information on those traits most widely studied by sociologists and deemed most important, such as career, profession, and education, was supplied by virtually all listees in the biographical reference books, providing ample data from which to select representative samples. Despite the limitations of biographical reference books as sources for social demography—incomplete facts or missing names—the volumes prove to be rich sources of data in social demography. For the reference librarian, the books provide information far beyond the most frequent use given these sources—the quick look at the life history of a contemporary celebrity. Used creatively, biographical reference books contribute to an understanding of past and present elite groups and their roles in society.

REFERENCES

1. See, for example, C. Wright Mills, *The Power Elite* (New York: Oxford University Press, 1958) and Thomas R. Dye, *Who's Running America* (Englewood Cliffs, N.J.: Prentice-Hall, 1976).
2. Michael Patrick Allen, "Continuity and Change Within the Core Corporate Elite," *The Sociological Quarterly* 19 (Autumn 1978), 510.
3. This section draws material from the following studies: Ibid., 510-21; E. Digby

Baltzell, "'Who's Who in America' and 'The Social Register': Elite and Upper Class Indexes in Metropolitan America" in Reinhard Bendix and Seymour Martin Lipset, eds., *Class, Status, and Power* (Glencoe, Ill.: Free Press, 1953), 266–75; Thomas R. Dye and John W. Pickering, "Governmental and Corporate Elites: Convergence and Differentiation," *Journal of Politics* 37 (November 1974), 900–25; Peter J. Freitag, "The Cabinet and Big Business: A Study of Interlocks," *Social Problems* 23 (December 1975), 137–52; Doo-Seung Hong, "Retired U.S. Military Elites: Postmilitary Employment and Its Sociopolitical Implications," *Armed Forces and Society* 5 (Spring 1979), 451–466; Peter Mariolis, "Interlocking Directorates and Control of Corporations: The Theory of Bank Control," *Social Science Quarterly* 56 (December 1975), 425–39; Priest, Thomas B., "Education and Career among Corporate Chief Executive Officers: A Historical Note," *Social Science Quarterly* 63 (June 1982), 342–49; Priest, Thomas B., "Elite and Upper Class in Philadelphia, 1914," *The Sociological Quarterly* 25 (Summer 1984), 319–31; Priest, Thomas B., "A Note on *Who's Who in America* as A Biographical Data Source in Studies of Elites," *Sociological Methods & Research* 11 (August 1982), 81–88; Michael Soref, "Social Class and a Division of Labor within the Corporate Elite: a Note on Class, Interlocking, and Executive Committee Membership of Directors of U.S. Industrial Firms," *The Sociological Quarterly* 17 (Summer 1976), 360–68; Michael Useem, "The Social Organization of the American Business Elite and Participation of Corporate Directors in the Governance of American Institutions," *American Sociological Review* 44 (August 1979), 553–72.

4. See Mariolis, 428, for examples of sources used to find names of holders of elite positions.

5. Priest, T.B., "Note" (1982), 85. See also Adele Hast, "Leadership in American Society 1899–1982" in Adele Hast and Jennie Farley, *American Leaders Past and Present: The View from Who's Who in America* (Chicago: Marquis Who's Who, Inc., 1985), 11.

6. The following studies are cited: Janet Saltzman Chafetz and Barbara Bovee Polk, "Room at the Top: Social Recognition of British and American Females over Time," *Social Science Quarterly* 54 (March 1974), 843–53; Persis M. Cope, "The Women of 'Who's Who': A Statistical Study," *Social Forces* 7 (December 1928), 212–23; Jennie Farley, "Women Leaders in America 1607–1982" in Hast and Farley, *American Leaders Past and Present*, 25–36; Clyde V. Kiser and Nathalie L. Schacter, "Demographic Characteristics of Women in 'Who's Who'," *Milbank Memorial Fund Quarterly* 27 (October 1949), 392–433; Amanda Carolyn Northrop, "The Successful Women of America," *Popular Science Monthly* 64 (January 1904), 239–44; Mary J. Oates and Susan Williamson, "Women's Colleges and Women Achievers," *Signs* 3 (Summer 1978), 795–806; M. Elizabeth Tidball, "Perspective on Academic Women and Affirmative Action," *Educational Record* 54 (Spring 1973), 130–35; M. Elizabeth Tidball, "Women's Colleges and Women Achievers Revisited," *Signs* 5 (Spring 1980), 504–17; Stephen S. Visher and Gertrude Hoverstock, "'Who's Who' among American Women," *The Scientific Monthly* 15 (November 1922), 443–47.

7. Edward C. McDonagh, Muriel C. Schuerman, and Leo A. Schuerman, "Academic Characteristics of Presidents of Major American Universities," *Sociology and Social Research* 54 (April 1970), 356–70.

8. Edward G. Weston, "Social Characteristics and Recruitment of American Mass Media Directors," *Journalism Quarterly* 55 (Spring 1978), 62–67.

9. Dr. Scott Nearing, "The Geographical Distribution of American Genuis," *The Popular Science Monthly* 85 (August 1914), 189–99; William S. Ament, "Religion, Education, and Distinction," *School and Society* 26 (September 1927), 399–406; Ellsworth Huntington and Leon F. Whitney, "Religion and 'Who's Who'," *The American Mercury* (August 1927), 438–443; Richard L. Zweigenhaft, "Recent Patterns of Jewish Representation in the Corporate and Social Elites," *Contemporary Jewry* 6 (Spring–Summer 1982), 36–46.

Small Press Reference Books

Kay Ann Cassell

Small press/publisher reference books have an important place in any reference collection. They cover in-depth subject areas which are superficially, if covered at all, by standard reference works. For the purposes of this discussion of small press reference works I have chosen to define small press in the very broadest sense. A small press is a press which publishes to serve a special audience. It might be an independent press, but it might also be a press connected to an association or organization. This last category is particularily important to reference librarians since many small organizations have the ability to survey and collect some specific area of information and then to publish it in whatever format it can afford. This kind of information is most valuable since it is collected by people who know a particular area of information well and have the right contacts. They produce an up-to-date work with fewer than average errors. It can often make an important contribution to many reference collections.

In this article I want to explore how to locate small press materials for reference collections, some review sources or listings, distribution sources and some examples of titles you'll want to consider. It has been most interesting to me to find as I have worked in reference departments that a great deal of needed information was not to be found in standard reference works. There are a variety of reasons for this:

1. the information was too specific for the reference works in the collection,
2. the information was of a regional or local nature, or
3. the information was on a subject not dealt with in any standard work.

The author is Director, Coordinating Council of Literary Magazines, 666 Broadway, New York, NY 10012. Also, she is an experienced and well known librarian.

For these and other reasons it is always amazing to me that many information requests were not to be found in what should have been a very adequate reference collection.

This is where small press materials come in. The small presses have always served a somewhat different audience. The works they publish are for a specific and usually smaller audience. There is no fear that a small audience will not produce a large sale since the purpose of the work is to fill a need. These works often provide more current information on a regular basis since they are produced in less elaborate formats, in a quicker time frame and often at a low cost.

HOW TO LOCATE THE MATERIAL

Although I will discuss review media and listings as it relates to small press reference material, much of the material which could be useful to the librarian will not be found in these channels. So how do you locate it?

First of all, read listings of new reference materials as well as reviews. Often you can tell by the title if it will serve your purpose. To be sure you have to take some chances.

Second, no matter where you go, pick up flyers announcing new publications or listings of a series of publications. They are usually not printed in any slick format since most small presses and organizations cannot afford to spend much on the marketing of their publications. Ask friends and colleagues to do likewise if they're going to any kind of an exhibit or association meeting.

Third, when you have problems answering questions in a particular area, look up a likely association in the *Encyclopedia of Associations* and contact them to see if they might have publications which would help you to respond to these queries. They may have a publications list they can send you.

Fourth, talk to colleagues in a special library in the subject area in question. Since they are collecting in a more in-depth fashion, they may have found sources you have missed. If you can get to the library, browse their shelves—that's the best. But if not, write or call them. For example, I found one of the best regional funding guides by browsing the shelves of the Foundation Center Library.

Visit regional and local bookstores and don't forget to check out bookstores when you're traveling. Many small presses place their books in bookstores near home since they have few inexpensive ways to distribute their publication. Some of the best material can only be found in bookstores. Regional travel books are an obvious example. But I also found a wonderful New York area writers' guide published by the City of New York's Department of Cultural Affairs in a local bookstore which I never saw listed anywhere. At the most it was probably mentioned at some point in local newspapers. Don't forget specialized bookstores when you get to large cities. They are often a goldmine of material.

If friends go on trips, ask them to look around for those good local travel guides—in bookstores and on newsstands. That's the only way you'll ever get them since they aren't distributed out of the region.

Read local newspapers for mention of new small press reference books. They could be in any section—the business section, a column on food, an article on travel or a how-to-do-it article.

Finally talk to local people who work in a particular field. Find out about their professional associations and what publications these groups publish. Sometimes you'll have to get them to order a publication for you if the association only sells to its members. And don't forget to talk to people who have hobbies and might belong to groups or organizations related to their hobbies. Yet another source of specialized publications.

Above all, keep your network broad if you want to expand your reference collection and include those elusive small press items. That perfect book that fills a gap could be anywhere. So keep your eyes pealed and be prepared to purchase it any way you can.

REVIEW SOURCES AND LISTINGS

Certainly reviewing of small press books has taken giant leaps forward since the early 70s when it was very difficult to get any reviews. Some journals finally provided separate column space to small press books to give them visibility. Articles were written about small press material. But it took several years to get them integrated into the regular reviewing media. Today many more small press books get reviewed as do small press reference books. *Library Journal, Booklist, Choice* and *Wilson Library Bulletin*, to name only a few, do regular reviews of small press materials.

Listings and reviews of new small press reference books are available from many sources. One of the most important sources of new small press reference books is the magazine, *Small Press*, which is published bimonthly, ($18/yr). It is chocked full of listings of new small press books (some of which are reference books), reviews of small press books and articles featuring the publications of a particular press. All in all it is a first choice for finding a large number of listings in one place. Reference books I found listed in a recent issue included: *Parental Kidnapping: An International Resource Directory*, Margaret Strickland, comp. and Joe Teague Caruso, ed., Rainbow Books $19.95. This is a country by country survey of the laws that affect the rights of children taken abroad; *Intellectual Property Law Dictionary*, by Stephen R. Elias, Nolo Press $14.95. This is a dictionary of definitions for legal words and phrases commonly used in relation to trade secret, copyright, trademark, patents, contracts and warranties; *Filmmaker's Dictionary* by Ralph S. Singleton, Lone Eagle Productions $5.95. This work includes over 1,500 words and terms used in professional motion picture and television production; and *The New Consciousness Sourcebook: Spiritual Community Guide No. 6*, edited by Daniel Ellsberg and Marilyn Ferguson, Arcline Publications $8.95. This sourcebook includes information and addresses for thousands of new-age centers, schools and businesses in such fields as health, meditation and therapy. Another excellent source is *New Pages* ($12/6 issues) which is a triannual publication reviewing and listing small press materials. It even has a reference section making it easy to spot small press reference material although more may be lurking in other sections. *Small Press Review* ($22/year) is a monthly publication which supplements Dustbooks' *International Directory of Little Magazines and Small Presses*. New small press books are reviewed and new presses and their publications are listed. In a recent issue, for example, is a short review of three poetry market books comparing the coverage in each. Another new source of reviews is *Small Press Book Review* ($20/year) which has just published its fourth issue. It reviews a potpourri of small press books and is yet another source of reference books. *Sipapu*, edited by librarian Noel Peattie, is a newsletter on small presses with an eye to the needs and interests of librarians. A number of reference items are reviewed in each issue. Finally don't miss the resource sections of the major library periodicals which list many small press reference publications in each issue. Although they do not formally review them, one can usually tell from the description how useful they will be.

DISTRIBUTION

Libraries like to order from library jobbers, and this is not always possible with small press material. So there needs to be some flexibility on the part of the library if these materials are to be purchased. Some of the smaller book jobbers do handle some of the material such as Quality Books which carries a large line of non-fiction small press materials, as well as Bookpeople, Bookslinger and Inland Books. Librarians should write them for their catalogs and try to ascertain what titles can be purchased from each of them. But some important titles will require direct orders, and others will require having the ability to pay by check or even cash. This is really difficult in larger libraries but some consideration must be given to this if a reference collection is to be more than a collection of standard titles from larger publishers.

SMALL PRESS ARTS REFERENCE BOOKS: A CASE STUDY

Just to give the reader an idea of the vast array of reference material available in one field, I have chosen the arts and literature area as a case study.

Dustbooks is the publisher who publishes the most definitive works on small presses. Their *International Directory of Little Magazines and Small Presses* is a must for libraries. It lists small presses and small non-commercial magazines and will be useful in locating that literary press or magazine which you cannot find in *Books in Print*. They also publish the *Small Press Record of Books in Print* which lists 18,000 books, broadsides and pamphlets from 1,500 presses ($29.95) and the *Directory of Small Magazine/Press Editors and Publishers* ($14.95) which is a companion volume to the *International Directory*. The first edition of a *Directory of Poetry Publishers* ($9.95) is now available which includes over 1,000 listings of presses and magazines and information on submissions policies, payments, rights and special interests. Any library with a budding group of writers should have some of these publications to help them find publishers with whom to place their work.

Poets & Writers, a New York-based organization, which has begun to expand nationally, publishes several important reference books which many libraries serving a community of writers will find invaluable. A first choice is *The Directory of American Poets and Fiction Writers*, 1985–86 edition, which lists the names, addresses and telephone numbers of 6,020 poets and fiction writers who publish their work in the U.S. with information on each author's publications. In many cases this will be more useful for finding correct addresses of writers than some other standard reference works which are not updated so frequently ($19.95). Poets & Writers will also answer questions about the currect addresses of writers by telephone (212) 757-1766. Other Poets & Writers publications of reference value are *A Writer's Guide to Copyright* which summarizes the law relating to copyright in layperson's terms ($4.95) and *Literary Agents: A Writer's Guide* which provides information on rights and fees as well as a selected list of agencies interested in handling literary work ($5.95).

The American Council for the Arts is an umbrella arts organization which has a very large publications program. Libraries may be familiar with its *Guide to Corporate Giving 3* which contains up-to-date information on the giving policies of over 700 major corporations. It provides a profile of each company, the type and level of support offered in the arts, health, welfare, education and civic philanthropy and application requirements ($30). But there are a number of other ACA publications you won't want to miss. The *Directory of Matching Gifts Programs for the Arts* contains information about 255 businesses which operate matching gift programs for the arts ($5). The *Survey of Arts Administration Training 1985–86* describes in detail each of the graduate degree programs in arts management ($7.50). It's often very useful to have specialized pamphlets to help people looking for educational information in a special field. The *National Directory of Art Internships* by Warren Christensen lists 350 on-the-job internship opportunities nationwide in dance, theater, music, art, design, film and video. You could look a long time to accumulate such a list yourself ($25). *The Dramatists Sourcebook 1985–86* is a comprehensive guide to professional theatre opportunities which lists over 200 theatres producing new plays, 90 playwriting contests, 35 developmental workshops and conferences and service organizations that aid playwrights. Ted Crawford's *Legal Guide for the Visual Artist: The Professional's Handbook* provides the artist professional with information on how to deal with sales, reproduction rights, publishing and dealer contracts, taxation, hobby losses, estate planning, donations to museums, etc. ($16.95).

Another useful reference book for writers is published by the PEN American Center. *Grants and Awards Available to American Writers 1986–87* (14th ed.) is a comprehensive list of grants and awards available to American writers for use in the United States and abroad. An additional section for grants and awards available to Canadian writers is also included. Each grant and award is described with information on any restrictions, deadlines and address for application. There is also a subject index by type of literature ($9.50).

The Coordinating Council of Literary Magazines (CCLM) publishes an annual *Directory of Literary Magazines* which provides information on about 350 literary magazines including the type of material they publish, their advertising policies, their policies on submitting material, and examples of some of the writers they publish ($5.95). This is a good beginning source for the writer trying to break into print as many of these editors make a special effort to read unsolicited material.

The Associated Writing Programs is an organization mainly of faculty and students in writing programs. They publish the *AWP Catalogue of Writing Programs* which lists over 250 institutions in the U.S. and Canada which have creative writing programs. The faculty, degree requirements and narrative descriptions of creative writing programs are listed as well as writers' colonies and support organizations ($10).

In "The Source" section of *American Libraries* I recently found this listing—*Alternative Press Publishers of Children's Books: A Directory* which lists 150 independent publishers of children's books in the U.S. and Canada and was published by the Cooperative Children's Book Center (CCBC) $8.

These few selections will give the reader some idea of the large number of small press reference items currently available and most useful to librarians. I hope this sampling will encourage readers of this article to search out those small press items which will be most useful in their collections. The users of your library will appreciate your extra efforts on their behalf.

ADDRESSES

American Council for the Arts, Dept. 24, 570 Seventh Ave., New York, NY 10018

Arcline Publications, Box 1967, Berkeley, CA 94701

Associated Writing Programs, Old Dominion University, Norfolk, VA 23508
Bookpeople, 2929 7th Street, Berkeley, CA 94710
Bookslinger, 330 E. 9th St., St. Paul, MN 55101
CCBC, P.O. Box 5288, Madison, WI 53705
CCLM, 666 Broadway, New York, NY 10012
Dustbooks, P.O. Box 100, Paradise, CA 95969
Inland Book Co., P.O. Box 261, East Haven, CT 06512
Lone Eagle Productions, 9903 Santa Monica Blvd. Suite 204, Beverly Hills, CA 90212
New Pages, P.O. Box 438, Grand Blanc, MI 48439
Nolo Press, Box 544, Occidental, CA 95465
PEN American Center, 568 Broadway, New York, NY 10012
Poets & Writers, 201 W. 54th St., New York, NY 10019
Quality Books, 400 Anthony Trail, Northbrook, IL 60065
Rainbow Books, Box 1069, Moore Haven, FL 33471
Sipapu, Rt. 1, Box 216 Winters, CA 95694
Small Press, 11 Ferry Lane West, Westport, CT 06880
Small Press Book Review, P.O. Box 176, Southport, CT 06490
Small Press Review, P.O. Box 100, Paradise, CA 95969

Major Business Reference Works

Thomas P. Slavens

Although a well-stocked library will have many reference works of value to the person interested in the provision of information about business, some of the more useful data are published by Standard & Poor's, Moody's, Predicasts, as well as Dun & Bradstreet.

Standard & Poor's, for instance, publishes a *Daily Stock Price Record* devoted to data on the New York Stock Exchange, the American Stock Exchange, and Over-the-Counter issues. In the daily price histories provided are included the high, low and closing prices in addition to bid and asked prices on non-traded securities. Other information furnished for stocks includes ticket symbols, shares outstanding, dividends, earnings, short interest positions, relative strength ratios, and averages for the preceding thirty weeks. Other stock market indicators are provided in these volumes.

Daily Action Stock Charts, also published by Standard & Poor's, provides data on the price and volume of popular stocks on the American and the New York Stock Exchange. Published weekly, it gives retrospective information as well as earnings estimates and trends.

Credit Week, published by Standard & Poor's, provides news and analyses for those people interested in commercial paper, preferred stock, and bonds. The work provides credit tables, calendars, and updated ratings. This periodical is of interest primarily to those people involved with fixed income investments.

Current Market Perspectives is published by Standard & Poor's on a monthly basis and provides facts and action on hundreds of stocks. Both industries and individual stocks are ranked.

Another publication of Standard & Poor's is *The Outlook*. In this weekly periodical, specific stocks are treated; and recommendations are made for investors. In the same issues, general articles of

---

The author is Professor, School of Library Science, The University of Michigan, 580 Union Drive, Ann Arbor, MI 48109.

© 1987 by The Haworth Press, Inc. All rights reserved.

interest to investors and statistics on indexes and percentages are included.

Standard & Poor's also publishes a *Statistical Service* which is updated each month. Included in the hundreds of series provided in this work are data on income, population, sales, inventories, rates of interest, prices, securities, bank reserves, and issues in many fields.

Standard & Poor's also publishes a monthly *Bond Guide* for people interested in buying or selling fixed income investments issued by many types of organizations. This work provides descriptions of, statistics for, and ratings of thousands of bonds.

Standard & Poor's *Stock Guide* is published monthly and provides statistics on thousands of stocks. These data include price ranges and volume, earnings, and dividends. Another important element of this work is its rankings and ratings.

Another of Standard & Poor's works is its *Dividend Record*, which is published on a quarterly basis, and which covers thousands of stocks and bonds. In this work appear announcements of dates with lists of redemptions and tenders, split actions, and rights.

Standard & Poor's *Industry Surveys* provide data on industries and hundreds of companies. A *Basic Survey* published each year is supplemented by *Current Surveys* published three times a year. In the *Basic Survey*, the industries are discussed within the context of their future in the economy. In the discussion of the financial condition of the industries and their companies charts and tables are provided. The *Current Surveys* described recent developments and make projections. The latter provides information on sales, profits, dividends and recommendations on investments for various companies. Another part of the *Industry Surveys* is the *Trends and Projections Bulletin*. Not only are leading economic indicators evaluated, but many projections are included. In charts, trends are presented on bond and treasury note yields, employment, housing, production, and sales.

STANDARD AND POOR'S GUIDES

This publisher also issues the *Stock Market Encyclopedia of the Standard & Poor's "500."* Issued twice a year, this work has stock reports on corporations. Each page includes a summary of the firm's activities and factors in the economy which may influence its future. Statistical tables including information on shares, income, and balance sheets for the past decade are also included. Earnings and dividend rankings for common stocks are also included. Some of this information is taken from annual reports. Similar data are provided in the *OTC Handbook* and the *Energy Stocks Handbook* published by this firm.

Standard & Poor's *Corporation Records* is another useful source of information. The major part of this set of books is composed of descriptions of corporations based on their annual reports. For these organizations, news stories are published on a daily basis compiled from news releases, reports to stockholders, newspapers and SEC documents. These accounts provide updated information on earnings, new products, personnel changes, mergers, and acquisitions.

Standard & Poor's Register of Corporations, Directors and Executives

This register provides information on thousands of companies. These data include addresses, telephone numbers, lists of staff, relationship to other companies, and descriptions of products and/or services, as well as information on sales and employees. In addition, banking, accounting, and legal firms for the corporations are often listed. Biographical data for executives in these firms are also included. In the indexes, the corporations are listed by cities and by products and services. The *Register* is updated three times each year.

Moody's Municipal and Government Manual

This annual covers nearly 15,000 municipalities along with state and U.S. government agencies. All entries are arranged geographically by state, county and then municipality. Information such as bond debt, tax collections and bond ratings is provided. The special features section has information on bonds, debts and securities. It includes an alphabetical index. *The Moody's Municipal and Government News Reports* updates the manual twice weekly, and it has the same arrangement.

Moody's Bond Record

The monthly record provides statistical information on fixed income securities along with Moody's bond ratings. The record covers over 32,000 corporate issues and it also covers government and municipal issues, commercial paper, convertible and other stocks. This work includes a monthly cumulative index.

AND FROM MOODY'S

Moody's Transportation Manual

This annual covers a wide variety of transportation companies from airlines to tunnel and bridge companies. The companies are arranged by type of transportations, and such information as financial statements and bond ratings is provided. A special features section provides such information as transportation income bonds and air transport data. The work includes some transportation maps. *The Weekly Moody's Transportation News Reports* updates the manual.

Moody's Public Utility Manual

This manual covers over 475 U.S. publicly held electric and gas companies, gas transmission companies, telephone companies and water companies. Companies are arranged alphabetically under the type of coverage, for example, complete coverage or full measure coverage. Information such as mergers, bond ratings and financial statements is provided for each company. More financial information is found in the special features section. It includes an alphabetical index and maps of public utilities. The twice-weekly *Moody's Public Utility News Reports* updates the manual in the same format.

Moody's Industrial Manual

This manual covers the industrial companies listed on the New York, American and regional stock exchanges. The entries are arranged alphabetically, providing such information as the companies' histories, officers, subsidiaries and capital stock. The special features section gives such information as bond ratings and commodity prices. The work includes an alphabetical index and a geographical index. The manual is updated twice-weekly by *Moody's Industrial News Reports*.

Moody's Bank & Finance Manual

This manual covers over 10,900 banks, investment companies, insurance companies and other financial institutions worldwide.

Volume one contains American banks and trust companies, savings and loans associations, international banks, federal credit agencies and other financial institutions. These are arranged alphabetically. Volume two is separated by insurance, finance, real estate or investment companies. The same type of coverage is given. Both volumes include an alphabetical index and a special features section. The manual is updated twice-weekly by *Moody's Bank and Finance News Reports.*

Moody's Dividend Record

The record provides up-to-date information on dividends on a twice-weekly and an annual basis with eight cumulative issues during the year. Included are preferred and common stocks, income bonds, mutual funds and foreign securities. The work includes a list of company meetings.

Moody's OTC Industrial Manual

This manual is a companion to *Moody's Industrial Manual* by covering over 2,700 over-the-counter companies unlisted on the national or regional stock exchanges. Broad coverage such as financial statements and histories are given for each company. The companies are arranged alphabetically under the type of coverage, for example, complete or standard coverage. Special features include a geographical index, classification of companies by industries, and products and stock splits. An alphabetical index is given. The manual is updated twice-weekly by *Moody's OTC Industrial News Reports.*

Moody's International Manual

This manual has business and financial information on over 3,000 corporations and national institutions in over 95 countries. The entries are arranged alphabetically in one of three sections: (1) sovereigns, municipalities and companies, (2) other sovereigns, and (3) world corporations. Information such as company's history is provided. A special features sections offers more business and financial statistics. The work includes a geographical index and an alphabetical index of corporations and institutions. The manual is updated with bi-weekly news reports, which are arranged alphabetically by company name with an index.

THE PREDICASTS GROUP

Predicasts F & S Index: International Annual

This reference source provides corporate and business information on the countries of the world except for the U.S. and European nations. The information is derived from over 500 business publications. The work is divided into 3 sections: Industries and Products, Countries, and Companies. The entries give short titles and a citations to publications. Major articles are indicated by a large dot.

Predicasts F & S Index: Europe Annual

This work indexes articles dealing with many forms of business in Europe. It includes both Western and Eastern Europe, including the Soviet Union. The annual is divided into three sections: Industries and Products, Countries, and Companies. Citations are derived from more than 750 business-oriented publications. Short titles and publication information are provided. This index is updated by monthly issues, which are cumulated quarterly.

Predicasts F & S Index: United States Annual

This work indexes more than 750 business publications to provide entries for U.S. corporations and industries. The citations are divided into two sections: Industries and Products, and Companies with alphabetical listings for each. The entries provide short titles and publication citations. A list of publications indexed is provided. The index is updated by weekly supplements, which are cumulated quarterly.

Dun & Bradstreet also publishes many services of interest to businesspeople. The *Million Dollar Directory*, for instance, provides basic information for about 115,000 U.S. business firms whose individual net worth exceeds $500,000. Volume I contains 43,000 businesses with a new worth of over $1,670,000; Volume II contains 36,000 businesses with a net worth ranging from $847,000 to $1,670,000; Volume III also contains 36,000 businesses with a net worth between $500,000 and $847,000. Types of businesses listed include industry, transportation, utilities, banks and trusts, as well as mutual and stock insurance companies. Each of the three volumes is arranged in the same manner: green pages comprise the alphabetical master index for easy volume and page reference to every company listed in the set, white pages comprise an alphabetical listing by name of business, yellow pages list businesses alphabetically within their geographical unit, and blue pages which group businesses by their numerical industry classification codes.

Entries provide such information as address, telephone number, type of business, Standard Industrial Classification (SIC) number, D-U-N-S number (a unique computer identification number), and names of executives. Other features include a list of symbols and abbreviations used throughout the work with their meanings and a numerical listing of SIC numbers and their meanings.

MARKETING DIRECTORY

Principal International Businesses

This world marketing directory offers up-to-date information on some 50,000 major companies in 133 countries. Selection of those establishments included is based on the firm's size, as determined by annual sales volume, and the company's national and international prominence. The work is divided into three main sections: the white pages which list businesses by country, the yellow pages listing businesses by product classification (e.g., heavy construction, textile goods), and finally the blue pages, providing a single alphabetical listing for all 50,000 firms.

Entries in the geographical section provide the most complete record of information about the company. In addition to the firm's full legal name and address, entries supply a unique, universal identification number (D-U-N-S Number), indication of import/export activities, name and location of any parent company, sales volume, number of employees, Standard Industrial Classification Number (SIC) to identify the company's specific function and its product/service category, a brief description of activities, and the firm's chief executive. The following two sections give basic information in their entries, mainly company name and address.

The table of contents and other introductory material are presented in four languages—English, French, Spanish, German— but directory listings are given only in English. A list of abbreviations and their meanings is provided along with a numerical index of SIC numbers. Also included is an alphabetical index of product classifications and SIC numbers, and a table of international statistics for each of the 133 countries.

Europe's 10,000 Largest Companies

This work is a continuation of *Europe's 5000 Largest Companies* reporting financial and statistical data for 11,900 companies in 16 West European and Scandinavian countries. Compilers depend heavily upon companies to supply information about themselves and this becomes a major factor for inclusion.

The main section consists of a listing of the 8,000 largest industrial firms ranked according to total sales. Information given includes ranking, yearly increase or decrease of net sales, total export sales, number of employees and shareholders, balance sheet data, location of headquarters, and industrial activity code. Headings for the numerical data tables are given in English, German, and French. Explanatory tables precede this section to define financial headings, country codes, exchange rates, and activity code numbers.

The next segment is a series of 26 secondary listings of data contained in the first section. These lists organize information under such headings as the top 500 profit makers, the top 100 profit losers, and the largest companies in terms of sales for each country. The section following provides the same type of information as the first section for the 2,500 largest European trading companies. Concluding the volume is a series of specialized lists providing statistical data for such sectors of business as transport, banking, insurance, advertising, and hotels and restaurants. Also included is an alphabetical index to all companies appearing in this work.

WHO HAS WHAT

Who Owns Whom: North America

The *Who Owns Whom* series of publications provides up-to-date information concerning parent corporations and their ownership of associate and subsidiary companies. A large portion of the data is furnished directly by the firm in question. Section one provides an alphabetical listing of parent companies for the United States and includes only those business enterprises whose activities are international in scope. Each entry gives the office address and an indication of the firm's major business activities. Entries also indicate the structure of the company body, including all member companies and their link to the larger corporate group.

Sections two and three follow this same format, providing information for Canadian and foreign parent companies. Definitions of all abbreviations and industry codes are given as introductory material. The index section comprises roughly 2/3 of the volume. It is arranged alphabetically by name of the subsidiary or associate company and gives reference to the parent company.

Who Owns Whom: Continental Europe

Volume I of this set provides separate listings for European parent companies and foreign parent companies situated outside of Europe but with subsidiary and associate firms in the region. All entries give an office address, an industry code to indicate major business activities, and an indication of the overall structure of the extended company body. Introductory material is given in English, French, and German and includes a list of industry codes and definitions.

The index is contained in Volume II. It is arranged alphabetically by name of the subsidiary and associate company and indicates the parent company. A separate one page index for numeric titles is appended. This volume also includes a list of abbreviations for company names.

Who Owns Whom: Australasia and Far East

Section I of this work groups businesses by country and lists them alphabetically by company names. Although the title of this publication varies, the countries and regions included therein are Australia, Hong Kong, Indonesia, Japan, Malaysia, New Zealand, Papua New Guinea, Philippines, Singapore, South Korea, Taiwan, and Thailand. Entries supply the office address, main business activities, and an indication of the structure of the company body, including member companies and their link to the larger corporate group.

Section II is entitled "Foreign Investment" and lists all parent companies located outside of Australia and the Far East which maintain subsidiary and associate firms within the region. Data contained in each entry complement that appearing in the first section. Concluding the volume is an index of subsidiary and associate companies with reference to the parent company.

Who Owns Whom: United Kingdom and Republic of Ireland

Volume I of the set is divided into four sections. The first two sections provide information concerning subsidiary and associate firms whose parent company is located in a country outside of the region. The final section provides a listing of consortia groups with reference to member companies, and also an alphabetical index arranged by member company and indicating their consortium.

Entries typically give the main office address and telephone number, major business activities, and an indication of the structure of the company. Introductory material includes a listing of industry codes and their definitions, as well as company abbreviations and their designations. The index is contained in Volume II and is arranged alphabetically by subsidiary and associate company name, with reference to the parent body.

Publishing Reference Works in the Electronic Age: Information Delivery Through Multiple Channels

Phyllis B. Steckler

The benefits and the difficulties of publishing reference works in the electronic age begin and end with computers. Today, in order to survive, reference publishers must compile, store, relate, and retrieve information electronically, using innovative production procedures and technology; the information must then be delivered to end users in the most usable and cost-effective print or non-print formats.

The three basic applications of computers in publishing are:

1. To compile, store, relate, and retrieve information electronically which is delivered to end users in traditional print formats;
2. To compile, store, relate, and retrieve information electronically that is delivered electronically, online; and
3. To compile, store, relate, and retrieve information electronically that is delivered to the end user on tapes, floppy disks, or some sort of laser optical format, where it is accessed via other computers, i.e., distributed electronic formats.

The three applications listed above seem to suggest that the computer offers a single, simple, unified solution to publishing reference works—whether bibliographic information, directories, or encyclopedia information—in the electronic age. It would appear that if data are compiled and stored electronically, the publisher can simply choose the appropriate publishing format for a given market

---

Ms. Steckler is the founder and Director of the Oryx Press, Suite 103, 2214 North Central at Encanto, Phoenix, Arizona 85004.

© 1987 by The Haworth Press, Inc. All rights reserved.

and proceed with publication. It's not that simple, however, although a single, unified database is essential for cost-effective and timely information publishing.

Let's look at the three principal formats—print, online electronic, and distributed electronic—and consider the advantages and disadvantages of each as part of a unified database electronic publishing program.

PRINT

Books and periodicals have been "computer typeset" since 1963, when the *Index Medicus* was issued by the National Library of Medicine. The first commercial utilization of the new technology, however, was in 1967, when the R. R. Bowker Company produced *Paperbound Books in Print*. Electronically produced printed output, therefore, is the most familiar publishing application of the electronic age. To produce a print product from a database, however, requires a specific file extraction including typesetting codes, especially when the printed pages include sophisticated typographic elements— multiple fonts and typesizes, non-Western alphabets, scientific and mathematical characters, charts, tables and sidebars, illustrations, and even photographs. Each of these elements requires special codes; in fact, even paragraphs, pages, headings, running heads and footnotes, line breaks, and hyphenation and justification require specific codes. Files can be extracted from the host database and have to be prepared differently from the print product just described if they are to be used for online searching.

ONLINE PUBLISHING

Large databases of time-sensitive information are very well suited to online access, and according to the several directories of online databases there are thousands now available to users. These databases must be specially prepared for this use however. They must be "searchable," for example, which means that essential elements must be specifically coded so that they can be retrieved. The publisher must provide searching tools (including a thesaurus!) to minimize the end user's cost to access the database. Unfortunately, very few database producers (also called "information providers'') are making money from the online publication of their information. Most of them cannot provide direct access to their databases but must send data to an online vendor. This means that not only does the information provider have to share the income which results from end users accessing the database, but they must—more often than not—incur the cost of interfacing their database with each online vendor's format.

The high online charges paid by the end users include the vendor's fees, telecommunications costs, and a royalty to the information provider, the latter being a small portion of the equation! But online remains the most suitable form of publication for certain types of information to which ready access is essential for a good information product. Online access to databases with good retrieval systems provides a much more powerful and timely means of accessing information than does looking up the information in printed indexes.

DISTRIBUTED DATABASE PUBLISHING

To circumvent high telecommunications costs and to gain a better return than online vendors offer, publishers can physically distribute their own databases—or portions of them—by publishing on magnetic storage devices such as floppy disks, or on laser optical disks, particularly CD-ROM. This option puts the publisher directly in touch with end users. It affords the user the same powerful access to the database as online, but it alleviates the fear of running up high telecommunication charges. However, at the time of this writing, for the publisher the cost of converting (actually "inverting") a database so that it is a retrievable file which can be searched using a PC and/or a CD-ROM player is very high. This in turn makes the cost to the end user also very high; however, knowledge of all costs to the end user is determined in advance, a decided advantage.

For many types of relatively static information, distributed database publishing offers a good alternative to both online and print publishing. Databases can be published on both floppy disks and CD-ROM with user friendly retrieval software that facilitates end-user access. Data can now be compressed to augment the amount that can be stored on a single floppy disk. With the large number of PCs now in libraries, these electronic publications can be accessed using equipment that is already in place. CD-ROM offers publishers much larger capacity than floppy disks, but certain standards are not yet established and CD-ROM players are not yet common as pieces of library hardware. None of these formats (print, floppy disk, or CD-ROM) is as attractive to end users as online, however, if ready access to timely data is an essential aspect of searching a database.

ELECTRONIC PUBLISHING AT ORYX PRESS

A brief history of one of our firm's reference publications illustrates much of what has gone on in electronic publishing in the last 12 years. In 1973, William K. Wilson (then director of the grants office at SUNY, Fredonia, NY) put together a card file of information on post graduate research and demonstration grants. In 1974, Oryx Press converted that card file to a magnetic tape database and published a series of monthly *Faculty Alert Bulletins* in various subject areas. Those monthlies were combined and cumulated into a quarterly report, entitled *Grant Information System*. Eighty-eight separate publications (in print format) were produced from that database which was updated in a batch process mode each month by an outside service bureau. The end users for those publications were college and university grants offices. A year later, a hardcover annual volume—*Directory of Research Grants*—was produced from the same database for sale to libraries. And a year after that, the GRANTS file went online.

As online usage increased, however, the market for the printed monthly bulletins declined, and they were discontinued in 1984. In the meantime, market research showed a need for subject-oriented annual printed volumes, and Oryx published—in 1985—the first edition of *Biomedical and Health Care Grants*. In 1986, *Directory of Grants in the Humanities* and *Grants in the Physical Sciences* were also published, as was the first edition of *The Grants Thesaurus*, for use by searchers of the online database, which is accessible through SDC and Dialog. These volumes were produced by Oryx using our own in-house typesetting equipment, the Autologic APS Micro 5, supported by the Prime 2550. The same computer produces the monthly tapes for the online vendors.

At this writing, Oryx is actively investigating two distributed database publishing opportunities for its GRANTS database. New compressed floppy disk technology may be the next publication format used, this time to publish subject-oriented weekly or monthly publications. The CD-ROM publishing format is being researched and may be used to publish quarterly cumulations.

The various publication formats used to provide end users with information about research and demonstration grants illustrates the benefits and difficulties of publishing reference works in the electronic age. Multiple channels have been used over the past 12 years to satisfy the information needs of the several end user groups who require access to this data.

Like many publishers, The Oryx Press will continue to investigate the most efficient and useful ways to deliver information to its customers.

Online Searching— Reference Librarians and Reference Publishers Meet the Challenge Together

Jon Clayborne

Few librarians would argue with the benefits online searching has brought to information management. Information specialists were quick to recognize the tremendous potential offered by this technology for easy access, rapid data retrieval, faster patron satisfaction, and an end to laborious manual searches. Similarly, reference publishers have welcomed the opportunity to expand current product lines and to create new modes of information transfer. However, the initial enthusiasm with which reference librarians greeted online searching has been moderated by serious practical and philosophical concerns. These same concerns must give reference source producers pause, because they affect the acceptance and use of electronic searching by librarians. There are solutions to the new challenges reference librarians face which arise from online searching, and meeting these challenges successfully is a task reference librarians and reference source producers can most effectively face together.

Working together, reference librarians and publishers have been able to satisfy the information needs of a diverse population of library users, and have kept pace with the huge volume of facts, figures, and statistics that are produced annually. Access alone is not sufficient, the speed of delivery is equally important. Computer technology has offered the promise of handling an infinite amount of information, offering traditional reference book publishers an opportunity to extend their product lines into online data retrieval while providing an entry for new electronically oriented manufac-

Mr. Clayborne is Library Relations Coordinator for The H.W. Wilson Co., 950 University Ave., Bronx, NY 10452.

© 1987 by The Haworth Press, Inc. All rights reserved.

turers into the field of information sources production. Unfortunately, for all the obvious benefits that online searching provides, it has resulted in some unsettling problems for reference librarians.

The introduction of online searching promised success for reference librarians in their continuing attempt to transfer information from myriad sources to their patrons. Not only can computer networks retrieve data from sources previously unavailable to all but the largest research and national libraries, online retrieval provides convenient and rapid access to that information. One can easily envision a scenario in which a library patron rushes up to the reference desk and requests many references on the latest development in some obscure, but vital research. A flick of a terminal switch, a few words typed on a keyboard, and within seconds a monitor screen displays the exact citations the patron wants. Moments after his anxious request, a calm and satisfied patron walks out of the library with a complete bibliography in hand. Surely, online searching would quickly become the dominant mode of handling reference desk inquiries as more and more libaries subscribed to computer database networks.

Computers have become an integral part of many library operations. Automated circulation procedures have relieved staff members of the manual drudgery and tedious record keeping associated with charging out library material. In technical services departments, the cataloging of library collections has been made easier through computer link-ups to bibliographic networks. Several online systems exist to allow acquisitions departments to verify and place orders. Many reference departments have offered their patrons online searching options for a number of years, but computerized services remain the exception in the reference department rather than the rule.

COST DISCOURAGES

Aside from reference librarians in corporate and legal settings, most online searchers cite the costs attached to online usage as a discouraging factor. Actually, the financial cost incurred through connect-time, telecommunication charges, and printout fees is not the real issue. Whether supported by public funds or student tuition, public and academic libraries have tried to guarantee equal access to information by providing reference services for free. This was not a difficult policy to maintain as long as reference services were an entirely manual operation; material costs were drawn from the book budget and search costs were assumed in librarian's salaries. Assigning responsibility for the costs of online searching, however, presents a completely new problem to librarians.

Some libraries have decided to handle online searches as though they were traditional searches and have appropriated library funds to cover the costs. Conversely, some libraries have required their patrons to support the cost of their own searches on a pay-as-you-go basis. In other cases, partial payment formulas have been devised: some libraries charge the patron a flat fee to subsidize costs; others charge the patron for all costs above a certain dollar amount; still others charge the patron if the search lasts longer than a specified number of minutes, and then only for the additional time. The option of choosing from a variety of fee arrangements can have predictable results. In one New Jersey city, the public library offers county residents free online searches, while a nearby college library charges students full cost. It should come as no surprise that the reference librarians at the public library are busy scheduling searches, and just as unsurprising, the reference librarians at the school rarely use their online resources.

The costs associated with actual searches are not the only financial considerations. A library embarking on computerized data retrieval services must purchase the equipment necessary to interface with a database network. While the price of computer hardware is relatively inexpensive—a CPU, monitor, keyboard, modems, and printer can be priced for less than $5,000—current budget restrictions, austerity measures, and other cutbacks have forced many librarians to proceed with caution in requesting items that cost in the thousands of dollars. Also there is a natural hesitancy to venture into anything new, unless there is complete confidence in the outcome.

STAFF TRAINING

Staff training in online search techniques draws on both library funds and time. Not only do prospective searchers have to attend a formal training session to acquire basic search skills, but in order to develop more sophisticated abilities, additional training in the use of specialized commands and features is necessary. Added to the costs of training sessions is the time devoted to training and practice. The loss of time that would otherwise have been devoted to existing reference staff responsibilities is another factor to consider.

The expenditure of time becomes more obvious when actual searches are initiated. Depending on the search inquiry, the techniques and commands used can range from the simple to the complex; consequently, the amount of time involved in preplanning the search varies widely. The assumption that all that would be required to initiate a search would be the knowledge of a few key words has deceived some librarians into conferring capabilities on the computer that it does not possess. Unlike Hal, the spaceship-borne artificial intelligence in Arthur C. Clarke's *2001: A Space Odyssey*, the current generation of computers do not think for themselves, but are programmed to respond in a logical sequence to the data they receive from a searcher.

Confronted with any but the easiest requests, a searcher has to develop a strategy to obtain the desired information using an online system. Searchers use printed indexes and thesauri to create the best pathway to obtain a desired response from the computer. Of course, some reference librarians feel that if they have to spend so much time developing a search strategy and deciding on which words, phrases, and possible subject headings they need to key into the computer, then they might as well conduct the search manually.

While many of the complaints about actual or perceived flaws in online searching are valid, occasionally the complaints conceal the personal anxiety some reference librarians feel when confronted with computer usage. On one hand, just mentioning the word "computer" arouses a sense of fear, especially among some reference librarians who did not anticipate using computer services in their work assignments to any considerable extent. Furthermore, possessing broad knowledge and feeling very comfortable and secure with their proficiency in using printed sources, some reference librarians question the necessity of learning new search techniques and the accompanying jargon. Not a few reference librarians have voiced a concern about whether or not they have the stamina to acquire online searching skills, and have expressed their hope to avoid any major transformation in the delivery of reference services before they retired. The prospects of having their research skills appear inadequate is justifiably disconcerting.

PERCEPTIONS

What will be the effect of online searching on the role of the reference librarian? In general, the public has an incorrect perception of what librarianship entails or lacks any perception at all. Aside from the stereotypical image "librarian" conjures in many minds, often the first comment a layperson makes upon being introduced to a librarian is, "You must read a lot of books," as though the primary responsibility of every librarian is to have read all the selections on *The New York Times* bookseller list. Whatever accounts for the public's misconceptions about librarianship, it has frequently resulted in a sense of low esteem and jeopardizes professional recognition.

Into an already uncertain situation comes online reference services to further blur the picture. Despite initial misconceptions about reference librarians, as library patrons use library facilities and services they develop an appreciation for the librarian's skills. Will the use of online systems at the reference desk lower the value of the librarian's search skills in the eyes of library patrons? If all the patron knows about online searching is that he makes an inquiry and later is given a computer printout of citations, the patron is apt to draw the conclusion that the computer did all the work. Indeed, why does he need a librarian to type in words, when he could do it just as easily? The disquieting alarm that such a train of thought poses has intensified with the development and introduction of online software systems, like WILSEARCH, BRS/After Dark and Knowledge Index, that are designed to enable library patrons to conduct their own computer searches. As Dalrymple noted in a 1984 article, "the commercial promotion of end-user systems . . . suggests that the existence of a human intermediary is unnecessary, even undesirable." A recent television commercial for a computer manufacturer extends this idea by implying that a student can have complete access to her college's library collection after hours, just by using a computer. Undoubtably, even those reference librarians who enthusiastically welcome online searching must wonder about the consequences of computerized data retrieval on their profession.

The implications of online searching for reference librarians are important to reference source publishers as well. The computer has offered opportunities within the field of information management to traditional reference book publishers, as well as to new electronically oriented companies. Online information retrieval networks were created partly out of the need to contain an ever incrreasing volume of information efficiently, partly in response to demands for rapid access to this huge quantity of information, and partly as a result of the technological advances that made easy access and affordability possible. While companies like DIALOG and BRS were able to enter the library market for the first time, reference publishers that had previously provided only printed information sources, like The H. W. Wilson Company, were able to extend their product line to include the new technology. Online information retrieval was envisioned as an enhancement in information management that would benefit all library professionals, reference librarians in particular.

REACTIONS

Initial reactions to online searching muted many of the qualms that some reference librarians expressed concerning computerized reference services. Despite personal apprehensions about the online process, a reference librarian would defer to a directive from an administrator or the expectation of library patrons. Thousands of libraries in the United States have linked their reference desks to one or several online networks.

For online information service vendors, obtaining accounts however has proven to be the easy part. It has become evident that merely having the capability to do online searching does not ensure usage of the systems. Unless online retrieval can be established as an integral component of reference service, online network producers could witness a stagnant—even declining— market.

Reference librarians at the John C. Hughes Undergraduate Library of the University of Tennessee (Knoxville) initiated a study to determine the role online should play in the library's reference service. The final report cited several findings, including the realization that "more substantial conclusions could have been gathered with the presence of a computer terminal at the Undergraduate Library reference desk" (McCully, p. 85). If usage levels of online searching are below anticipation, one reason may be the low profile of the service. Public exposure of online hardware goes a long way in encouraging use of the retrieval networks: "At the Science-Engineering Library (University of Arizona), a T1745 portable was placed on a desk next to a reference desk, which made it both handy and highly visible to both staff and patrons'' (Brownmiller, p. 321). Not only are patrons unaware that online searching is available, but when terminals are out of sight, reference librarians do not readily think to consult the databases. How many reference librarians want their patrons to be aware of the availability of online searching, however, is open to question given the undefined role of the reference librarian vis-à-vis computer services.

Solutions to the problems encountered as a result of the introduction of online retrieval systems are possible. As Dalrymple points out: "While some of the problems will simply disappear with the passage of time, research and critical analysis are needed to come to grips with others" (p. 182).

Through studies and articles library professionals are developing criteria to promote the fullest use of online searching in reference departments and demonstrating that online does not diminish the role of the librarian. In a report developed by a Computer Assisted Reference Services (CARS) group at the University of Arizona, the group proposed three situations which justify the use of online ready-reference (Brownmiller, p. 321):

1. When the available printed index is inadequate because it is not current enough or cannot be used conveniently.
2. When the library either does not subscribe to the printed equivalent of the database or no equivalent exists.
3. When the time spent to obtain similar references from print sources is significantly higher than from using an online system.

The CARS study indirectly brought up a point frequently ignored in the promotion of online searching and which has led to some unnecessary anxiety among reference librarians. The printed indexes and other hardcopy reference resources that librarians are adept in using are not being programmed into extinction. There are justifications for using print instead of online, and vice-versa. A ready-reference search may be relatively inexpensive, but not every inquiry directed to the reference librarian can be handled quickly. More involved requests command additional time in planning and searching. There is a finite amount of time and funding that reference departments can allot to online searching, which precludes using database retrieval networks to answer every question and argues for the continued use of printed indexes in many instances.

Not even end-user systems, in which online searching is designed to be performed by library patrons, eliminate contact with the reference librarian. Reference librarians do not feel a sense of unease when patrons learn how to use indexes, abstracts, encyclopedias, and other printed reference resources on their own and no longer require the assistance of professionals to complete basic research. Regardless of the simplicity of the end-user system, there is still a need for reference librarians to teach library patrons the basic concepts of online searching. Indeed, reference librarians will be kept busy refining their search skills in order to maintain their edge as instructors and problem-solvers.

The development of online searching has presented reference librarians and reference source producers with a host of challenges even as they have sought to up-grade information management. The potential for the increased use of online systems is so evident, as are the benefits, that the best interests of library patrons will be served by the efforts librarians and systems producers make together to meet these challenges.

REFERENCES

1. Brownmiller, Sara, A. Craig Hawbaker, Douglas E. Jones, and Robert Mitchell. "On-line-Ready-Reference Searching in an Academic Library," RQ, Spring (Spring, 1985):320–326.
2. Dalyrymple, Prudence W. "Closing the Gap: The Role of the Librarian in Online Searching," RQ (Winter, 1984):177–184.
3. Hilchey, Susan E. and Jitka M. Hurych. "User Satisfaction or User Acceptance? Statistical Evaluation of an Online Reference Service," RQ (Summer, 1985):452–459.
4. McCulley, Lucretia. "Computerized Reference Service in the Undergraduate Library: Determining the Need," Tennessee Librarian (Summer, 1984):82–86.
5. Pruitt, Ellen and Karen Dowling. "Searching for Current Information Online . . . How High School Library Media Centers in Montgomery County, Maryland are Solving an Information Problem by Using DIALOG," Online (March, 1985):47–60.
6. Kaplan, Robin. "Online Searching: Introducing the Inevitable," (May, 1985): 122–123.

Old Books— New Technologies

Davie Biesel

Well, here we go again. We publishers (packagers, producers, new product developers, pick one) are going to repackage some old material and sell it to you in a new medium. I think we're going to call the medium CD-ROM but, by the time this old medium (the printed word on paper) reaches you we may have gone beyond that to something even newer and more fantastic.

Now, don't get me wrong. I love technology, either as the way to deliver, store, retrieve, sort (or even mangle) information or as the facility to provide a new way to analyze the substance of the information. All of this to ensure the advancement of knowledge.

And new technology has made it possible to reduce greatly the cost of producing books and journals. (Did I hear someone ask why the prices don't go down if the cost of production is cheaper. Please, one question at a time.)

However, in my profession the temptation to repackage information runs deep and somehow we assume that the same data should be sold in all medias or formats. Do we need *Books in Print* available in print, microform, online, computer tape and CD-ROM formats? If so, what is the proper variation and frequency for each? At what point in time do we drop or change an existing format or frequency? Does the new format reduce costs and provide a lower price? All too often, we don't ask these questions. (Or if we do, we ignore the answers.)

Let's take a moment to look at this new technology and define it because by the time you get to the end of this article, there may be another technology.

In general, we can lump most of this new technology under the category of optical disc. It includes a number of variations but let's

---

The author is Editorial Director for M.E. Sharpe, Inc., 90 Business Park Dr., Armonk, NY 10504.

© 1987 by The Haworth Press, Inc. All rights reserved.

limit our discussion to CD-ROM (compact disc-read only memory). In one format, this technology gives us the ability to store up to 550 megabytes of information (equal to 1500 floppy discs or 220,000 pages of typewritten double-spaced text). All of this on a small disc 4-3/4 inches in diameter that you can use as a frisbee. However, you can't change the data once it is on the disc, thus it is a "storage" device. These discs can be mass produced very inexpensively and all you need to use them is a microcomputer and a compact-disc player. Both of these items of hardware are cheap, but producing the master disc, from which you can reproduce multiple discs, is not cheap.

Inexpensive (or cheap) comes from the ability to market and sell a substantial number of copies to cover all costs (direct and indirect) and to make a profit. Although there are some parallels to the "plant" costs of producing a book, all the newer technologies—including CD-ROM have a cost and selling price that is based on producing a "master" from which all copies are made. In essence, microforms (fiche, film, etc.), data bases, all have economics tied to the "master," no inventory concept.

How often have you seen a microform publisher or a database publisher holding a remainder sale? Could a microfiche "best seller" come out in a cheaper "paperback" edition? Our new technology just has a different set of economics and if we are aware of that and if we are inventive with this new technology, we may surprise ourselves with something really good.

LET'S BE INVENTIVE

But are we going to be inventive with this new technology? Rockley Miller, editor of *The Videodisc Monitor*, stated in an interview in TechTrends (Nov.–Dec. 1985, page 72)

> It should be a huge boon to researchers once we start thinking how to package it to make it most useful to them. The trick, again is to break out of these constraints of how we've always done it and to start reevaluating how we would *like* to do it, now that we've got the potential to really achieve those benefits.

The benefits he was referring to include adding layers and levels of indexing, making data more accessible, and relating different types of data in new ways. That will cost money, but could produce excellent new products. How many of us will take that option and how many of us will opt to repackage old material, is the question yet to be answered. Unfortunately, it is far too easy for the unimaginative to simply redo the old in new garb. I believe librarians have caught onto that ploy!

Not that repackaging of old material is bad. Far from it. Properly done, and fairly priced, it can be an excellent use of technology to provide new access to data and to preserve data that would be lost in its current format. For example, let's look at serials storage which is an area that is touted as one of the best prospects for our new technology.

Suppose that I am a graduate physics (or advanced undergraduate) student at MIT or Stevens. Why couldn't I go into the library and check out "all the back volumes of *The Physical Review*, please." Suppose that the American Institute of Physics produced an "archival" collection from 1985 and back. Suppose the American Chemical Society, the IEEE, etc, did the same for any of their major professional journals. I'm not excluding the commercial publishers. In fact, we (M. E. Sharpe) could easily put all the back volumes of our seven Asian Studies journals on one CD-ROM disc. However, the professional society journals, in most cases, have the longest continuous sequence and the greater volume of material.

ADVANTAGES

There are obvious advantages of putting a continuous sequence of a journal on a CD-ROM disc.

1. It saves valuable shelf space, hopefully for books and serials that *should not* be on a CD-ROM disc.
2. It can aid in the preservation of material that, in some cases, is rapidly deteriorating. It may even be cheaper in the long run but that is far from proven as yet.
3. It can allow greater flexibility in inter-library loan, *if* you have several copies of the disc to circulate. (You don't want to lend your entire file!)
4. Students or instructors can check out the complete file.
5. Students or instructors can even *buy* the complete file.

It is that last item that can be the key. If we can sell enough copies the price per disc could be pegged much lower than the current high price of journals. Remember, at this point in time, each journal is priced to meet what the publisher feels is his maximum market. (And I will agree that the publisher can be wrong!) If we are able to project a market based, to some degree, on consumer sales and if we can resist the temptation to go only for a library sale, then the use of CD-ROM technology can be a boon to librarians and to publishers especially for archival serials collections.

However, I do not believe that it will have an immediate advantage for serials (or books) that stress current awareness, unless we are discussing a very large body of new data (such as in indexing services like ERIC, PAIS, etc). The cost of producing the master and updates (which are themselves new masters) will limit the price flexibility and only the larger libraries will be able to afford it. That may be a mistake.

But let's return to that item 5 we listed above. When I was in college (and when we had free time from fighting the Indians!) you could easily spot the engineering student because he was the one with the slide rule attached to his belt. Not only were those slide rules replaced by far more powerful shirt pocket calculators, but now some colleges have made the purchase of a computer a mandatory requirement for entrance. Five years ago, Carnegie Mellon University started the practice and now such schools as Drew, Stevens Institute of Technology, Clarkson, Virginia Poly and even the Dallas Baptist University, require computers.

Each of these—the slide rule, the calculator, and the computer—is an advancement in technology, but each needs to be programmed with data (software) and used effectively. Each can "manipulate" far more data than its predecessor. (Despite what some computer commericals would have you believe, you won't get higher SATs because your parents bought you a computer at age 8 or 9). Just as each of these has gained wide acceptance on the college campus, the compact disc is no exception. The trail has been blazed by the music industry. (Compact audio disc sales are expected to hit 23 million in 1986 from only a million or so a few years ago.)

In other words, much of the hardware is now in the hands of the college student or is easily obtainable. It is also easy to use. (It does not have the problem of early unacceptability that the microform industry faced.) Only the software (or data) is not yet there.

LET'S IMAGINE

Can you imagine what an MBA student could do with an econometic forecasting model using a database stored on a CD-ROM disc? It would put the current floppy disc model in the trash bin. Or suppose a pre-med student could have the complete run of the *Journal of the American Medical Association* or *The New England Journal of Medicine*? But, if we start out by pricing on the assumption that *only* the library will buy it, then we'll price it out of reach. And it will stay there. Unfortunately, there are those who believe that if you can sell a publishing product (I hate that word) for $75, then why sell it for $60.

But where else besides serials do we go to be inventive?

Let's take a look at an area that causes great problems in publishing, specifically the distribution and returns for mass-market paperbacks. In this respect, I am talking not so much about the best-sellers of the "current" year, even though this system might work there, but more so about the ongoing "best sellers." Guys like Shakespeare, Dickens, etc.

Using existing technology—or technology that could be easily developed—in combination with CD-ROM, we could create the following situation.

Suppose I walk into my local supermarket, bookstore, or library, and want a copy of my favorite mystery author: John Dickson Carr. Possibly I would find a few of the titles available but if you're a Carr afficionado (or Christie, Queen, Chandler, Doyle, Sayers, etc.) you'll find a very small percentage of the total. Why? Well if we're in a book store or supermarket, it costs too much to keep all the titles in print available, especially the slower movers. Also, it is obviously impossible to have it in stock if it is out-of-print. And if we're in a library, it costs (in dollars and in space) to acquire and retain.

I collect Carr, but I don't want to carry my collectibles on a train or subway, plane, etc. And I long ago learned the secret of survival in New York City is to carry a paperback with you at all times. You're always waiting on a line somewhere. Like many readers, I'm not interested in the graphics of the cover if it is just a reading copy that I want.

Or suppose I'm a college student and I need a copy of *King Lear* or *A Tale of Two Cities* for an English course, I don't care what it looks like. I'll take whatever paperback I find in the college bookstore. The point is that in many cases, the *content* and its *availability* are the most important considerations for the buyer.

CARR ON CD

Now as a publisher (packager, producer) let me apply the new technologies to this problem. Suppose we were to store *all* of Carr, Christie, Sayers, Chandler, Gardner, etc. on a CD-ROM disc. (Let's assume we could get only 100 250 page books on one disc.)

Now as a reader, suppose I walk over to a large Pepsi or Coke-like machine which I have called the "Insta-Book". I read the titles on a computer (CRT) terminal. Suppose I select Carr's *Seeing is Believing* (New York, William Morrow, 1941) or perhaps I wish to reread *The Lost Gallows* (New York, Harper & Bros, 1931.)

"Ah, here it is, Carr is K563 and costs $2."

The first version of the machine will be slow and I'll probably have to pay at the "Insta-Book" counter, where a nice young high school student will take my money and operate the machine—a very sophisticated gadget with 8 different buttons to push and a waiting time of about 20 minutes. No problem, I have other shopping to do so I'll pick up my book on the way out.

Later, high-speed machines will be operated by fools like me and I'll get my book in 2 minutes or less. Of course, there will be a red panic (service) button that will summon someone if I need help. (It will probably be the same white-gowned gentleman who emerges from the back of the store when I press the red button for help or special service at the meat counter!)

What is this "Insta-Book" machine? Well, it includes 100 discs (let's say 10,000 books but newer technology may increase that number.) In the machine is a high-speed web-fed laser printer. As the paper roll (8-1/2 inches wide) is fed through it is printed on both sides. (Page imposition is not a problem because each title has been preprogrammed.)

Or, the machine might use cartridge prepacks of paper—in 250, 275, 300 page lengths—that require that once a week someone open the machine, restock it (like any soft drink machine), and collect the money.

There are no "signatures" in these books and the books are all perfect bound with a fast drying adhesive. (The same adhesive that is used to apply labels to cans at high speed.) The covers are all the same stock and my laser printer gives me a variety of different designs. I can even have a list of "related titles" printed on the inside back cover. These instant books will not be expected to have a lifetime of more than a few years. (But how long do many of today's paperbacks last anyway?)

With my "Insta-Book" machine, I am able to give you any "old" book without having an expensive inventory, without a complicated and costly returns and distribution system, and at the same time I can keep track of the payment (royalty) due both publisher and/or author.

Will there be problems with the machines? Did you ever have a problem with a copier or soft drink machine? But you didn't stop using them, did you?.

Let's add another "inventive" use of CD-ROM to our list.

Suppose you could put all those scholarly books that can't be reprinted (because of the economics of standard book publishing techniques) on the same kind of equipment that I have in my "Insta-Book" machine. Here again we are not trying to compete with beautifully hand bound first edition. Rather we wish to make a reading copy available for study—not for resale on the rare book market through *AB Bookman's Weekly*.

This will not be the last time we are faced with a new technology that begs for applications but let's let the dust settle first and see how we can best be its master, instead of its slave.

Do you think we could put a complete set of the world's postage stamps on a compact disc? Or what about all the baseball cards ever produced. . . .

By the way, have you heard about this new technology called CDI (Compact Disc-Interactive)?

The Medium Must Match the Message

Kathy Niemeier

Reference librarians are direct recipients of many of the marvels of modern technology. A decade ago, much of their information searches led directly to print sources or to very dated microfilm files. In that ten years, the librarian has added to his or her tool kit, computer-output-microfilm which offers timely data as well as retrospective files, online information delivery which provides an organized and rapid search of vast repositories of information which is as fresh as today's news headlines or can yield facts published over 20 years ago. Now, a new medium, optical disc storage with computer retrieval, adds yet another option for periodical reference.

The proliferation of publishing media and the awesome speed and flexibility of computer-aided searching, threatens to make the medium more intriguing than the message. There's a predictable frustration among adventurous librarians who do not have some of the newest reference aids at their fingertips; but what was not predictable was the librarian who has the state-of-the-art systems available and chooses to use familiar print or microform sources more frequently than today's electronic library systems. Publishers of reference products have been so dazzled by new technology that at times they've lost sight of fundamental library needs and those ever-present cost constraints. It is the publisher's responsibility to develop reference products that bring new efficiency, completeness and/or timeliness to researchers and then to deliver that product in a medium match to the library's need.

The author is Marketing Manager, Information Access Co., 11 Davis Drive, Belmont, CA 94002.

DEVELOPING THE MEGADATABASE

As an example, at Information Access company, we index, index and abstract, or index and provide full text of more than 2,000 periodicals. Database developing and publishing is our concentration. We are not committed to any specific delivery media.

We view this huge volume of information as a prism. It is the user's need beamed through this monumental collection of data that reflects actual products and the media in which they are delivered. Few of our products have a print version because timeliness has always been the driving force in product development and delivery. The print production cycle is just too long to provide timely periodical reference aids. IAC chose to address problems that print cannot: currency, cumulation and comprehensiveness.

A single citation covering the details of an article which appeared in a magazine, for instance, will appear in microfilm and microfiche products, be offered in an online database and as part of the digital data on optical disc. Yet, none of these product needs have identical contents. Each was developed toward a specific need and, though some libraries may have a demand for all products in the line, they have, based on their use and budget, the ability to select the media most appropriate to their application.

Publishers of reference works also operate within economic constraints. The projected demand for a new product must be widespread enough so that the effort can ultimately be a profitable endeavor. The creation of any reference product is a labor intensive task—intellectually labor intensive. At Information Access Company, more than 100 professional librarians devote their full workday to indexing the more than 2,000 newspapers, magazines and journals which are covered in our databases. A comparable number of keyboard operators and filmers work full time to prepare the full text files for online and microform delivery. Because of the huge investment in a new reference product, publishers carefully assess the size of the ultimate market for any proposed concept. Though cost is a significant consideration, content and media is equally important.

Some of the new delivery media has clouded publishers' vision and encouraged the creation of products for which there is no viable application. For instance, a company which provides online data on corporations, began offering portions of its files on optical disks so that users could have constant on-site access to the information without running up online charges for each use. The media didn't match the message. This company's customers wanted up-to-the-minute data on which to base investment and other economic decisions. The lag time between the availability of the data online and the creation of a video disc rendered the information almost useless because timeliness is its primary attraction. The online service is excellent and has attracted many users. This is a case in which the delivery mechanism was at fault, not the value of the data.

Other cases in which the media wasn't suited to the message are recent attempts to offer an online patent file, which had to offer graphics as well as words. The technical difficulties in mounting and maintaining the file, in addition to the special printers needed to capture permanent records of relevant material made the system cost-prohibitive when print sources were far easier and less expensive to use. Caught up in the online technology bandwagon, several publishers have tried to launch online versions of their print publications. In some cases, the cancellation rate for the print version proved counterproductive to profitability; in others, the timeliness of the data did not demand the immediacy of online availability so the electronic delivery went virtually unused.

The Media is Dictated by the Market

To be successful, any reference product must reflect the practical needs of the market for which it is intended in its content, design and the medium in which it is delivered. Some reference products can be delivered in many media each addressing a specific market niche. Information Access Company's most widely used product, MAGAZINE INDEX^{tm}, is distributed on microfilm, is available online, and is incorporated in InfoTrac^{tm}, an extensive database for optical disc delivery. Mounted in a reader, the microfilm product is used by library patrons throughout the United States and Canada to search for citations on articles contained in more than 400 widely-read publications including issues indexed back five years. This product addresses most routine periodical research needs. Its limitations are timeliness, capacity and single topic searching. There is a lag of up to six weeks between the publication of an issue of a covered magazine and delivery of the microfilm containing its indexing. This is a dramatic improvement over print, yet not fast enough for the person searching for the article which was published in Fortune or Forbes last month. Because of the capacity of a reel of microfilm, the earliest citations must be dropped in order to add new material, therefore, five years' of indexes is maximum for this product. Of course, there is no opportunity for the searcher to "and", "or" or "not" is using microfilm.

The online counterpart of MAGAZINE INDEX overcomes these limitations and offers the librarian or other trained searcher the opportunity to access very fresh citations or material that is up to 20 years old. The database is updated online daily and the computer capacity allows the database to be cumulated indefinitely and the searcher can use Boolean logic. Using an online media presents other limitations, however. The user must be trained in online searching and there must be a budget for telecommunications charges and database access. Even though it may be more cost-effective to do an online search than attempt to gather the needed information from any other media, dealing with online costs can be a real barrier for many libraries. Manual searches are buried in the personnel budget, while online charges show up as a direct cost item, so online isn't for everyone. Librarians who have passwords to several online services may rarely use them rather than fighting the battle of the budget.

Much of the contents of MAGAZINE INDEX along with citations to an additional 700 magazines are contained in IAC's optical disc system, InfoTrac^{tm}, which is updated monthly with the delivery of a disc containing the full cumulated database. This product offers the flexibility of online searching without the unpredicatability of cost usually associated with computer-assisted reference. A single video disc playback system can support up to five computers and printers, allowing simultaneously access to the database by multiple users. This has proven to be the medium of choice for very active public and academic libraries which need the speed of computer access to support the heavy demand made on periodical reference systems, while offering a service that can be used without training and usage-based pricing. The cost of the system is justified in this setting, because it would require 20 or more microfilm indexes and readers to duplicate the service of a single InfoTrac system.

The Faulty Embrace

Yet, a video disc reference system would be an extravagance in a small library where microfilm or print reference aids are used only a dozen or so times a day. The rush to embrace some of the new media just because it is there, threatens to displace some of the print and microform products while not providing practical reference tools in their place.

Options in both the content and delivery media are vital if libraries are going to be able to find the reference aids that meet their specific applications and budgets. Market research has to take the developers out into the libraries to understand how librarians think and work, to understand the logic the patron employs in searching for data, and the technical expertise of the people who will actually use the reference product. The design of InfoTrac is an excellent example of a product that grew out of recognized need within major libraries. The content of the database closely reflects the periodicals collections of the libraries themselves, so that patrons can usually expect to find the publications containing the cited articles in the library's archives. The software programming was developed to reflect the logic of the user and is designed to coach the patron in its use so that professional staff members do not have to assist in the search. The professionals, therefore, can attend to projects which demand their training, as they are free from most routine periodical searches.

Because a product is introduced in a new media does not mean the developer should abandon the traditional medium, if a need continues to exist. An increasing number of print reference works are now being offered online, yet there remains a good market for the print version even in those libraries that regularly conduct online searches. Information Access Company has generally concentrated on developing reference aids to periodical literature, and then delivering those products in media that fit specific market need. Our indexes of business publications, national newspapers and legal journals, exist both in microfilm and online. For timeliness, NEWSEARCH[tm] which is available online only contains the daily update of indexes for all of our databases, so searchers tracking a specific timely topic can be assured of a source of very fresh information.

Information Access Company has been developing products for library use for more than nine years and, though its concentration has been on applying new technology to information delivery and we can be as dazzled by bits and bytes as anyone. Our regular visits to real, working libraries keeps us in touch with reality. Though optical disc is the hot, new medium, our pragmatism keeps us developing microform products, as well. One of our most popular recent products didn't, at first glance, seem to have any need to exist. IAC has offered MAGAZINE INDEX and BUSINESS INDEX™ in microfilm since the company was formed. Why not full text microfilm coverage of the most frequently accessed publications in those two indexes? The negatives appeared to outweigh the positives. Would libraries want a system that duplicated in microfilm many of the publications that were contained in print in their archives? Many reference librarians said they would. Would publishers give rights to reprint their magazines and journals risking that libraries might end their subscriptions? Libraries said it was unlikely that they would discontinue any subscriptions. So where is the gain, we asked? For every library that indicated interest in an automated, full text system which will allow the patron to either read a desired article on a screen or print it out for future reference, the answer was: eliminating a great deal of the staff drudgery in locating and refiling archival material. Many other urban libraries cited space savings as a major benefit; being able to house a collection of hundreds of magazines on microfilm in a few square feet of space would allow them to move their print collection off-site to less expensive storage. Virtually every library stated that an automated periodical delivery system would eliminate the recurring problem of lost or stolen issues of magazines and journals. Both Magazine Collection™ which contains some 300 magazines, and Business Collection, with more than 500 journals and other periodicals, may both be used in an urban library in a business district while Magazine Collection alone may be offered in suburban branches of the same system. Libraries made it very clear that options and comprehensiveness were more important that a single system containing a combination of general interest and business publications.

And, yes, this same library system may regularly access the online version of MAGAZINE COLLECTION or BUSINESS COLLECTION when someone is in search of very current material in periodicals to which they do not subscribe.

Advantage of Database Matches

A publisher that is able to draw from the same information database to create products to serve a number of needs, is able to contain the cost of products as development expense can be spread over several applications. Many of the familiar print reference products which are now offered online allow the publisher to draw on editorial work already being done to offer the online version. This expands the library's reference options relatively economically.

Understanding that principle, just after IAC introduced the optical disc system, it went back to its origins and created a new microfilm product, TOM (Text-On-Microfilm), which is scaled in content and price to high school libraries. The information the product contains—indexes to 100 magazines frequently use to support high school class studies with the full text of many of those magazines on microfiche—was already available to us in other forms. So we pulled together from the megadatabase that we support, information which is specifically applicable to high schools and the delivery media was selected based on typical high school budgets. The product design also offers easy reference so that librarians minimize hand-holding. It's a self-explanatory product. The temptation to desert more traditional reference media in favor of computer-assisted products would keep a practical products, such as TOM, from being created. TOM isn't revolutionary, it doesn't draw gasps of admiration when it is demonstrated—but it does serve a real reference need, one that is not addressed in any other way.

As new reference technology has been introduced, we're continually hearing that "print is dead" or "microfilm is dead"—this is the "Chicken Little" syndrome at work. Reference plurality is the ideal. Today, many large library periodical sections use print index, microfilm indexes and full text delivery systems, online index and full text searching, and optical disc index databases; and no one reports that any single form has been abandoned in favor of the more recent technology. Patrons' need for information appears to expand to meet whatever resources are available. Our mistake—as database publishers and as librarians—is to assume the need for information is finite and can be fully satisfied in any single medium.

Ready Reference Using Online Databases

Barbara E. Anderson

If we accept the role of the reference librarian as one of bringing the inquirer and the reference sources together, i.e., serving as the communicator in translating the information needs of the library user into the sources of information available, then online databases are simply another source in the information pool. Typically, reference librarians provide various responses to inquiries—some requiring quick lookups of factual information, others a much more detailed knowledge of sources and further in depth study. The role of the reference librarian in the latter is often that of teacher and instructor to set the library patron in the right direction seeking the information needed.

This paper will concentrate on the use of online sources to respond to the first type of reference question, i.e., the quick lookups of factual information. Typical questions of this type are: dates and/or details of an event, an address of an organization or company, a piece of biographical information, a fact about a product, the tracing of an acryonm, the completion of a bibliographic citation, a review of a movie or product, etc. Online services provided by large vendors such as DIALOG Information Services, Inc.; Bibliographic Retrieval Services (BRS); System Development Corporation (SDC); and Mead Data Central provide reference librarians with millions of sources beyond those that may be directly available in library reference collections to respond to these questions. No longer is the reference librarians' capability limited by the reference materials available in the local collection or via the network of connections to other libraries for with access to online sources each librarian can become the librarian of a vast reference collection numbering millions of records.

The author is Manager, Dialog Customer Services, 3460 Hillview Ave., Palo Alto, CA 94304.

Using online sources for ready reference requires the same skills as currently used by the traditional reference librarian of an all print collection—a knowledge of what is available in each of several hundred databases. This is exactly what reference librarians now know with printed reference collections of several hundred (or thousand) printed works. There is also the need to know the various idiosyncracies of each of the several hundred databases available, such information as when particular sources started being indexed, when the vocabulary of the subject headings changed, when new source data began being included. Experienced reference librarians already know these things about the reference sources in their collections. Online databases have similar quirks and idiosyncracies which can be learned and acquired through regular use to a degree that the casual user of online services will rarely experience.

Another similarity between ready reference with printed works and online sources is that of translation of the query into the selection of the source of information. Experienced reference librarians, already skilled at taking inquiries, can, with a few deft questions, get to the heart of the information being requested. They then mentally cycle it through their knowledge of reference works and the special features of each to come up with the ideal source or sources. Where this process breaks down is when the library does not have the resource needed to provide the answer. Online database services can help to close this gap or at least provide a bridge to other sources. A reference librarian in even a very small library can have access to a vast collection of the world's secondary sources through a computer terminal.

ONLINE DATABASES AND READY REFERENCE

What types of ready reference information can be located through online databases? Following is a review of what is currently available to assist in responding to various categories of ready reference questions. Remember, more and more databases are being published and the sources mentioned here will continue to grow.

Biographical Information

The common sources of biographical information in reference library collections are the Who's Who type of biographical directories and other biographical dictionaries and indexes of biographical information. When these fail to provide the requested information, a library patron may be turned away.

Who's Who directories are now available online as well as some biographical indexes. In addition to these, other online sources can offer a much wider range of possibilities for locating biographical information quickly and efficiently. The current affairs news databases (e.g., UPI NEWS, AP NEWS, REUTERS, WASHINGTON POST, NEW YORK TIMES, CHRISTIAN SCIENCE MONITOR, etc.) are rich full text sources of information, many of which are biographical, or may give leads to further sources of information. Each significant word in these articles is indexed, thus even a small mention of an elusive personality may be found.

The secondary source databases also often provide information relating to author affiliation and/or author's address. The data is included by many of the major indexing and abstracting services as part of the standard information with each article indexed, offering an ever wider range of possibilities for locating an address of an individual.

Some of the major business directory databases include listings of key executive officers and members of boards of trustees. These too can be leads to biographical information that might be found elsewhere. In addition, there are directory databases such as the ELECTRONIC YELLOW PAGES which give nationwide listings of names and addresses of professionals such as physicians, attorneys, etc.

Suggested databases for biographical information:

Biographical Directories
    AMERICAN MEN AND WOMEN OF SCIENCE (R. R. Bowker)
    BIOGRAPHY MASTER INDEX (Gale Research Company)
    MARQUIS PROfiles (Marquis Who's Who, Inc.)
    MARQUIS WHO's WHO (Marquis Who's Who, Inc.)

News
    AP NEWS (Press Association, Associated Press)
    UPI NEWS (United Press International)
    NEW YORK TIMES
    WASHINGTON POST

Bibliographic Databases
    <Bibliographic Databases by Subject Category. See Appendix.>

Business Directories
STANDARD & POOR'S REGISTER—BIOGRAPHICAL (Standard & Poor's Corp.)
D&B—INTERNATIONAL DUN'S MARKET IDENTIFIERS (Dun & Bradstreet Corp.)
ELECTRONIC YELLOW PAGES (Market Data Retrieval, Inc.)
DISCLOSURE MANAGEMENT (Disclosure Information Group)

Current Events

Where to find details on an event that happened within the past month, or past week or past few days? The printed indexes for such data are often not available at the time the questions are asked. Online databases can provide newsbriefs of today's information today, indexed articles of the major U.S. newspapers from yesterday on back and full text data of the actual stories within 24 hours of the event. With the ever widening array of newspapers online, local events of some metropolitan areas can be found in such newspapers as the Los Angeles Times, the Chicago Tribune, etc. The reference librarian no longer needs to be completely restrained by budgetary limitations which allow only a few print or microfiche copies of subscriptions to newspapers, now a large collection of these materials are readily available at what may be a small fraction of the cost of storing and maintaining even microprint versions of these materials.

Information in current news magazines is also readily found through databases in either index or full text form. Events reported in Time, Newsweek, etc. are easily located, though subject indexing helps as well as full text views of the articles.

Suggested databases for current event information:

Newspaper Indexes
NATIONAL NEWSPAPER INDEX (Information Access Company)
NEWSEARCH (Information Access Company)
FACTS ON FILE (Facts on File, Inc.)

Newspapers—Full Text
WASHINGTON POST
NEW YORK TIMES

Wire Services
AP NEWS (Press Association, Associated Press)
UPI NEWS (United Press International)

Magazine Indexes
MAGAZINE INDEX (Information Access Company)
PAIS INTERNATIONAL (Public Affairs Information Service, Inc.)
<See Current Affairs in Bibliographic Databases list. Appendix)

Bibliographic Verification

Regardless of the subject, most of the world's major secondary sources of bibliographic information are available in machine readable form. Through these indexes and abstracts, a complete citation can be located in minutes. Using databases of secondary sources does not require having an approximate date or even the correct spelling of the author or the exact subject heading, for with online sources every word of the title (and sometimes abstract) can be searched. For uncertain spellings of author names, displays of author names with similar spellings can be seen—most covering 10–15 years or more in one display. For this type of ready reference question, the online database search is more efficient than manual lookups.

Suggested databases for bibliographic verification:

<Bibliographic Databases by Subject Category. See Appendix.

Associations, Societies, Acronyms

Online databases provide good sources for locating obscure and hard-to-find names of societies and associations, as well as acronyms which may represent the same. Traditional sources such as the Encyclopedia of Associations are also available online and are indexed for online searching so that every word of the name of the association/society can be searched as well as every word of the text of the description of such societies including their publications, conference dates and sites, and number of members.

Other sources of information leading to data on societies and organizations may be found using the bibliographic databases of secondary sources. Often acronyms of societies can be unscrambled by searching a database of the known subject content, for the acronym may appear in a title, an abstract, a corporate source, and even in the subject descriptors. The value, of course is that each word of these parts of the bibliographic descriptions is searchable. Often, just one such lead can open up additional means for locating further information.

A third, but perhaps less direct, source of this type of information are the current news databases. Societies and organizations currently making news through their conferences and/or recent policies are often discussed in the wire services and such as AP (Associated Press) and UPI (United Press International). Newspapers also follow with similar stories. Several types are available: indexes to several newspapers such as the NATIONAL NEWSPAPER INDEX and NEWSEARCH which index the New York Times, the Wall Street Journal, the Christian Science Monitor, the Washington Post, and the Los Angeles Times and online versions of the complete text of some newspapers such as the Washington Post.

Information about the activities of societies and organizations of a particular region which are often difficult to locate with a small reference collection, can be located through databases indexing regional journals and newspapers such as those magazines of a particular large city or metropolitan area. Such sources provide the reference librarian a major new source of information that can rarely be found in all but the very largest of reference collections.

Suggested databases association/society information:

Directories
   ENCYCLOPEDIA OF ASSOCIATIONS (Gale Research Company)

Bibliographic
   Bibliographic Databases by Subject Category. See Appendix.

News
   AP NEWS (Press Association, Associated Press)
   UPI NEWS (United Press International)
   NEW YORK TIMES
   WASHINGTON POST (full-text)

Regional news
   PTS REGIONAL BUSINESS NEWS (Predicasts, Inc.)

Historical Data

There are a few online databases of encyclopedias in which the entire text of every article is made searchable. Elusive sources of information which may have been missed in the manual indexing of the printed work may be located in the online version.

There are also a few bibliographic index databases that can provide clues to historical information. HISTORICAL ABSTRACTS and AMERICA: HISTORY AND LIFE are two indexes to specialized historical journals. Indexing in these two databases began in 1973 and 1964 respectively, but the articles covered in the journals indexed cover the range of human history.

Historical data on technical fields can often be found in the bibliographic databases for the specific subject. For example, the Journal of the History of Medicine and Allied Sciences is indexed in MEDLINE and the Journal of the History of Biology is indexed in BIOSIS PREVIEWS (Biological Abstracts). Historical indexes of literature of the arts can be located through databases such as ARTBIBLIOGRAPHIES MODERN, ART LITERATURE INTERNATIONAL (RILA), and RILM ABSTRACTS (music).

Suggested databases for historical data:

Encyclopedias
   ENCYCLOPEDIA BRITANNICA
   ACADEMIC AMERICAN ENCYCLOPEDIA (Areta Publishing Company)
   EVERYMAN'S ENCYCLOPEDIA (J. M. Dent & Sons)

Historical
   AMERICA: HISTORY AND LIFE (ABC-Clio Information Services)
   HISTORICAL ABSTRACTS (ABC-Clio Information Services)

Technical
   <Bibliographic Databases by Subject Category. See Appendix.>

Reviews

Traditionally reference librarians have relied on indexes to locate reviews of books, movies, and drama. Indexes to these are also available in online databases. In fact, a wide range of reviews of all sorts can be found online: book reviews, movie reviews, music reviews, drama reviews, new product reviews, etc. Whatever is reviewed in the major newspaper and magazine sources, can be located through the online databases. Search on a type of product or brand name, e.g., "video tape recorders" or "Sony VCR" to locate reviews of this type. Most databases provide a generic subject subheading such as REVIEW which can be added to the name of the book, movie, restaurant, music, product, or whatever, for ease of location.

Suggested databases for review information:

Reviews
    BOOK REVIEW INDEX (Gale Research Company)

Periodical Indexes
    MAGAZINE INDEX (Information Access Company)
    NATIONAL NEWSPAPER INDEX (Information Access Company)
    MAGILL'S SURVEY OF CINEMA (Database Publishing)
    TRADE AND INDUSTRY INDEX (Information Access Company)
    <Bibliographic Databases by Subject Category. See Appendix.>

Company and Product Information

All manner of information about companies can be found in online sources. The directories of the major producers of financial data about companies are all available: Disclosure, Dun & Bradstreet, Moody's, Predicasts, Standard & Poor's, Thomas, Trinet. They can be used to locate addresses, financial data, product data, mergers, etc.

Suggested databases for company information:

Public Companies
    DIALOG QUOTES & TRADING (Trades* Plus)
    DISCLOSURE(r) FINANCIALS (Disclosure Information Group)
    DISCLOSURE(r) MANAGEMENT (Disclosure Information Group)
    DISCLOSURE(r)/SPECTRUM OWNERSHIP (Disclosure Information Group)

INVESTEXT(r) (Business Research Corporation)
MEDIA GENERAL DATABANK (Media General Financial Services)
MOODY'S(r) CORPORATE PROFILES (Moody's Investors Service, Inc.)
MOODY'S(r) CORPORATE NEWS—U.S. (Moody's Investors Service, Inc.)
PTS ANNUAL REPORTS (Predicasts, Inc.)
STANDARD & POOR'S NEWS (Standard & Poor's Corporation)
STANDARD & POOR'S CORPORATE DESCRIPTIONS (Standard & Poor's Corp.)

Corporate Directories
ADVERTISED COMPUTER TECHNOLOGIES (tm) I (ACT 1) (Data Courier, Inc.)
D&B-DUN'S FINANCIAL RECORDS(sm) (Dun & Bradstreet Corporation)
D&B-DUN'S MARKET IDENTIFIERS(r) (Dun & Bradstreet International)
D&B-MILLION DOLLAR DIRECTORY(r) (Dun & Bradstreet Corporation)
ELECTRONIC YELLOW PAGES (Market Data Retrieval, Inc.)
ELECTRONIC DIRECTORY OF EDUCATION (Market Data Retrieval, Inc.)
STANDARD & POOR'S REGISTER—BIOGRAPHICAL (Stand. & Poor's Corp.)
STANDARD & POOR'S REGISTER—CORPORATE (Standard & Poor's Corp.)
THOMAS REGISTER ONLINE(tm) (Thomas Publishing Company)
TRINET ESTABLISHMENT DATABASE (Trinet, Inc.)
TRINET COMPANY DATABASE (Trinet, Inc.)

International Companies
D&B-INTERNATIONAL DUN'S MARKET IDENTIFIERS(r) (Dun & Bradstreet Intl)
ICC BRITISH COMPANY DIRECTORY (Inter Company Comparison, Ltd.)
ICC BRITISH COMPANY FINANCIAL DATASHEETS (Inter Company Comparison, Ltd.)

INVESTEXT(r) (Business Research Corporation)
MOODY'S(r) CORPORATE NEWS—INTERNATIONAL (Moody's Investors Service)

WHAT CANNOT BE FOUND ONLINE (YET)

Some data simply are not yet available online or cannot be found as easily online as in print form. World Almanac information of the type that gives lists of sports, weather, and historical records in a manner that is easy to find and efficient to scan is not yet available online. Similarly, some historical that precede the development of databases is often more easily found in the older Statistical Abstract, Almanac, and Yearbook type reference works. Literary analyses and reviews that precede the development of databases.

ONLINE BIBLIOGRAPHIC DATABASES AS READY REFERENCE SOURCES

The recurrent theme throughout this paper has been that the traditional periodical indexes and abstracts can be used in a ready reference mode in their online forms with an ease never considered in their print form. As noted, they can be used for biographical information, society and organizational information, historical information, bibliographic verification, etc. Reference situations which require time and effort to search through many volumes of printed works for something that there may only be a slight chance of location are often never undertaken. However, in their online form such indexes provide ease of access over 10 to 20 years simultaneously, thereby making what may previously have been a prohibitively time consuming activity one easily achieved. In addition, the multiple access points provided by full indexing of every word of titles, abstracts, corporate sources, etc., allow for far more detailed searching than use of the printed versions. Most online services provide a cross-index to their databases, e.g., DIALOG's DIALINDEX, BRS' CROS, and SDC's DATA BASE INDEX allowing ease of determination of which of many databases may have information on the topic desired. These databases serve as an easy index to clusters of databases on specific subjects allowing use of a single command to determine in advance which database has the desired information.

SUMMARY

Published sources of bibliographical and historical information, current events, societies and associations, companies, products, reviews, are now available in online versions. The online versions of these publications often provide additional access points beyond that of the printed works providing reference librarians with rich sources of information that can be tapped in a ready reference mode. In addition, some bibliographic secondary sources are available only in the form of an online database. The reference librarian needs to become as familiar with the coverage and idiosyncracies of several hundred databases to parallel similar knowledge of printed reference sources.

Movements to bring online searching to the end user, whether within a library or at home, are not likely to change the traditional role of the reference librarian with regard to ready reference lookups. As noted earlier in this chapter, the experience and knowledge of the reference librarian of the specialized details and differences between databases is similar to that which already exists for searching printed reference books. Today's reference librarian is the professional who knows the sources of information whether they be published in traditional printed form or in online database form. The reference librarian will continue to be the one who best knows the sources and can efficiently select which book or database to use for any particular information need. With online databases, the resources for such assistance are expanded beyond the size of the local reference collection. Almost the entire range of printed matter can be available at the reference librarian's fingertips using online databases.

The Reference Services From Mead Data Central: Combining Index Terms and Free Text Searching for Saturation Retrieval

Sharon K. Peake

A pioneer in the development of full-text online information for professionals, Mead Data Central (MDC) has taken a determined step into the business of providing bibliographic services as well. Although the company still stresses its full-text offerings as its primary products, bibliographic abstracts and structured files in MDC's new Reference Service have been added to complement and extend the value and utility of full-text material.

The beginnings of Mead Data Central's growth into the bibliographic database business began in 1983 when the company became sole distributor of databases produced by The New York Times Information Service.

The New York Times Information Bank or "INFOBANK" (whose general news and business abstracts are now known as ABS in NEXIS^R and INABS in The Reference Service) and the Advertising and Marketing Intelligence (AMI) database were already recognized as excellent online information sources produced by one of the best news organizations in the world. Besides broadening the coverage of MDC's existing databases by abstracting numberous publications not included in NEXIS, the addition of ABS and AMI also introduced many NEXIS users to databases of synthesized information and the option of using a controlled vocabulary for structured searching. At the same time, long-standing users of The New York Times' services learned to appreciate the reliability and

---

The author is Manager, Public Relations at Mead Data Central, 9393 Springboro Pike, P.O. Box 933, Dayton, OH 45401.

© 1987 by The Haworth Press, Inc. All rights reserved. *237*

ease of using those services with Mead Data Central's user-friendly software.

All in all, it was a good marriage and first step for MDC into the reference information market. The resulting success and increasing demand from customers to add other bibliographic services brought about the development of The Reference Service, which was introduced to the public early in 1985.

The Reference Service (REFSRV™) is a collection of bibliographic databases and structured files produced by well-respected business and government organizations. The bibliographic files contain abstracts of and references to journal articles, books, research reports and government documents. The structured files consist of almanacs, statistical sources, directories, handbooks and specialized research data. The files, which vary widely in content and format, currently emphasize science and technology, defense, energy, banking and finance, business, management and marketing, social and political background information and regulatory trends.

ADVANTAGES OF THE REFERENCE SERVICE

Although many of these databases are also available through other online services, Mead Data Central believes accessing them through The Reference Service offers users numerous benefits.

Perhaps the most important advantage is that users can supplement the wide-ranging information in REFSRV's bibliographic files with the timely, in-depth, detailed coverage provided by NEXIS^R, EXCHANGE™, LEXPAT^R and the other full-text services unique to Mead Data Central. Once a user has located relevant bibliographic abstracts in one of The Reference Service's files, he or she can find more information on the topic by scanning the full text of relevant documents found in one of MDC's other services.

REFSRV users also benefit from the fact that each of its files offers the ease and freedom of unlimited searching throughout each document, not just in specified segments. Every word of the text is searchable, so segments do not have to be specified. This can be an advantage if users are uncertain what index terms are most applicable or if they wish to conduct a more highly focused, precise search.

For example, by searching "pharmaceuticals industry AND japan!" in ABI-INFORM, a user would find over 60 abstracts discussing this topic. The exclamation point after "japan" picks up additional terms, such as "Japanese."

Segments that are found in these databases available from other vendors are also similarly searchable in Mead Data Central's REFSRV. Because the full index-term searching capability of each database is retained, users who prefer structured searching and the more focused results it can often provide can use REFSRV in the way that is the most comfortable for them.

To cite another example, the SOURCE segement in the ABS file of INFOBK could be searched to limit retrieval to a specific publication (*Current News*) in the following search for abstracts of articles dealing with counterterrorist activity:

"Counterterroris! OR counter terroris! AND SOURCE (current news) Again, the exclamation point picks up all terms that begin with the given root, including terrorist, terrorism, etc.

Although each of the REFSRV files can be searched separately, users also have the option of searching in group files that combine several of the databases instead of having to search each desired file separately.

Segmentation and the names of particular segments (or "fields") are made as consistent as possible among files to make it easy and efficient for searchers to find valuable information in an assortment of different databases.

The Reference Service also offers advantages in displaying documents. Segment labels are displayed within each document to make information easier to identify. The choice of display formats is broad, including (1) full text; (2) KWIC or "Key Word In Context" format, which highlights search terms and displays them in context with 15 words on either side; and (3) various REFS (references) formats, which display specified segments of information in a list of retrieved documents. There is no extra charge for displaying either an entire document or portions of it.

REFSRV users can also take advantage of Short Cut, a feature that enables them to bypass menu screens and certain command sequences by stringing command together in a series, separated by semi-colons. This recent software enhancement applies to all Mead Data Central services. Short Cut is a popular feature that allows librarians, information specialists and other experienced intermediaries to save time searching so they have more time to evaluate results.

ECLIPSE™, Mead Data Central's *electronic clipping service*, enables users to track trends and topics of special interest to them automatically on a daily, weekly or monthly basis. Each of the files available in The Reference Service (as well as other files in each of Mead's services) can be used with ECLIPSE.

An ECLIPSE of a BILLCAST search, such as:

COMM(house committee on agriculture) AND FODD>50

will constantly update a search for bills referred to the House Agricultural Committee that have a probability greater than 50 percent of passing the house floor. This is one way that researchers could easily and quickly keep on top of pending legislation. (COMM is a "committee" segment.)

The Reference Service was developed to complement MDC's existing services by providing many new sources and kinds of information for subscribers. While several sources, such as INFO-BANK's ABS and AMI databases, were already part of MDC's services, a variety of other databases have been added to enhance the depth and breadth of the full-text information. The following are descriptions of these databases, grouped by subject area.

ONLINE USER AIDS

Because the subject coverage of The Reference Service files is so diverse, and because the files are so much more highly structured than those in other MDC's services, the company has developed a unique group of files to help researchers effectively use each database. Called PROFILES, these "how to" files offer details on the contents, features and search techniques of each individual database. Each PROFILE contains:

— a detailed description of the file's subject coverage, contents and applications,
— a list of the publications indexed,
— a sample document,
— a description of each segment's contents,
— search examples and hints
— an explanation of subject terms used to describe document topics,
— a list of printed user materials available for the file,
— and instructions for ordering the full text of a document.

Each PROFILE is an automatic display file. As soon as the file name is entered (e.g., PFDOE for the PROFILE of the Department of Energy database) a tabel of contents is displayed. Users can browse through all of the PROFILE topics or display just the topics that interest them most. PROFILES are available free except for telecommunications charges ($10 to $15 per hour). Normal offline printing charges apply if any material is printed, but no connect time or search charges are billed. PROFILES can be updated or revised quickly if changes occur in a database, unlike printed documentation.

Several other features are also available online to help searchers develop and perfect their skills. These include a computer-assisted instruction exercise, a practice library, and TUTOR—a series of subject-specific lessons in which the user can focus on either LEXIS^R, NEXIS or LEXPAT. Each of these features is also available at no charge except normal telecommunications charges.

THE BASIS FOR GROWTH

Mead Data Central made a name for itself in the electronic publishing industry as creator and distributor of the LEXIS computer-assisted legal research service, which was the foundation of the company's entry into the online industry in 1973, and NEXIS, the general news and business information service launched in 1980. LEXIS and NEXIS provide the full text of source material, rather than abstracts or references. The services were designed not only to allow users to search, but to immediately *retrieve* the full text of a document, rather than only directing a user to where the answer might be found.

LEXIS and NEXIS are recognized for their user-friendliness and the free-text searching capability they provide, benefits of the sophisticated software developed to support these immense databases. The reliability and responsiveness of a powerful computer center and communications network have also contributed to the Mead Data Central's continued growth and success. To date, Mead Data Central has trained over 300,000 people in the United States and in more than 40 foreign countries to use its comprehensive services.

The amount of data in Mead's services keeps pace with the growth in subscribers. In 1985 alone, more than 32 billion characters of information were added to Mead Data Central's online services.

This data is accessible through a wide variety of terminals and personal computers, including equipment from IBM, AT&T, Apple, Wang, Rolm, DEC, Hewlett Packard, Xerox, TeleVideo, and many others. Mead Data Central no longer requires customers to lease a dedicated, custom terminal to use with its services, though terminals and printers may still be obtained from the company.

Mead Data Central pricing is simple and predictable. The cost of searching each individual file in The Reference Service is the same, including $20 per hour connect time and reasonable search charges that are discounted by a third during off-peak hours.

Mead Data Central also offers a large and well-trained marketing and support staff with offices in 44 cities, 24-hour Customer Service via an 800 number, and the superior reliability of a dedicated telecommunications network and state-of-the-art computer center.

OTHER SERVICES FROM MEAD DATA CENTRAL

LEXPAT, introduced in 1983, offers the full text of U.S. patents issued since 1975. The only online library with patents in full text, LEXPAT is a significant resource for technical researchers in R&D functions, patent lawyers, and other professionals who need current information on the latest products and technology developed in the United States.

EXCHANGE, a financial and competitive information service, provides full-text company and industry research reports written by expert analysts at Merrill Lynch, Paine Webber and about 40 other leading brokerage, investment banking and research firms in the U.S. and abroad. The full texts of 10-Q and 10-K reports filed with the Securities and Exchange Commission, plus abstracts of other SEC filings from Disclosure II, are available for portfolio managers, market researchers, business analysts, strategic planners and financial officers to search and read online.

Mead Data Central's newest service, MEDIS™, provides the full text of more than 60 prestigious clinical journals, textbooks and newsletters, as well as leading reference databases, such as the National Library of Medicine's MEDLINE, Drug Information Fulltext and the National Cancer Institute's Physician Data Query. The MEDIS medical information service contains valuable information for physicians, researchers, medical librarians, public health officials, hospital executives and other professionals who need current, accurate information on everything from surgical procedures to medical practice management.

As Mead Data Central continues to add new full-text services and expand its existing ones, users can expect to see The Reference Service grow, too. New bibliographic databases will be added in a continuing effort to provide customers with the broadest possible coverage in their areas of interest. Additions will generally be selected in response to customer demand and with the objective of complementing and supplementing existing services. By increasing the value and utility of NEXIS, EXCHANGE, LEXPAT, MEDIS and other full-text services, The Reference Service will play an important role in helping Mead Data Central continue to set the pace for the online industry.

APPENDIX

BUSINESS AND FINANCIAL DATABASES IN THE REFERENCE SERVICE

FINIS—Financial Industry Information Service

This bibliographic database focuses on financial service marketing, banking regulation and financial industry trends. It contains abstracts from over 200 banking journals, newsletters, Federal Reserve Board publications, bank marketing plans and other sources. Abstracts are produced by an in-house staff at the Bank Marketing Association, an affiliate of the American Bankers' Association. Online coverage begins in 1982, and updates are monthly.

INAMI—Advertising and Marketing Intelligence

The Advertising and Marketing Intelligence database is designed to offer up-to-date surveillance of key marketplace changes that affect daily business decisions. It covers new products, test marketing, product safety, market research, consumer behavior, and FTC, FCC and FDA regulations. Special emphasis is given to statistical information related to sales, market share, ad expenditures, promotions and demographics. Articles are selected from over 50 advertising and marketing-related publications, and abstracts are written by The New York Times Company. Online coverage begins in 1979, and the file is updated daily, Monday through Friday.

INDASO—Industry Data Sources

With marketing and financial data on 65 key industries, this bibliographic file is designed for those who need information on a specific industry, industry sector or product. Articles selected from over 2,000 sources—including business, trade and government publications—are abstracted and indexed by Information Access Company, a division of Ziff Corp. The file also contains abstracts of unpublished materials such as financial and market analyses, economic studies and technical reports. Coverage begins in 1979; the file is updated monthly.

FORBAD—Forbes Annual Directory

Forbes Annual Directory contains analyes and tables on companies ranked in the Forbes 500, with such detail as company sales, profits, cash flow, assets, market value and number of employees. FORBAD also includes an alphabetical summary of rankings and a directory of the Forbes 500 with company phone numbers, addresses, ticker symbols, CEO's and industry groups. This file contains the 1984 directory published by *Forbes* magazine. It is updated annually.

MGMT—Management Contents[R]

This bibliographic database focuses on business and management topics by providing abstracts of information from over 700 business periodicals, international journals, newsletters, proceedings and transactions. A broad range of business topics is covered, including corporate intelligence, labor relations, business law and market research. Management Contents is produced by Information Access Co., a subsidiary of Ziff Corp. Online coverage begins in January 1980.

COMPUT—The Computer Database™

Also produced by Information Access Co., COMPUT concentrates on computers, electronics and telecommunications. Abstracts of material from more than 650 journals, newsletters, tabloids and proceedings are included, as well as coverage of computer-related books and self-study courses. The database is designed to answer questions about hardware, software, peripherals, services, communications and the financial stability of computer companies. It includes the results of rigorous product evaluations and comparisons. Online coverage begins in January 1983; the file is updated twice monthly.

ABI—ABI/INFORM^R

This file focuses on management concepts by providing bibliographic citations and abstracts of articles from more than 500 management and business journals. It covers such topics as competitive intelligence, finance, human resources, computers, marketing and new product development. Articles typically describe a business method or strategy that is of value to managers or administrators. The file is produced by Data Courier, Inc. Coverage begins in 1971, and updates are monthly.

SCIENCE AND TECHNOLOGY DATABASES IN THE REFERENCE SERVICE

DOE—Department of Energy

DOE is a bibliographic file containing abstracts of multi-disciplinary domestic and international literature on energy. It includes research and development information, regulatory and legal information, and practical reports and case studies of energy problems in industries and corporations. Coverage includes conservation methods, energy markets, nuclear waste disposal techniques, DOE funding and regulation, public utility regulations, and waste treatment related to industrial uses of energy. The Department of Energy's Office of Scientific and Technical Information produces the DOE database. The file's coverage begins in 1980, and it is updated monthly.

NTIS—National Technical Information Service

NTIS contains information on virtually every topic covered by the varied research interests of the federal government, its contractors and foreign groups conducting related research. Its coverage of the sciences, technology and defense is especially thorough. This bibliographic file includes reports on government sponsored research as well as other analyses prepared by federal agencies, their contractors and grant recipients. Coverage begins in 1980; the file is updated twice monthly.

FRIP—Federal Research in Progress

The FRIP file is a descriptive directory of current, ongoing federally-funded research projects. The majority of the projects listed are from the physical sciences, life sciences and engineering areas. Research summaries include start and completion dates, investigators, sponsoring organizations and project progress status. Although FRIP is not a bibliographic file, some project descriptions list publications that resulted from research efforts. The file is produced by the National Technical Information Service of the U.S. Department of Commerce, which also produces the NTIS file. FRIP will be reloaded twice a year.

HAZARD—Hazardline^R

HAZARD contains regulatory, health and precautionary information on more than 78,000 industrial chemicals. The file covers each chemical's physical properties as well as emergency procedures, labeling requirements and waste disposal. It also has comprehensive references to regulatory standards of OSHA, NIOSH, the Code of Federal Regulations and others. The file, produced by Occupational Health Services, Inc., is updated quarterly.

AERO—The Aerospace Database

The Aerospace Database offers worldwide coverage of aerospace research, engineering and technology, with an emphasis on basic and applied research in aeronautics and space sciences. Compiled over the past 20 years by the American Institute of Aeronautics and Astronautics (AIAA) Technical Information Service, it also covers such multi-disciplinary fields as satellite communications, laser and robotic technologies, and material sciences. The file is updated twice monthly.

BIOSIS—BIOSIS^R Previews

BIOSIS Previews provides comprehensive worldwide coverage of research in the life sciences. Its citations from *Biological Abstracts*, *Bioresearch Index* and *Biological Abstracts/Reports, Reviews, Meetings* offer information contained in basic research papers published in nearly 9,000 biological and biomedical journals.

BIOBUS—BioBusiness™ is also available in REFSRV.

MSDS—Material Safety Data Sheets

Occupational Health Services Inc.'s Material Safety Data Sheets provide online access to information that is critical for compliance with new OSHA regulations on the handling, use and labeling of hazardous chemical substances. These data sheets, which OSHA has declared its de facto standard, are available exclusively on The Reference Service. They contain details on the chemical's manufacturer or importer (name, address, telephone); the substance's chemical and common name and identity, as labeled; ingredients in a chemical mixture; physical and chemical characteristics of the hazardous substance; health hazards; emergency and first aid procedures; and other generally applicable precautions for safe handling, storage and use.

CURRENT AFFAIRS DATABASES IN THE REFERENCE SERVICE

AMPOL—Almanac of American Politics

The results of the 1980 Census and more recent population estimates for the early 1980's are in AMPOL, as well as a profile on each of the 535 members of Congress and each state governor. The AMPOL files of structured information also have descriptions of every state and congressional constituency, assessments of redistricting, political analyses and predictions.

The *Almanac* is published annually each summer by the Government Research Corporation, which also published the *National Journal*. The file contains the current edition of the *Almanac* and will be updated annually with each new edition, although some documents may be revised during the year.

INABS—The New York Times Information Bank

Also known as ABS, this bibliographic database is produced by The New York Times Company. It focuses on current affairs, business, economics, and social and political information, with abstracts of selected articles from about 60 newspapers, magazines, and scientific and technical periodicals. Coverage begins in 1969, and the file is updated daily, Monday through Friday.

BLCAST—Billcast™

Billcast is a comprehensive listing of all public bills currently pending in the U.S. House and Senate. Besides listing the bill number, title and sponsor, the file provides statistical odds for a bill's success in Committee and on the House or Senate floor with a historical accuracy rate of 94%. The statistical model was developed by a staff of political economists at the Center for the Study of Public Choice, George Mason University. Billcast currently covers the 1985–86 congressional session.

DDWA—Deadline Data on World Affairs

The DDWA file contains geopolitical data on 250 countries, the 50 states, Canadian provinces, territories and major world intergovernmental organizations. Each profile includes geographic data, population statistics, economic data, government structure and officials, and information on topics such as health care, transportation, communications, armed forces and culture.

DFAHBK—Defense & Foreign Affairs Handbook

This structured information file contains up-to-date historical, political and demographic data for the majority of countries, colonies and territories in the world. It contains alphabetical lists (including addresses) of military equipment manufacturers around the world; a "Who's Who in Politics and Defense"; and tabular information on missles, arms transfer, petroleum production and prices, standard arms, etc. The file currently contains the 1984 edition of the *Defense & Foreigh Affairs Handbook* produced by Perth, Inc. It will be updated when the new edition is issued.

WORLD—World Information

This file contains a synthesis of current information on international finance, economics, banking, trade, labor and currency for approximately 125 countries. It also includes political, social, statistical and general information on these nations. The file is produced by ENFORM—a division of Multinational Computer Models, Inc. Coverage consists of the current 18 months of documents. The file is updated daily, Monday through Friday.

EXPERT—The Forensic Services Directory

The EXPERT file contains biographical data and credentials for over 5,000 experts in more than 3,500 areas including engineering, biomedicine sciences, accident prevention, damage valuation, housing, public utilities, recreation, social sciences, humanities and fine arts. The file currently contains the 1984 fourth edition of the Directory issued by the National Forensic Center. It will be updated three to four times a year.

RECENT ADDITIONS TO THE REFERENCE SERVICE

WHDRCT—White House Phone Directory
LGIND—Legal Resource Index
NWSIND—National Newspaper Index
MAGIND—Magazine Index
TRDIND—Trade and Industry Index

Optical Disk—
The Electronic Library Arrives

Sandra Sinsel Leach

The publishing of databases and reference sources on optical disk is a recent and significant development in electronic publishing. Reference departments must understand the nature of this event in order to take advantage of the opportunities it offers. Information Providers (IPs) are closely watching developments in the market.

THE TECHNOLOGY

Optical disks were originally developed to distribute motion picture films (videodisks) and sound recordings (compact disks). Both the videodisk and the compact disk are reliable and inexpensive to reproduce. It was soon discovered that this same technology could be used to encode digital data, the same data residing on the magnetic tapes used in the printing process to produce books and journals, which we also search online as databases. Optical disk can store pictures as well as text, so it is an ideal publishing medium. It has vast storage capability, and individual frames can be randomly accessed in less than one second.

Both videodisks and compact disks are produced by laser technology, which etches data onto a master disk and reads it back using a laser beam of flashlight intensity. The master disk, which costs in the neighborhood of $5,000 to $10,000, can be reproduced quickly and accurately by a stamping process for under $20 each. Both are highly durable, unaffected by moisture, and do not chemically deteriorate. Disks are read by a laser beam and the disks are protected by a plastic coating, so they are relatively resistant to damage. Archival lives of ten to twenty years are claimed. It is

---

The author is Database Searching Coordinator, University of Tennessee, Knoxville, TN 37996.

© 1987 by The Haworth Press, Inc. All rights reserved.

projected that by the end of this life span, copies of the information stored on disks can then be transferred to whatever new storage medium is available and appropriate.

Videodisks Pave the Way

Until this year the main optical medium used to store databases was the videodisk. A videodisk, at 8", 12", or 14" diameter, can hold more data than a compact disk, which measures 4.7" across. However, videodisks have a costly conversion factor which requires data to be converted to analog signals to be stored, and then back to digital form to be read. The videodisk can hold the equivalent of a million pages of text or a billion characters (1 Gigabyte) per side.[1] The videodisk is ideally suited to the needs of archival storage and other applications which do not require updates. Any frame of the audio and/or visual material can be accessed within seconds. It is excellent for use in interactive training sequences. Its larger size does make it and its player bulky and space-consuming, and the lack of standards for videodisk makes product compatibility unlikely.

Both compact and videodisks are read by a disk player which plugs into a microcomputer. A projected development is a CD player which plays both audio and digital CDs. Presently, an average player costs about $2500. It is projected that costs will drop dramatically.

CD ROM: Promises for the Future

The information on a digital compact disk, called CD ROM for Compact Disk Read-Only Memory, is already in digital format, so it doesn't need to be converted. A compact disk holds the equivalent of 275,000 pages.[2] Once information is written on to a compact disk it cannot be recorded over or removed; thus it cannot be edited or corrected. CD ROM's advantage is that it is a standard, co-developed by Phillips and Sony as to format and digital recording techniques. This standardization insures that any CD ROM will play in a standard CD ROM microcomputer peripheral player. Now that the physical format has been standardized, efforts are underway to try to standardize the information format so that libraries and other information users can retrieve data from many CD ROMs using one operating system and one software retrieval package. Since, however, sixty companies are currently estimated to be involved in product development for CD ROM, file format and software standardization may be a distant goal. The Compact Disk Data Format Standards Committee of the National Information Standards Organization is currently at work on the task.

Other Optical Media

Other optical storage media available or under development include the Write Once Read Mostly (WORM) disk, which can be written onto once. This is primarily a medium for archival use, since its copying cost is not competitive with CD ROM.

A recent entry into the optical disk market is the DREXON LaserCard, a credit card-sized format capable of holding the equivalent of 800 pages on a magnetic strip. It is predicted that in future we will each carry a LaserCard encoded with vital and pertinent personal data.

Erasable Direct Read After Write (DRAW) disks are still at a developmental stage, but are expected to someday replace floppy disks, as they will incorporate also the storage and durability aspects of CD ROM.

THE ENVIRONMENT

Microcomputers have become commonplace in libraries, information centers, workplaces and homes. This equipment base is a prime factor spurring the development of information products on optical disk. Given that a relatively inexpensive disk reader can be attached to a microcomputer to enable it to read optical disks, a ready market of information users has been created. In 1983 sales of computer-based workstations were over $4 1/2 billion and sales of electronically distributed information (database access) were over $1 billion.[3] The availability of databases on optical disk, especially CD ROM, will extend access to information to any user with a properly equipped workstation. Optical disk access to databases and reference sources will free users of online connect charges, telecommunications charges and complications, and the physchological pressure of timed access to information. Waiting for offline prints to arrive will be eliminated. Information will be immediately available and novice users can take time to learn databases and familiarize themselves with content and technique. The more often a disk is used, the less expensive each use becomes. The medium encourages unlimited browsing. Optical disk will penetrate the library, the office, eventually the home—wherever people work, or think. It is easy to see how John Messerschmitt of North American Phillips could reach such levels of exaltation as to predict that CD ROM "will have the same effect on modern society as the Gutenberg Bible had on its era."[4]

The Hesitant Marketplace

Given the above, why has *PC Week* as recently as December 1985, observed that acceptance of optical disk technology is slow?[5] While standardization has been reached for the production of CD disks themselves, software and file format standards are still being considered. In the arena of videodisks, standards are even further away. There is of yet also limited application of the technology, and thus relatively few products are currently available, although many are promised. Many IPs are hesitant to commit resources to publishing on CD ROM until the market establishes itself. CD ROM producers identify information and software distribution and electronic publishing as the medium's primary applications.

Software to access the information on the CD ROM is another complicated problem. Pete Rudnicky of Digital Equipment Corporation describes it as the classic chicken-and-the-egg dilemma: "No hardware has moved because there isn't much software; however, the software developers can't provide programs because there isn't an installed base of hardware in the field."[6] Dan Tonkery of Horizon Information Services, speaking at the Optical Information Systems in Libraries Seminar, estimated that as of January 1986 there were about 500 CD ROM drives purchased and installed.[7] Around half of this number were users of Library Corporation's Bibliofile, a version of the Library of Congress catalog. This is the first CD ROM application delivered to paying customers.[8]

Intrepid IPs who have jumped into the marketplace have met this challenge by offering, or planning to offer, integrated products which combine the software, database and equipment in a single package, guaranteeing the product against potential technological advances or change. A typical workstation includes a keyboard, monitor, printer, CD reader, and microcomputer, plus the compact disks containing the database, indexes and search software. This approach to the library market allows libraries to buy into the new technology by purchasing a service and avoiding costly investment in potentially obsolete equipment.

IPs Are In Control At Last!

For the time being, then, the IPs seem to hold the cards. The marketplace is active with entrepreneurs who have developed optical disk drives or the capability to produce masters and then replicate them. But without the products and customers of the IPs, a vital link is missing. And the IPs are biding their time; since "databases will have to be distributed to at least 100 sites to be economically feasible,"[9] no one wishes to misjudge the market and thereby make a costly mistake.

An obvious target for the market is the end user, the students and professionals with the computers—be they doctors, lawyers, teachers, nutritionists, engineers—who need information and would readily purchase it if it were packaged attractively as personal databases. Several IPs have proposed products along these lines.

THE PRODUCTS

There are some companies with optical disk products in the field. The previously mentioned *Bibliofile* from Library Corporation is accompanied by other "look-up" products like Brodart's *Le Pac*, a public access catalog, and Faxon's CD ROM-based *MicroLinx* serials control system. Some reference source products debuted in 1985, and many are promised for 1986.

Information Access Corporation's InfoTrac and LegalTrac

Information Access Corporation's (IAC) Morry Goldstein stated, "CD ROM is just simply not here yet,"[10] to explain his company's choice of 12″ videodisk as medium for distribution of IAC's *InfoTrac* and *LegalTrac* databases. *InfoTrac* is a business and current affairs database made up of citations from nearly 1000 journals and newspapers already indexed in one of the company's other products: *Magazine Index*, *Newspaper Index* and *Business Index*, which are available both online and in microfilm. *InfoTrac* contains over a half million citations on a single disk, which is reissued monthly. *LegalTrac* is IAC's *Legal Resource Index* on videodisk, providing access to over 720 legal publications. The company is planning to add a version of the *Monthly Catalog* called *Government Publications Index* to its videodisk line early in 1986. At the 1986 Midwinter meeting of the American Library Association in Chicago, IAC announced an *Enhanced InfoTrac* which adds downloading, word processing and dial out access to remote online databases. Although IAC's January 1986 press release states that five access stations may be used for each system configuration, subscription prices released a week earlier list prices for a maximum of four workstations.

One of *InfoTrac*'s most attractive features is its ability to support more than one user on a system. A four station system including all hardware and support of the hardware and access to either *InfoTrac* or *LegalTrac* is $16,000. After five years, the subscriber owns the hardware, and the subscription price drops to $7,500 if IAC continues to supply the control unit (player) and $4,000 if the customer provides all hardware. InfoTrac has obvious advantages, in addition to the multi-user capability mentioned above and the characteristics inherent to all optical disk media discussed earlier. User acceptance and enthusiasm are phenomenal. Patrons who have used *Reader's Guide* for ten years and still call it the "green books" know *InfoTrac*'s name. There's no other source in the library that people stand in line to use. This event was previously reserved for copying machines, and there is some similarity in *InfoTrac*'s queuing, for the single most attractive feature for the user is the fact that *InfoTrac* prints out the citations, eliminating the need to remember to bring a pen or pencil to the library. *InfoTrac* shares the advantages of IAC's older products, the databases in the rom readers, especially the reverse chronological cumulation of citations and the subdivision of subject headings. It also shares IAC's tendency to index publications and editions that no one has or can get access to, as for example manufacturer's editions of journals or newspaper editions which are not available on microfilm. Quality control of indexing and the attendant editing of input records continue to take a back seat to the goal of currency, so the user does find such references as that to the "Aluminum Company of Aluminum." *InfoTrac* is a look-up database for there is no software in place to enable Boolean searching using logical operators. Users must find subject headings just as though they were using more mundane sources like the card catalog or paper indexes, although it is granted that once found, it is a marvel of ease to move to or among citations listed under the headings. It is supposed that for the time being, IAC has abandoned efforts to make *InfoTrac* searchable (substituting the dial-up capability mentioned earlier), in favor of a quick entry to the market, and thus also avoiding the issue of cutting into its own revenues from online connect royalties by not making a searchable product locally available.

InfoTrac's keyboard is that of the familiar IBM PC with the function keys programmed to accomplish all tasks necessary to find headings and citations, get help, print references, and begin again. Directions are very clearly presented, and keys are clearly labelled as to functions, but of course few read them, whether librarian or patron, and most stumble around, using the system in a manner short of its capability. One need only wander by the machine to see a user printing out screen after screen of subject headings to surmise that some sort of misunderstanding is taking place. It would be nice if IAC could change the print function to a different place on the keyboard, or enable it only with an additional command, since a significant additional expense for libraries is the provision of paper and ink for print capability.

The message of course is that *InfoTrac* is here, and that it is serving a large number of users, to their satisfaction. But don't listen to the logic that says, "We couldn't hire another librarian for $16,000, and look at all those people who are helping themselves." Like most library automation, *InfoTrac* will not decrease your workload. It is likely to increase it, as librarians teach, explain, demonstrate, and find alternatives when the marvel fails.

The Grolier Academic American Encyclopedia

The *Academic American Encyclopedia* is available on a CD ROM for $199. The disk holds the 9 million words contained in the 21-volume set. A search program lets the user search for topics by keyword anywhere in the article.

Digital Equipment Corporation's CDROM Database Publications

Digital Equipment Corporation (DEC) is another company said to be shipping CD ROM products. DEC's line includes ten databases from five publishers, divided into subsets of information along lines of professional interest. From COMPENDEX we have *Electrical &*

Computer Engineering, *Chemical Engineering*, and *Aerospace Engineering*. Chemical Abstracts offers *Health & Safety in Chemistry*. National Technical Information Service offers *Environmental Health and Safety*; *Computers, Communications and Electronics*; *Medicine, Health Care and Biology*; and *Aeronautics, Aerospace & Astronomy*. From the Royal Society of Chemistry we have *Current Biotechnology Abstracts*, and from Fraser Williams the *Fine Chemicals Directory*.

DEC has apparently gone after the professional end user, creating database subsets and becoming an integrated systems distributor, providing the user with all necessary hardware and software in addition to the databases. Each database is sold as a yearly subscription with quarterly updates. Cost of the titles is between $995 and $1395 for the database alone, or between $3285 and $3685 if DEC supplies the CD reader.

DATEXT INC.'S CORPORATE INFORMATION DATABASE

Since Fortune 500 companies spend a significant amount of money on online time each year, it is no surprise that many of the available and announced products are targeted to this lucrative market. Datext Inc. seems to have been one of the first, if not the first entry. The monthly *Corporate Information Database* is a compilation of business news and financial information from Disclosure, Business Research Corporation's *Investext*, and Predicast's *F & S Index*. Subscription prices, including the reader, range from $9,600 to $19,600. Disclosure has also announced availability of *Compact Disclosure*, including the use of a CD player and annual or quarterly subscriptions. Educational or public library rates are $2,200 for the annual disk and $3,200 for the quarterly; commercial rates are $3,500 for the annual and $4,500 for the quarterly.

IPS ARE MAINTAINING FLEXIBILITY

IPs, including those like IAC who are already in the market, are attempting to gauge the potential demand for disk products and offer sample products while retaining the flexibility to change formats should the market demand stabilize for a particular format. IAC's

Goldstein stresses that they aren't selling the technology, just the product, and that IAC would be willing to change to which ever technology proves to be most economical.[11] Many IPs subscribe to this theory, and many with products under development (Wilson and UMI among them), are concurrently experimenting with development of products in both videodisk and CD ROM format.

The remaining products discussed in this section are promised as this is written, but by the time it is read, many of them will have become available. Some of them are among the titles most eagerly awaited by librarians. Libraries will undoubtedly begin by experimenting with one or two disks, most likely CD ROMs, containing databases for which there is currently a high expenditure for online connect time. Even if your library is not one to rush to embrace new technology, you will have ample opportunity to explore the nature of these products in the exhibit areas of what ever library or online meetings you attend. IPs are sincerely looking for feedback about their products and their capabilities. Share with them your impressions and your needs.

University Microfilms International's Information Delivery Workstation

In September 1985 University Microfilms International (UMI) announced the optical disk prototype for its *Information Delivery Module* (IDM). Designed to provide search and retrieval as well as document delivery capabilities at one workstation, the demonstration videodisk provided access to the Institute of Electrical and Electronics Engineers (IEEE) 1984 INSPEC database on optical disk, along with stored facsimiles of the 1984 issues of 42 IEEE journals. Thus the user can search the database and retrieve and print full text articles at one workstation. Should the retrieved citation be from a publication not available on the disk, the workstation provides the communication capability to request document delivery from an online system or the OCLC ILL subsystem, and includes a facsimile interface to enable telefacsimile reception at the workstation. The videodisk is searchable with full Boolean capabilities at lightning-quick speed. Three disks are required to hold the indexes, software and full-text. This presently requires some handling of the disks, but more sophisticated technology is being explored to eliminate this problem. Demonstrated at the Midwinter meeting of the American Library Association in 1986, the IDM is expected to be commercially available in the third quarter of 1986. An important feature of the IDM is Billing and Royalty Tracking (BART), which gives the IDM the ability to track billing and royalty data for printing of copyrighted documents. The company will bill the user each time an article is printed from the disk, after collecting the data by monthly electronic polling of workstations. UMI has thus effectively developed what the company calls the "information vending machine." Many IPs will be interested in this development. UMI's future plans call for it to equip similar workstations with libraries of core journals in selected fields.

UMI Also Demonstrates DAI/CDI Disk

UMI has also developed a database consisting of *Dissertation Abstracts International* (since 1980) and the entire *Comprehensive Dissertation Index* on a 12" videodisk. Online ordering of cited titles from UMI is possible from the same workstation.

SilverPlatter Information Services

Some of the most anticipated CD ROM products will be forthcoming from SilverPlatter this year. Béla Hatvany, President of SilverPlatter, assures his company's intention to concentrate on the provision of reference materials to the academic market. The first products, *ERIC* and PsycLit on SilverPlatter, are expected in the second quarter of 1986. *PsycLit* will be priced at about $5,000 for coverage retrospective to 1974 of the printed *Psychological Abstracts*. The *Eric* file, due to its massive size, will be more complicated, as it will require distribution on one or more archival disks that do not require updating. *Current Index to Journals in Education (CIJE)* and *Resources in Education (RIE)* will be distributed on separate disks. Another disk will contain current year data, updated and reissued on a quarterly basis. Each disk from SilverPlatter will be searchable with full Boolean capability, will allow truncation, proximity searching, selection of print formats, and will offer context-sensitive help information. In addition SilverPlatter will supply users with integrated stations for viewing, reading and searching, and will support search activity with a telephone Hotline. Many SilverPlatter subscriptions can be supported on one workstation. Other databases expected from

SilverPlatter within the year include Public Affairs Information Service's *PAIS International*, the Library Association's *LISA* (Library and Information Science Abstracts), and Elsevier Science Publishers' *EMBASE*. Since these databases represent many of those most frequently searched in academic libraries, it is likely that many of us will soon be owning SilverPlatters. The market is not without competition, however, as other IPs are also considering issuing releases of these databases. Oryx Press is testing market desires for *ERIC* on CD ROM, and it is said that Information Access Corporation is looking at making many other databases available on its videodisk system.

NewsBank, Inc. Announces CD Product

A recent announcement of the availability of *NewsBank* on CD ROM follows its demonstration at the ALA Midwinter meeting. Delivery is anticipated in the summer of 1986. All NewsBank products: The *NewsBank Index*, *Names in the News*, and the four divisions of *Review of the Arts* will be contained on a single CD ROM. Disks will be updated monthly, and NewsBank will make available a subscription which includes lease or purchase of equipment.

Bowker Announces CD ROM Products

R.R. Bowker will release CD ROMs for *Books in Print* and *Ulrich's International Periodicals Directory* by June 1986. Other Bowker products on CD ROM are expected to follow shortly. Online Computer Systems, Inc. will offer Bowker customers a hardware package.

What Are the Online Vendors Up To?

Obviously this will all have a very large effect on the giants of the online industry. It is a fact of the marketplace, however, that the IPs don't know who their customers are. Until now, they have turned over their tapes to vendors for use by customers identified by password. Really savvy IPs have built a list of probable customers by offering free newsletters covering online features. Others have no idea who uses the products. Because of this situation, and because the online information distributors already have in place massive marketing networks, some IPs may find it wise and convenient to join with these vendors to distribute disk products. BRS sees a definite market for CD ROMs to distribute backfiles which are currently taking up expensive computer space while accounting for relatively little revenue from use. Bill Marovitz, BRS president, predicts that BRS will have a CD ROM product ready sometime in 1986. It is possible that it will be a "hot topic" database compiled from a number of databases on topics for which no dedicated database exists.[12]

The Wilson Company, latecomer to the online field, is forging ahead with its optical disk product. Although concurrently developed on CD ROM and videodisk, the medium of choice appears to be leaning toward the CD ROM demonstrated at the ALA Midwinter meeting. Wilson has chosen to integrate local search and online search capabilities into a single workstation. A user can decide to search a database owned in CD ROM format, or can choose to go online to one less frequently used and thus not owned. Each station has three modes of searching to provide access for those with all levels of proficiency. Wilsearch is available for those wishing to search by responding to menu items. Wilsonline is available for those who know how to use it. In addition an expert mode of searching which provides the capability of using some of the screen-handling capabilities and intelligence of the microcomputer will be made available. If Wilson chooses to release disks with a single database, a disk can hold five years of a file the size of *Readers' Guide* or fifteen to twenty years of a file the size of *Index to Legal Periodicals*. In developing the product Wilson decided to emulate its online product rather than its printed index; therefore, a display of all citations found under a particular index term, as is available on *InfoTrac*, will not be found. Wilson reasons that this approach utilizes the storage capabilities of optical disk medium, but does not take advantage of the information systems capabilities. The Wilson CD ROM system literally replicates the online databases, it does not convert them. Cost is presently estimated at $7500 including the player and other hardware. Wilson has 12" disk capability in-house, but believes that the economies that are perceived for the future of CD ROM will not come with videodisk. However, Wilson is ready to switch disk format if the market demands it.

OCLC has also been investigating the feasibility of distributing certain portions of its database on CD ROM. In addition a user friendly public access version called the Micro Enhancer Reference

Services (MERS) software is being developed in response to reference librarians who asked for a version of OCLC easier for patrons to search.

Dialog, if Roger Summit's annual December letter to the masses is any indication, seems to be aware of the technological horizon, but unwilling or unable to identify to the rest of us the direction it chooses to take. At the Online '85 meeting in New York this past November I asked a Dialog boothperson what plans were afoot for CD ROM products and she replied that they didn't know and even if they did they wouldn't share such industry secrets with me. So perhaps egos are a little tender at certain places in the online industry, or perhaps it was a bad day. Nevertheless, Dialog seems pretty quiet on its plans, although as the largest online vendor it will surely be affected by this new development.

If the press releases of IPs and optical disk manufacturers and masterers are to be believed, the advent of optical disk technology will not compete with either the online or the microformat market. Instead, these people say, each format will capture the portion of the market representing what that format does best. In addition the widespread public distribution of databases on optical disk will familiarize new users with the capabilities of these databases and create a new market of users who have discovered that they need the most current information online.

THE EFFECTS OF OPTICAL DISK TECHNOLOGY

On Information Providers and the Online Industry

Information Providers are seeing the dawn of a new age. They are being tantalized with the prospect of every businessperson's dream: a new market. One of the decisions which must be made is how to price the new products on optical disk. Following the advice of Martin Hensel, CD ROM pioneer, they would be wise to price products at a level that results in the highest potential volume of sales, in order to get new products into the marketplace. A likely gauge of this level would be an analysis of the number of hours per year IP's products are used per online searching password.[13] If CD ROM is to become an additional marketing vehicle, IPs must decide how to identify and reach their users. They must also identify ways to obtain new revenues from new users. If CD ROM is to be complementary to existing online services, the parameters of each must be determined. Realities of the existing marketplace must be realized. One thousand billing locations provide the majority of use hours to online services.[14] Eighty percent of all use is accounted for by 25 files.[15] If as mentioned earlier products need to be placed at 100 sites to be economically feasible, the necessity for development of new markets and new users is clear.

We can expect the IPs to go after the end user with even greater enthusiasm than has been shown by the online vendors. They will study their product mix and develop packages of complementary databases to be used as a point of first access in research. This focused information will have a high value to selected users. IPs should capitalize on the accurate perception that optical disk is more reliable, efficient and cost-effective than online access.

On the New Market, the End User

The new users should be concerned that the software offered with their optical disk products is adequate and sufficiently friendly. Since use of databases will no longer be restricted by high cost for online time, longer, more extensive use will result in greater familiarity with the database content and searching capabilities. New users can take time to learn. Access to information will be more convenient than ever before. Planners and decision makers will have more information on which to base their work. Owners of workstations will get even more use and value from their investment.

On the Library and Librarians

The most obvious effect will be on database seraching services. Managers will need to determine which databases should be purchased on optical disk to achieve the greatest economies, or the greatest volume of use, whichever is most compatible with the goals of the unit. The role of the librarian as intermediary can be expected to diminish in some instances, while the role of the librarian as teacher of search techniques and consultant on search strategies will increase dramatically in proportion to the number of sources made available to library users for direct access to databases. Reference librarians will need to adjust attitudes and roles as the future brings us a new format for publication of standard reference tools. The reference librarian as educator will identify a role beyond the teaching of mere search techniques as the patron who searches will learn new respect for the intricacies of subject headings and evaluation of sources. We may need to learn a new approach. We will probably work harder as we develop proficiencies and learn to transfer this knowledge to the library users. As always in discussion of the effects of new technology on libraries and information centers, the topic of money, funding, revenue must be addressed. As the figures cited throughout this discussion indicate, optical disk technology is very expensive. Few libraries will be able to afford more than a very few disk products at current prices. Although we are assured that the cost of hardware will continue to come down, the perceived value of the information contained on the disk is likely to rise. Librarians concerned with collection management will quickly see that unless there are further technological advances, few of the products currently available on optical disk can replace those added to collections for archival or research value. Disk products become extras rather than the only copy of a particular publication. This has implications for budget allocation, as libraries must move more of their dollars out of acquisitions purchases and into the purchase of services, such as those represented by optical disk products. The issue of charging for the service will become apparent as libraries begin using optical disk products. While charging for access to online services has become commonplace, it has been to my knowledge never suggested that someone pay, say, 25¢ to use *Reader's Guide*, or 75¢ to use a citation index. We must find new ways to support expenditures for these services. Perhaps given the success we seem to have had at finding millions of dollars to pay for online catalogs, the task is not as impossible as it may seem.

Optical disk technology will change the face of the library of the future. Its advent will be slow, its impact great. Reference librarians will rise to the challenge, and the world of information service will be greater for it.

KEEPING UP
WITH OPTICAL DISK DEVELOPMENTS

Several publications and knowledgeable spokespersons have emerged from this very fluid technology. Julie Schwerin writes a regular column on optical disk development in *Information Today*, the electronic information services industry tradepaper. Titled

"Optical Publishing," it keeps readers abreast of new developments yet manages to keep rumors and hype in perspective. Nancy Jean Melin is a regular writer and speaker on optical disk technology for publishing. She is editor of *Small Computers in Libraries*, *Library Software Review*, *M300 and PC Report*, and *Optical Information Systems in Libraries*, all of which carry articles on disk technology. A regular speaker, writer and consultant on optical disk technology is Nancy Herther of Robbinsdale, Minnesota. Nancy tries to speak enthusiastically yet realistically about this emerging technology, and her efforts to promote sensible thinking on the topic are appreciated.

Several publications in addition to those already mentioned focus on the world of optical disk technology. Since 1981 *VideoDisk and Optical Disk* has reported monthly on developments in the field. It is currently accompanied by a biweekly update. *CD Data Report* claims to be the only publication devoted exclusively to the compact optical disk storage industry. In addition articles on optical disk are regularly carried by journals such as *Library HiTech*, *Information and Technology in Libraries*, and *Online*. Run a quick search through your LISA or ERIC databases on CD ROM for a list of the latest citations.

REFERENCES

1. Harding, Jessica R., and William R. Nugent. "Library Applications of Optical Storage," *Encyclopedia of Library & Information Science*, Supplement 3. New York: Marcel Dekker, 1985, p. 257.
2. Herther, Nancy K. "CD ROM Technology: A New Era for Information Storage and Retrieval?" *Online*, 9(November 1985), p. 19.
3. Gale, John C. "The Information Workstation: A Confluence of Technologies Including the CD-ROM," *Information Technology and Libraries*, 4(June 1985), p. 137.
4. "CD-ROM revolution predicted," *Library Journal* 111(2), February 1, 1986, p. 33.
5. Freedman, Beth. "Optical-Disk Acceptance Is Slow Despite Advances in Technology," *PC Week*, 2(3), December 17, 1985, p. 3.
6. *Ibid*.
7. Tonkery, Dan. "The Potential for Library Applications of CD-ROM Technology," speech at Optical Information Systems in Libraries Seminar, Holiday Inn Chicago City Centre, January 18, 1986.
8. Littman, Jonathan. "Optical-Disk Databases," *PC Week*, 2(August 13, 1985), p. 32.
9. *Ibid.*, p. 33.
10. Herther, *op. cit.*, p. 23.
11. *Ibid.*, p. 22.
12. *Ibid.*, p. 24.

13. Hensel, Martin. "Optical Discs: Tool for Database Market Expansion," speech at the National Online Meeting, Sheraton City Centre, New York, May 2, 1985.
14. *Ibid.*
15. Kesselman, Martin. "Online Update," *Wilson Library Bulletin*, 58(10), June 1984, p. 732.

Online Services at the Reference Desk: New Technologies vs. Old Problems

Mary Boulanger

In the final decades of the twentieth century we have come to expect, though not necessarily accept, change in our environment. Library operations have been transformed by ever increasing levels of automation. Until recently, however, activities of the typical reference librarian at the desk were largely unaffected by the new technologies. The library might have online reference services, but they were likely to be located in a separate room, just off the main reference area or around the corner. If reference staff wished to verify a citation on OCLC, the nearest terminal to do this would most likely be in the cataloging department, acquisitions, or perhaps interlibrary loan office.

In 1975, Jean Kirkland expressed doubts that any library had "an electronic computer" at the reference desk.[1] By 1983 there were reports from some reference departments using various bibliographic utilities and databanks to answer patron inquiries.[2] During the past few years, several new products have been introduced or announced that could possibly accelerate the move to put high tech at the reference desk. We have seen and heard many predictions about how the latest technological breakthrough will revolutionize libraries. Any such claims that appear in this article will be given critical, if not skeptical treatment. The article will first review some of the products, with an eye to Wisconsin and other libraries' experiences using the new technologies. Then it will raise questions concerning the impact implementation of these products might have on libraries and reference services in particular.

The author is at the Golda Meir Library, University of Wisconsin, Box 604, Milwaukee, WI 53201.

© 1987 by The Haworth Press, Inc. All rights reserved.

GATEWAY AND FRONT-END SOFTWARE

In addition to new technologies, the appearance of gateway software has had an impact on reference departments. Gateway software, which first appeared on the market in 1983,[3] is used with microcomputers serving as terminals for database searching. The purpose is to make it easier for end users primarily, but also for professional searchers, to search various database systems or databanks. A gateway can be defined as, "an interface between the user and the databank that performs the functions of dialing the telephone call, selecting the communications network, connecting to the databank, and sending the user's password."[4] These software packages are sometimes called "front end" systems, though front end software capabilities usually extend beyond what gateway software can do. An ideal front end system might provide access to more than one databank, automatic dialing and logon, help features, presearch editing and uploading, database selection, downloading, and post-processing the search results.[5]

Typical of the front end packages, and designed with the needs of "librarians, information professionals, and online searchers" in mind, is Menlo Corporation's Pro-Search.[6] It is an enhanced version of In-Search, an end user product for searching DIALOG. Like gateway software, Pro-Search can provide access to both the DIALOG and BRS databanks with its automatic dialing and logon feature. It is much more powerful than gateway software, however, since it can also select databases, help formulate search strategies prior to going online, and will allow the searcher to use one databank's software and commands in other databanks being searched. This "emulator" capability is most helpful for those who are quite proficient in searching BRS databases and need to search DIALOG, or vice-versa.[7] Pro-Search can also provide detailed cost information with its Accounting Reports facility, that will produce a monthly or session report.[8]

A revent survey listed several Wisconsin libraries where Pro-Search is used. At the corporate library (information center) of Northwestern Mutual Life Insurance Company, Pro-Search gets high marks, with comments like, "Excellent, can do native and assisted mode. Accounting system is great."[9] The UW-Stevens Point Library, on the other hand, has problems becoming familiar with its operation saying, "Have not used very much. May be "front end," but requires some time to learn."[10] Quint notes some problems with the documentation as well, in an otherwise favorable review.[11] Additional front end software packages geared for the librarian or non-librarian professional include Sci-Mate, micro-Disclosure and microCambridge.[12]

END USER PRODUCTS

The end user is the intended market for other front end products such as IAC's SearchHelper and WILSEARCH from H. W. Wilson. SearchHelper provides entry to just seven databases, all produced by Information Access Corporation, but they cover a wide variety of subjects. Magazine Index, National Newspaper Index, Trade & Industry Index, Legal Resource Index, Management Contents, and Computer Database, are updated monthly. Newsearch, which contains "up-to-the-minute" references from newspapers, legal, business, and general periodicals, is updated daily.[13] The user chooses a database and then types search terms of one or more words, which can be linked with the Boolean operator "and." The software calls and connects up to DIALOG and the appropriate database. SearchHelper proceeds to run the search, with the result being a set of up to twenty citations. Other search refinements include limiting the search to a single periodical, a range of dates, or to article type, including play, book, film and restaurant reviews.[14] The Queens Borough Public Library has used Search-Helper since November 1982, and has found it an extremely valuable asset to their reference service.[15]

WILSEARCH came on the market in late 1985 and was designed to provide inexpensive direct patron access to the WILSONLINE databases. It is a menu-driven system, though a help command can be used at any time to give more detailed information. In addition each screen has a HELP window to explain the available options. The database selection menu lists the twelve available options. The database selection menu lists the twelve periodical databases and three book databases currently searchable. After the patron chooses one or two databases from the menu, the system prompts for subject terms. WILSEARCH will also suggest additional related terms after the search is complete, if appropriate. If the search does not find any references, there is no charge.[16] Though it is intended for the library patron, WILSEARCH can also provide ready-reference aid for librarians. Its use should save on the time and cost of other online searching, and save time librarians spend on patron assistance, according to its producer.[17]

A review of end user products would not be complete without a mention of BRS/After dark and DIALOG's Knowledge Index. With just a microcomputer and modem, the home computer owner can have access to a variety of databases and have citations printed on the monitor or printer, or download them. Primarily menu-driven these systems can frustrate the experienced searcher, but the low cost is an incentive to perhaps test out a difficult search and perfect the strategy before searching a more expensive version of the database.[18] Two other end user services, BRS/Saunders Colleague and BRS/BRKTHRU have special features and databases tailored for the medical and other non-information professionals.[19]

CD-ROM SYSTEMS

One of the latest media for the storage of data to be developed is the compact disk. Though its initial use has been in the recording of music, the compact disk is capable of storing digital data as well.[20] At 4.75 inches, the CD is smaller than the floppy disks used in IBM PC and Apple microcomputers, and has a data capacity of 550 megabytes.[21] There is no physical contact with the CD to read it; a laser beam tracks over the CD, reading the information from "pits" in the surface of data tracks. The actual surface of the CD is coated with a transparent layer 1.2mm thick. This means that the CD does not wear out, and scratches have almost no effect on the accuracy of the optical scanning. When the CD is used in a system that stores and reproduces digital datra, the system and disks are called CD-ROM, which stands for Compact Disk-Read Only Memory.[22]

One application with particular possibilities for the reference desk is the database loaded on a CD-ROM. In late 1985 Digital Equipment Corporation (DEC) announced they would market five chemical and engineering databases on CD-ROMs, using a CD-ROM reader compatible with DEC's Rainbow 100 microcomputer and the IBM PC.[23] According to DEC's promotional literature each CD-ROM contains either an entire database or a subset, as well as search and retrieval software called MicroBASIS. The databases include NTIS, Compendex, Chemical Abstracts, the Royal Society of Chemistry Current Biotechnology Abstracts, and Fraser Williams Fine Chemicals Directory.[24]

Another company offering similar wares is SilverPlatter. Available in mid-1986, SilverPlatter intends to market a version of Psychological Abstracts called PsycLIT,[25] as well as ERIC and Excerpta Medica. Current plans are to have material from 1974 to the present on CD-ROM, with quarterly updates. Subscribers would also have the option to lease, purchase, or use their own micros as workstations. Both SilverPlatter and DEC promise telephone hotline support.

1986 should be a big year for introduction of CD-ROM products, according to various company announcements. Dissertations Abstracts Online had a demonstration laserdisk at the ALA Midwinter Conference exhibits. WILSONLINE will be testing some of its databases on CD-ROM during the year as well. The list is even longer if you include other library applications.[26] There is another technology in use in libraries related to CD-ROM that has been around for a while longer: videodisk.

VIDEODISKS

Like CD-ROMs, videodisks can store graphics as well as textual data. Usually ten to twelve inches in diameter, they were developed over a decade before their smaller cousins, with a prototype of today's system in existence in 1972.[27] Their capacity is greater, about 800 megabytes, but other features are similar to the CD-ROM, including ease of maintenance and lack of significant wear.[28] Several libraries in the United States and Canada have developed videodisk projects, most often to create a database or graphics and text catalog of a particular collection.[29] One commercial videodisk system with reference applications has been available since March 1985, and has been in use in Wisconsin for almost a year.

In the summer of 1985, one of the librarians at the University of Wisconsin-Stevens Point won a free one year subscription to InfoTrak, a videodisk system from Information Access Company. InfoTrak provides access to millions of article citations drawn from IAC's array of index databases. It can support up to four work stations, each consisting of an IBM-PC, floppy disk drive, monitor, and one HP Thinkjet Printer. The central control unit includes one controller, a multihost interface, a videodisk player, and various interface cards and cables in order to attach the PC's. Each month subscribers get a freshly updated and cumulated videodisk, which contains the entire database of business, technical and general interest periodical citations.[30]

The system has been operational at UW-Stevens Point since October 1985 and has been proven to be very user-friendly. InfoTrak is located in the reference room, but the reference staff is rarely called upon to give instructions in its use. Library patrons spend an average of five to seven minutes at the access stations, leaving with a list of citations on their topic. There is a built-in thesaurus for locating precise search terms, but InfoTrak is so totally geared to the non-professional end user that it often takes longer for librarians to arrive at appropriate subject headings than the typical patron takes.[31] A major consequence of having InfoTrak available at no cost to patrons has been a sharp reduction in the number of fee-based online searches conducted at UW-Stevens Point, especially among undergraduates. Other libraries report having policy guidelines for determining when to do free ready-reference or quick reference online searches, as opposed to searches where the patron absorbs the cost. Each kind of service is distinct and does not interfere with the other in these libraries.[32] However, this has not been the case at UW-Stevens Point.

IMPLICATIONS FOR REFERENCE SERVICES

At a recent meeting of the Information Industry Association, an executive from a company which produces CD-ROM systems proclaimed that technology as, "the most significant advance in publishing technology in four hundred years."[33] This would put CD's right up there with the Gutenberg bible. Before a revolutionary idea can have much effect, however, certain questions would have to be answered. Are all or most manufacturers supporting their products with consumer hotlines, warranties, and the like? Are there future developments planned that would make the current hot technology obsolete quickly? Finally, are there well developed applications *and markets* for the technology?

A negative answer to the last question is the main reason many new technologies don't get off the ground. They are the victim of what Alan Veaner called "around the cornerism."[34] If a market is supposed to develop "any time now," it may never develop. Industry experts watching the CD-ROM think that its development has progressed to a point where it can positively answer the question of markets, and is likely to become more widespread.[35]

For most libraries, the cost of introducing and maintaining a technology is a large obstacle to be dealt with, especially if there is a substantial start-up or ongoing expense. At the UW-Stevens Point library, they are faced with the dilemma of how to find budget room for a popular service that was free for the first year, but will cost over $8,000.00 to maintain. WILSEARCH and SearchHelper have modest software costs to begin service, and each search costs from $1 to $3, but searches must be purchased in "search packets" of 700 or more.[36] Equipment, supplies, training and security costs must also be weighed.

The most critical concern for libraries and especially for reference departments, is that of staffing. Will everyone be trained to use the new product? If only some professionals will be using the technology, the rest of the staff must be at least knowledgeable enough to refer patrons when appropriate. There can be confusion and unevenness of service in the early stages of implementation, and beyond, if planning is not done well.[37] Guidelines should be developed to give criteria for making decisions regarding online searching.[38]

Another issue is level of service to library patrons. At the University of Wisconsin-Milwaukee Golda Meir Library, we have had fee-based online searching since 1975. With current budget and staffing levels, we do not anticipate being able to introduce ready-reference searching in the near future. The reference staff has even considered cutting back on the time allowed for interviewing individual patrons.[39] William Miller warns in an insightful essay in *American Libraries*, that if more services are created at a library without increased staff or more innovative staffing, the present staff will lose effectiveness as well as enthusiasm.[40] New technologies/ services are not likely to succeed without enthusiasm in their promotion.

SUMMARY

Is the reference desk soon to be transformed into a showcase of technological innovation? It is beginning to in many libraries, especially where there is philosophical and budgetary support for providing the best service possible to the library's user population.

Planning and study of that population's information needs, as well as planning for staffing and cost considerations are critical to new technologies' success. For many libraries, however, new technology may be an extremely long range goal.

REFERENCES

1. Jean Kirkland, "Reference Service and the Computer: an Experiment at the Georgia Tech Library," *RQ*, 14 (Spring 1975):212.
2. Some examples can be found in, *Information Resources on Online at the Reference Desk: a selected ERIC Bibliography*, ERIC Document ED254226, 1984; and the entire issue of *Reference Librarian*, no. 5/6, 1983.
3. Cynthia A. Kehoe, "Interfaces and Expert Systems for Online Retrieval," *Online Review*, 9 (November 1985):492.
4. Donald T. Hawkins and Louise R. Levy, "Front End Software for Online Database Searching, Part 1: Definitions, System Features, and Evaluation," *Online*, 9 (November 1985):31.
5. Ibid, p. 33.
6. "CLASS to Distribute Pro-Search Software," *Online* 9 (November 1985):75.
7. Hawkins and Levy, p. 34.
8. Barbara Quint, "Menlo Corporation's Pro-Search: Review of a Software Search Aid," *Online*, 10 (January 1986):18.
9. Wisconsin, Division of Library Services, survey of Wisconsin libraries, 1985.
10. Ibid.
11. Quint, p. 20.
12. Henry Pisciotta, "Sci-Mate: A Review," *Reference Services Review*, 13 (Summer 1985):11.
13. Information Access Company, SearchHelper marketing brochure.
14. Queens Borough Central Library Staff, "SearchHelper: the Queens Borough Experience," *Online* (November 1985):54.
15. Ibid, p. 53.
16. H. W. Wilson Company, WILSEARCH marketing brochure.
17. Ibid.
18. Robin Kaplan, "Knowledge Index: A Review," *Database*, 8 (June 1985):123.
19. For example, BRS/BRKTHRU has 65 databases compared to the 31 of Knowledge Index. In addition, BRKTHRU is available for almost the same hours as the regular BRS databank, while After Dark is only available after 6 pm weekday evenings. BRS/BRKHRU brochure.
20. Brower Murphy, "CD-ROM and Libraries," *Library Hi Tech*, 3(2):21, 1985.
21. Nancy H. Herther, "CD ROM Technology: A New Era for Information Storage and Retrieval?" *Online* 9 (November 1985):17.
22. Murphy, p. 21.
23. "Database Publishers Go CD-ROM Route with DEC," *Information Today* 2 (November 1985):21, and "The Printout," *Online* 10 (January 1986):13.
24. Digital Equipment Corporation, marketing brochure.
25. "Announcing PsycLIT on a SilverPlatter," *PsycINFO News* 5 (October 1985):1.
26. Some of these include BiblioFile Catalog Production System by The Library Corporation, Laser Quest (retrospective and new cataloging) available in April from General Research Corporation, and the CLASIX STA/F Text software system (local database production) by Reference Technology.
27. Judith Paris and Richard Boss, "Videodiscs," in *Conservation in the Library: A*

Handbook of Use and Care of Traditional and Nontraditional Materials, ed. Susan Garretson Swartzburg (Westport, CT: Greenwood Press, 1983), p. 188.

28. This applies to optical videodisks only. The capacitance type of disk, such as the one marketed by RCA as SelectaVision in the early 1980s, is read by a mechanical stylus which causes wear. See Peter B. Schipma, "Videodiscs," in *New Information Technologies—New Opportunities*, ed. Linda C. Smith (University of Illinois at Urbana-Champaign, 1981), p. 90; and Charles Sneed, "The Videodisc Revolution: What's Ahead for Libraries?" *Wilson Library Bulletin* 53 (November 1980):188.

29. For examples of videodisk projects, see Alfred L. Freund, "A Regional Bibliographic Database on Videodisc," *Library Hi Tech* 3(2) pp. 7–10; and Sabine S. Sonnemann, "The Videodisc as a Library Tool," *Special Libraries* 74 (January 1983):7–13.

30. Information Access Company, marketing brochure.

31. Interview with Jim Belz, University of Wisconsin-Stevens Point, Stevens Point, Wisconsin, February 1986.

32. See Kay Durkin and Donna R. Dolan, *Reference Database Use: A New Application of Online Seraching*, ERIC Document ED190054, 1980; Maruita Peterson Holland, "'Real-Time' searching at the Reference Desk," *Reference Librarian* (Video to Online) no. 5/6 pp. 166–168, 1983; and Russ Chenoweth, "The Integration of Online Searching in Reference Service," *Reference Librarian*, (Video to Online) no. 5/6 pp. 119–127.

33. John C. Gale, "The Information Workstation: A Confluence of Technologies Including the CD-ROM," *Information Technology and Libraries*, 4 (June 1985):138.

34. Barbara Magnuson, "Collection Management: New Technology, New Decisions," *Wilson Library Bulletin*, 58 (May 1983):741.

35. Julie B. Schwerin, "Optical Publishing: Evolution or Revolution?" *Information Today* 2 (November 1985):5.

36. WILSEARCH and SearchHelper marketing brochures.

37. Sara Brownmiller, A. Craig Hawbaker, Douglas E. Jones, and Robert Mitchell, "Online Ready-Reference Searching in an Academic Library," *RQ*, 24 (Spring 1985):325.

38. See Holland, p. 167; and Durkin and Dolan, p. 17.

39. The Data Base Services at UW-Milwaukee schedules patrons who wish an online search for 30 minute appointments. The interviews usually take less time, but are still much longer than the typical reference desk interview. Current department policy recommends answering reference questions in less than three minutes, if possible. This discrepancy was the subject of a staff meeting, but the issue was left unresolved.

40. William Miller, "What's Wrong With Reference: Coping with Success and failure at the Reference Desk," *American Libraries*, 15 (May 1984):321.

PUBLISHING POLICIES AND REFERENCE SOURCES

Keeping the Lid On: Approaches to the Control of Costs in Reference Book Purchasing in an Academic Library

Heather S. Miller

Everyone knows what a reference book is. Asked for an off-the-cuff definition, most of us would come up with some variation of the two succinct definitions given in *Websters Third*:

> reference book n 1: a book (as a dictionary, encyclopedia, atlas) intended primarily for consultation rather than for consecutive reading 2: a library book that may be used on the premises but may not be taken out[1]

The second is appealing in its simplicity, but the libraries I frequent have several categories of books that "may not be taken out," reference being only one of them. Webster's first definition seems at first glance to be inarguable, but the trick is in deciding what will be useful for consultation in a given library. One librarians's reference book might be another's circulating title. And sometimes we hedge our bets and put a copy in Reference and another in the circulating stacks.

Do librarians have a better definition, one that takes into consideration such ambiguities? The phrase "reference book" seems often used without definition. The two definitions found in the *ALA Glossary* essentially parallel those in Webster.[2]

Mudge gives perhaps the clearest definition of reference books in the introduction to the sixth edition of the *Guide to Reference Books*, reprinted in the 9th edition, saying that reference books are:

The author is Head, Acquisitions Department, State University of New York, The Library, Albany, NY 12222.

meant to be consulted or referred to for some definite piece of information. Books of this second class are called *reference books*, and are usually comprehensive in scope, condensed in treatment, and arranged on some special plan to facilitate the ready and accurate finding of information.[3]

Moreover, Mudge goes on:

There are other books, however, which, while intended primarily to be read through for either information or pleasure, are so comprehensive and accurate in their treatment and so well provided with indexes that they serve also as reference books.[4]

This comes closest to the truth, but no definition will overcome the differences between one library and another.

Having so defined our reference book it is clear that while most librarians might agree on a certain core of indisputable reference works such as *Websters Second* and/or *Third*, *Encyclopaedia Britannica*, zip code directory and certain almanacs to name a few, the bulk of the reference collection will be idiosyncratic. Books in the reference collection will reflect course and research priorities on campus, how the library defines its role in relation to these priorities, the library's relation to the community at large and other factors including the inevitable filtering of policy through the individual human beings who select the books. And then we must muddy the waters further by pointing out that we are not limited to books here but include all sorts of publications in all formats that serve our basic reference purposes, so we may include certain periodicals and serials, law sources, microfiche, microfilm, etc. As a result we now have "reference materials."

Now that we know, more or less, what we are talking about we can proceed to discuss some of the issues involved in obtaining and paying for this material that we call reference.

THE REFERENCE BOOK SITUATION

Increasing Numbers

It is not difficult to find references in the literature to the increasing volume of books available and to their escalating prices, although the rapid rise in both numbers and price may have levelled off a bit for American publishing as a whole. The most recent *Bowker Annual* states that

> American book title output continued its moderate annual rise in 1983, but average per-volume prices were holding steady or even beginning to drop slightly in a number of subject categories for the first time in several years, according to R.R. Bowker Company computations.[5]

Nevertheless, the volume is already so great that a modest increase still means a tremendous number of new books. The effects of this situation on libraries are graphically discussed by Audrey Eaglen in "Too Many Books? Publishers' Problems and Collection Building."[6] However, specific information on either the volume of publishing of *reference books* or their prices is hard to come by for precisely the lack of easy definition discussed earlier.

Statistical compilations such as those in *Publishers' Weekly*, *Library Journal* and elsewhere do not deal with reference books as a category; although some useful information can be obtained. Among such useful data was the Serials Services (including Wilson Indexes) statistics included in the *LJ* price indexes through 1984.[7] Similarly, book trade statistics appearing in the *Bowker Annual* include no category for reference books. In the 1984 volume, one finds "Dictionaries & Theasauruses" and "Encyclopedias" listed under "U.S. Book Exports, 1980–1982"[8] which again is no help to libraries trying to determine figures for reference materials.

Reviewing media for reference books are better sources of these data. *American Reference Books Annual* is the most comprehensive source of reviews of U.S. reference books although certain categories (e.g., U.S. government publications) are not included and non-reference library science material is. In 1970, its first year, *ARBA* reviewed 1474[9] titles. Since 1980 it has reviewed the following:

Year	Titles Reviewed
1980	1635
1981	1740
1982	1658
1983	1604
1984	1534
1985	1734[10]

Despite three years of declining numbers, it is clear that there is a significant increase in a number that was not unconsiderable to begin with.

Each *ARBA* issue includes reviews of imprints of the previous year. These are vast numbers for selectors to consider and they do not comprehensively represent non-U.S. reference publications or items not readily definable as reference.

The compilations entitled "College Book Price Information" published in *Choice* deal specifically with reference books, but only those reviewed in *Choice* and designated reference in the review. For some libraries, this will not be a major problem. Others will find that they include more than *Choice*-reviewed titles in their reference collections. This compilation for 1984 showed the following numbers of reference books reviewed:

Year	Number of Titles
1978	453
1983	506
1984	591[11]

Like the *ARBA* figures, those from *Choice* show a steady increase in the number of reference books being published.

Reference publications of the U.S. government must be considered separately. Until recently, their numbers too have proliferated, as shown by the figures in *Government Reference Books* which indicate that in the 1968/69 volume there were 600[12] reviews while the 1982/83 volume contained 1191.[13]

This is another large group of reference books which presents its own problems and will not be treated in depth here because most large academic libraries are depositories and incur negligible costs for this material.

Increasing Costs

Given the large number of new reference materials appearing each year and each year more than the last, total costs cannot but be high even assuming that not all will be favorably reviewed (although it seems that most are) and that not all will be suited to any given library.

The compilations of figures published in *Choice* are useful for those attempting to determine costs of reference materials because "reference" is one category used. But serial reference books, which can eat up a large part of the reference budget are not caught in this net unless newly reviewed.

Titles that were reviewed but were priced above $500 per title are also excluded from these statistics along with several excluded due to "format." Nevertheless, the excluded titles are identified and it is possible for libraries to refigure totals to include these expensive items.

This compilation is useful for anyone attempting to determine costs of reference materials. The first compilation included data for 1983 and, for comparison, 1978. The second compilation included data for 1984, 1983 and 1978.

These data indicate that the average price of the reference books reviewed in *Choice* rose from $34.15 in 1978 to $47.50 in 1984.[14] This represents an increase of 39% over the seven year period. By way of comparison, the consumer price index for all items rose from 202.9[15] in December of 1978 to 315.5 in December of 1984.[16] This is an increase of 55.4%.

Library journal also publishes a select list of the best reference books published during the preceding year. Figures for the past three years and 1978 are shown below.

	number of titles	total price	average price
1978	49	$2267.40	$46.27
1982	40	2499.10	62.48
1983	35	2567.85	73.37
1984	39	2592.60	66.48[17]

This average price is obtained from a very small number of books deemed to be "works that would be most valuable for a wide range of public and college libraries."[18] The average increased by 14% over the seven year period, by 4% between 1982 and 1984.

These figures, useful as they are, are only a first step in the process of coming to grips with reference costs. They indicate that numbers of new reference books and their prices have risen significantly during the recent past but prices may not have risen as rapidly as overall consumer costs. Although one could further collect and analyze data, what we have here is sufficient to indicate that keeping tabs on reference costs is a serious and challenging undertaking. Reviewing media only cover newly published materials, but even here numbers of new books and their costs are formidable. In perusing the 1984 *ARBA* volume, it is heartening to note titles that are definitely unsuited to one's own reference collections and the infrequent critical reviews. At least it cuts down on the choices a bit, but not enough to be of significant help. Hard choices must be made in order to build and maintain a quality reference collection within the confines of budget restrictions.

With this view of reference books in mind another outlook on the problem can be gained by examining the serial reference book situation.

Serial Reference Books

As librarians are fond of saying, serials are different and serial reference books are no exception. They too challenge the Acquisitions librarian in different ways than do monographic reference books due to their ongoing and changeable nature. Here at SUNYA we follow the definition of serial found in the *ALA Glossary*:

> serial 1. A publication in any medium issued in successive parts bearing numerical or chronological designations and intended to be continued indefinitely.[19]

This continuing nature of serials is not only a source of difficulty, but, potentially at least, also a means of control. Control may be desirable because there is some indication that prices of serial reference books may have risen in the last few years at an alarming rate, higher than monographic reference book prices.

Nancy R. Posel suggests that publishers may be "biting the hand that feeds them"[20] by increasing the prices of reference books beyond the ability of libraries to pay. She includes a chart showing seventeen standard reference titles, *all serials*, and their prices over a four year period. Price increases here are undeniable. All of the seventeen titles are normal components of academic library reference collections. The prices given by Posel are similar to those paid by SUNYA and, as she points out, some show increases of "60, 70, even more than 100 percent over three years."[21] The average price of the seventeen titles for 1984 is $336.82. Posel objects not only to price rises but also to the fact that: "Most of the works had not been significantly expanded."[22]

Returning to the *Choice* figures cited above, it is interesting to examine the titles excluded from the entire study which covers far more than reference books. Exclusions are due to format or prices over $500.00. Of the five titles excluded in 1983, three are designated as reference and have an average price of $410.00.[23] In 1984, seven of ten excluded titles are designated reference. Six of these have an average price of $405.00. No price is given for the seventh.[24] For 1983 all three reference titles are also serials. For 1984 six of the seven are serials.

These two sources indicate that the real killer of the reference book budget may be the serial reference book. The problem we have to deal with is two part (1) to document whether it is indeed the case that serial reference books are showing unreasonable price gains and doing so with little or no control, and (2) to try to gain some control over them.

Approaches to these two problems will vary from library to library. In an attempt to evaluate both the problems and possible means of control, I will describe some recent activities in this library. It should be noted that although this discussion focuses on serial *reference* books, many of the issues involved are applicable to serials as a whole.

The Situation at SUNYA

All serial materials received by the SUNYA libraries are checked in through a central kardex which contains, in one alphabet, all subscription and standing order receipt and billing information. There are some 13,500 entires in the Kardex of which 6572 are standing orders. Of these, 1567 are standing orders for reference material. During the 1985 calendar year 16,722 pieces were checked in as standing orders.

Control over this material in terms of budget ramifications has gradually increased during recent years when it became apparent that generous acquisitions budgets were a thing of the past.

A system of fund codes was devised by the Head of Collection Development whereby each of the various subject areas in which we collect (e.g., pathobiology, chemistry, computer science, reading) was assigned a three digit number. One code was also assigned to "Reference" for all material housed there regardless of subject. In addition, a system of account codes was established. These six digit codes relate to type of material rather than subject and include such categories as hard copy periodical backfiles, approval (a separate number for each plan), discretionary books (foreign and domestic separately), periodicals and standing orders, both subdivided. By utilizing both of these systems it has been possible to keep abreast of budgetary expenditures within subject areas as well as for specified types of material.

Although encumbrances (as opposed to expenditures) have been tracked using fund codes in an Osborne Executive I microcomputer[25] and a campus wide data processing system called MAPPER has been used since late 1982 to generate reports of expenditures (separately from encumbrances) based on the account codes, access to other data has been manual. Due to time constraints, the net effect of this has been the unavailability of much data.

During the second half of the 1984/85 fiscal year it became apparent that expenditures, if continued at the current rate, would outstrip available funds before the end of the fiscal year. Despite constant monitoring of expenditures this situation had not been foreseen. In addition to applying immediate brakes to spending at the time, several long range measures were taken to slow the rise in spending in the future. One such measure involved each bibliographer of the Collection Development Department in scrutinizing all standing orders carrying his or her fund codes. Since we had an integrated, manual alphabetical kardex, there was no easy means of identifying which titles were assigned to any given fund code even though fund codes had been recorded on most kardex entries.

It was decided to embark on a crash program to create a manipulable list of all our standing orders using an IBM PC. This was envisioned, not as an automated kardex, but simply as an admittedly rather primitive way to link titles and fund codes thereby providing each bibliographer with a list of titles sorted by fund code. The kardex had never before received such thorough scrutiny by the bibliographers and the aims were multiple: to identify titles linked to each fund code, to quantify expenditures for each fund code, to assign and change fund codes where necessary and finally to trim future expenditures by identifying and cancelling expendable titles. The list is being used for the latter purpose at this time by all bibliographers. Reference is only one area where this review is taking place.

Using D Base II, a simple template was prepared onto which staff members would enter the title, source (vendor), fund code and price for each standing order encountered in a title-by-title pass through the entire kardex from A to Z. This was done primarily by clerical staff although the program was set up and administered by professional staff members. Input took place over a two month period. When complete, the list was printed in fund code order and distributed to the bibliographers. It was never seen as anything more than a finding tool to guide a bibliographer to those kardex entries pertaining to his or her fund codes.

We were aware of a number of pitfalls. Price was particularly prone to error. Although we specified inputting the full price for one recent year (1983 or 1984) and using zero price for all other situations, errors and misinterpretations crept into the list. Prices listed in foreign currency had to be converted, prices covering several years had to be divided, multiple payments for a single year added up and so on. Zero prices were given for all titles for which payment was recorded elsewhere (e.g., the several titles received on a membership would show zero price).

Another limiting factor was the fact that two disks were required to record the entire kardex and allow indexing space. Thus it is not possible to manipulate the entire list at once. This means that lists printed in anything other than alphabetical order appear in two separate segments. The alphabetical sequence prints in sequential order because the list was input sequentially from A to Z.

Despite such difficulties, the list was found to be useful even beyond its original intent. Because the list could be sorted in various ways, it became possible to look at standing orders from new and long overdue perspectives. In order to examine the situation of reference books, quite apart from the use made of the whole list by Collection Development, the Acquisitions Department printed the reference list alone in two sorts for its own use.

One list printed in alphabetical order all titles fund coded for reference. This was done after fund code corrections had been made by the bibliographers and it could be assumed that a high degree of accuracy existed in the correlation of fund codes and titles. A second list was printed sorting titles alphabetically within price ranges.

Lists Provide Access

These lists provided access to and an overview of serial reference materials that had never before been available. The bibliographer had only been aware of the price for the first issue or year of a new order he or she was placing. Once established, a standing order was paid for each year by clerical staff. Prices were not as a rule questioned. This situation meant that we had no data on how much we were spending on serial reference materials. Moreover, it meant that no one was even spot checking or questionging invoices as they were processed unless obvious errors were noted. The inexorable climb of prices was simply accepted.

Even before our lists were available we instructed clerical personnel to give to the department head all invoices showing an unusually large jump in price over the preceding payment. Once the lists were in hand a more systematic review of serial reference book expenditures was possible.

The list totalled 1567 titles distributed as shown on Table 1. This Table shows that by far the greatest number of reference titles cost us less than $100.00. The "price O" category, as explained earlier, includes items included in other payments as well as inactive and problematic records. We receive virtually nothing that is free and have no gift and exchange program.

It was also decided to look more closely at a 5% sample of all 1567 titles. Time constraints precluded using a larger sample. Every twentieth record was chosen, given a total of 79 titles to be examined and categorized as shown in Tables 2–4. These figures were useful in identifying areas of greatest budgetary impact. Table 2 shows that, of the sample, 21 titles (27%) were foreign, 58 (73%) were domestic. Nevertheless of the ten titles that decreased in price 8 (38%) were foreign while 2 (3%) were domestic. Ten (48%) foreign titles increased in price while fully 47 (81%) domestic titles increased. Table 3 categorizes the domestic and foreign titles in terms of percentage of price increase over the period 1982–1985. Overall the greatest increase fell in the 1–25% range with 27 (34%) of the 79 titles increasing 1–25% and 22 (28%) increasing 26–50%. However, because percentages in these circumstances mean less than actual dollars spent, it is also useful to sort increases by dollar amount.

Looked at in terms of dollar amount of increase rather than percentage of increase, the figures show a similar distribution, as recorded in Table 4. This shows that 34 (43%) of the 79 titles increased $25 or less over the four year period, while 7 (9%) increased more than $100. Given this method of identifying and sorting reference standing orders, it is possible to target particular base price ranges, or particular ranges of percentage of increase or particular ranges of dollar increase for closer scrutiny.

Table 1: Total Number of Reference Standing Orders Subdivided by Price

price$	0	1-100	101-200	201-300	301-400
number	542	609	195	64	41

price	401-500	501-600	601-700	701-800	801-900
number	25	19	10	9	5

price	901-1000	1001+
number	11	37

Table 2: Price Changes of a 5% Sample of the Serial Reference Books on Standing Order at SUNYA 1982-1985

	inactive	increase	decrease	no change	total
domestic titles	5	47	2	4	58
foreign titles	3	10	8	0	21
Total	8	57	10	4	79

Table 3: Percent of Increase of a 5% Sample of the Serial Reference Books on Standing Order at SUNYA 1982-1985

	inactive	decrease	0%	1-25%	26-50%	51-75%	76-100%	over 100%	Total
Domestic Titles	5	2	4	25	15	3	2	2	58
Foreign Titles	3	8	0	2	7	0	0	1	21
Total	8	10	4	27	22	3	2	3	79

Table 4: Dollar Increases of a 5% Sample of the Serial Reference Books on Standing order at SUNYA 1982-1985

	inactive	decrease	$0	$.01-25	$26-50	$51-75	$101-200	201-300	301-400	401-500	501-600	601-700	over $1000	Total
Domestic Titles	5	2	4	29	4	9	1	1	0	1	0	1	1	58
Foreign Titles	3	8	0	5	3	0	1	0	1	0	0	0	0	21
Total	8	10	4	34	7	9	2	1	1	1	0	1	1	79

Simply looking at the figures in these tables it is interesting to note that, overall, the increases in reference standing order prices are essentially in line with the increase in our total allocation (27% over the four year period) and with the increase in the amount spent on all standing orders which increased 35% over the four year period.

The number of titles on standing order and the size of the budget do to some extent mask excessive price increases of certain reference titles. For example, while the titles that Posel lists do show price increase that are high in terms of percentage and/or dollars, the larger the collection and budget the less noticeable they will be. The 17 titles Posel lists increased an average of $103.35 or 48% over the four year period 1981–1984. Our sample of 79 titles increased an average of $60.25 or 28% over the period 1982–1985. The fact that a few of the commonest reference books have exhibited extreme price increases cannot be taken to mean that this is the norm for the entire reference collection. In a large library the fact that specific large increases can be obscured is fortunate in that they seem less painful, unfortunate in that size tends to protect such items from scrutiny and complaint. This means that even greater watchfulness is necessary on the part of those who oversee reference book expenditures for larger collections.

Further Study

One of the many categories that could be identified for further study is items priced over $1000. Do such very expensive items increase at a faster or slower rate than average? Obviously, a high percentage increase of an inexpensive item may have less budgetary impact than a lower percentage increase of a very expensive item. Table 5 shows the results of examining not a sample, but all, of the reference items priced over $1000. This table shows that in this price range, the bulk of the titles increased in the 26–50% range, resulting in fully 73% of these titles increasing over $200. The highest increase for a single title was $2279.94, with six titles increasing over $1000. Thus. the prices of the most expensive items increased at both a higher percentage and a higher dollar amount than the sample average.

Another category that should not be ignored is the group of titles that decreased in price. Of the sample of 79 titles only two domestic and eight foreign titles decreased in price. Foreign decreases ranged

Table 5: Price Changes of The 37 Most Expensive Serial Reference Books on Standing Order at SUNYA 1982-1985

a. Number of Titles Increased and Decreased in Price

	increase	decrease	Total
Domestic Titles	30	1	31
Foreign Titles	3	3	6
Total Titles	33	4	37

b. Percent of Increase

	—	1-25%	26-50%	51-75%	76-100%	over 100%	Total
Domestic titles	1	10	15	3	0	2	31
Foreign titles	3	3	0	0	0	0	6
Total	4	13	15	3	0	2	37

c. Dollar Increases

	—	$.01-25	$26-50	$51-100	$101-200	$201-300	$301-400	$401-500	$501-600	$701-800	$801-900	$901-1000	over $1000	Total
Domestic titles	1	0	1	1	0	11	4	2	1	1	1	2	6	31
Foreign titles	3	1	1	0	0	1	0	0	0	0	0	0	0	6
Total	4	1	2	1	0	12	4	2	1	1	1	2	6	37

from 3% to 25% while for the two domestic titles we recorded decreases of 4% and 5% on fairly inexpensive items. Thus, the decreases will not significantly affect total expenditures. The foreign decreases might be attributed to the strong dollar over this period of time, but why did most foreign titles rise rather than decrease? Many such questions can be raised, most unanswerable without full knowledge of publishers' and vendors' policies. Along these lines, it might prove interesting to print the list in vendor order so that, in cases where items are ordered direct from publishers, comparative data could be compiled on pricing patterns of various publishers. Unfortunately, at this point, we do not have the capacity to enter both publisher and vendor into our database so comparisons of publishers' pricing practices would only be valid on direct orders where the publisher is the vendor and appears in the vendor field. For those content to attempt to deal with the situation as it is instead of delving into whys and wherefores, we have access to the necessary data. From here we can pursue closer scrutiny of specific titles or groups of titles that most seem to warrant it.

APPROACHES TO CONTROL

Automation

In the computer we have a means of identifying and potentially controlling costs that we did not have a few years ago. Now we can collect, manipulate and study specific costs in our own library.

There are other ways in which automation can impact on the costs of reference books. Certain reference information is available on-line and indeed the computer terminal has become common at or near reference desks. A logical question is that asked by Tina Roose: "How do the costs of using computer databases for reference compare to the costs of using manual sources for references?"[26] As she correctly notes, not much has been done to try to answer it. Roose gives information from two public libraries that indicates that computer searching is considerably less expensive than manual answering of reference questions, largely because of the speed with which a computer retrieves information. The studies described by Roose determine average cost per question answered. They do not have much to say about the costs of specific reference materials in print vs. online form.

Here a multitude of questions arise. If we want to know whether a specific title is worth what it costs in print form we need to know its price as well as amount of use. We need to know whether it, or the information it contains, is available online and if so at what cost to the library. The latter will vary depending on whether online searches are free or fee based. In fact, the only one on one comparison would result from answering the *same* reference questions both manually and online and then computing costs for each, something that could only be done under highly controlled and therefore somewhat unrealistic circumstances.

Some items that are available both in print and online such as the Dun and Bradstreet services are far too expensive online for us to purchase. So far in this library there have been no reference books that have not been purchased or reference serials that have been cancelled due to their availability online.

So, at this point at least, we have not exercised much control over reference costs by eliminating subscriptions to printed materials that are available online. Statistics may give a general picture of the situation, but they do little to aid one in making title specific decisions.

Automation in the form of an automated acquisitions system offers greater promise in terms of closer control and more detailed financial reporting. This library expects to change from manual ordering and receiving and fund accounting on the MAPPER system mentioned above to a Geac Automated Acquisitions system with fiscal year 1986/87. All orders, receipts, claims, returns and payments will eventually be handled at the computer terminal. During the first year all invoices will be fed through the system even though serials checkin will remain manual. This will result in detailed financial reports for designated material types and account codes. Reference figures will be reportable in specific categories such as "approval monograph" or "standing order service." A number of budget reports will be available on whatever frequency we request and will essentially show at a glance amounts budgetted, encumbered and spent monthly and year to date. Once there is a succession of payments entered for serial publications, a summary of expenditures over recent years can be called up on the screen. The combination of online availability, screen dumping use of a printer and overnight report printing will provide us with detailed data on where the money is going for Reference as well as for all other types of material.

Nevertheless, we expect to maintain our two disks of standing order titles for some time to come because the automated acquisitions system will not permit us to manipulate the standing order titles and to print lists of them as we can on the IBM PC. The two methods of gaining control over reference costs, one highly sophisticated and powerful, the other more simplified, will be used in concert to produce as much information as possible.

Shared Resources

Another means of saving money which is often talked about is resource sharing, although putting it into practice can be difficult indeed. As Beth J. Shapiro points out in "Serials Resource Sharing and Public Services speed is critical in the delivery of information."[27] This is even more true for a reference collection where an immediate answer is sought. Few patrons would return to a reference desk where they found that the needed answer had to be obtained from another library. However, a certain amount of resource sharing can take place even in reference. If a library devoted to or having an unusually strong collection in a particular field is accessible to another library's clientele, the second library will likely obtain only the minimum of reference material in that field. An item in *Hotline* indicates success among four public libraries in the sharing of reference resources:

> Reference figures show that cooperative efforts among the four library systems involved are beneficial to patrons; Miller "concludes that the specialized collections in each of the four systems should be supported and further enhanced."[28]

In our case, there have been only a few large sets that we have not purchased because they were available at the nearby New York State Library. However, these have been extraordinarily expensive titles with significant budgetary impact. New York State Library holdings are taken into account when very expensive items are considered for purchase here.

In the end, resource sharing may be reduced to the need to save money *vs.* the need to have the book at hand. If patrons cannot be well-served long distance, the material will be purchased and cuts made in whatever other areas are deemed more expendable.

The Role of Acquisitions Personnel and Bibliographer

In this endeavor as in so many others, communication is critical. In a large academic library Acquisitions personnel and bibliographers may seldom see each other. It is the responsibility of those in Acquisitions to keep the lines of communications open, to alert the reference bibliographer to problems and price increases etc. of reference materials. Placid acceptance of a renewal invoice should be replaced by a critical eye and a questioning mind.

The responsibility of Acquisitions personnel for helping to keep the lid on prices begins with vendor selection. All vendors like to think (or have us think) they are the best. Vendor studies we have done indicate that service is similar among the vendors we frequently use and therefore the critical factor to us is price. We will go where we can get the best price without sacrificing service.

Of course, for many serial reference books no discount is possible. Here vendor selection must be based on service including speed of delivery and accuracy of reporting, particularly for foreign titles.

Acquisitions personnel are on the front line when it comes to receiving reference materials. In serials especially their vigilance is critical in keeping costs down. It is they who see invoices and can bring excessive increases to the attention of the reference bibliographer. Any other peculiarities should be noted as well. Information of this sort, screened through a professional staff member, has always been welcomed by bibliographers at SUNYA.

Acquisitions personnel also are responsible for the collection of statistics on pricing and price increases. During the past year we have undertaken the collection of standing order data described earlier and an extensive vendor survey. With the advent of the automated acquisitions system collection of much data will become automatic, but there will still be a need for staff members who can identify such problems as unusual price increases and who can channel questions and comments in the right direction. The same kind of vigilance needed today will be needed then.

The bibliographer in turn has certain responsibilities in the area of cost control as well. He or she should be alert to overlap between reference materials and carefully consider what the collection really needs. Nancy Posel's comment that many of the expensive reference books had not been significantly expanded should prompt critical examination of them. The bibliographer cannot ignore price as the purview of acquisitions. Recent budget crises here at SUNYA have made bibliographers all too aware of prices and the limitations of funding. If a cancellation project is planned, bibliographers need to become aware of renewal schedules so that cancellation notifications are timed prior to, not just after, the titles are renewed. Much of this is based on the existence of a coherent collection development policy. This is a subject about which much has been written so it will not be discussed here.

CONCLUSION

It appears, from reading the literature, that a considerable problem exists in the pricing of reference books and that many have undergone exorbitant price increases. Examination of data collected here at SUNYA indicates that extremely high increases have not been the norm, but that vigilance over reference costs is certainly justified. The responsibility for this vigilance is shared by acquisitions personnel and the bibliographers who build the collection. Open lines of communication between the two are a must. Careful collection and study of data, judicious use of automation, communication and watchfulness by all involved in the acquisition of reference will go a long way toward keeping the lid on the cost of this essential material.

REFERENCES

1. *Webster's Third New International Dictionary of the English Language, Unabridged* (Springfield, Mass.: G. & C. Merriam, 1981), p. 1907.
2. *The ALA Glossary of Library and Information Science* (Chicago: American Library Association, 1980), p. xiv.
3. Sheehy, Eugene P., *Guide to Reference Books*, 9th ed. (Chicago: American Library Association, 1980), p. xiv.
4. Ibid.
5. *The Bowker Annual of Library and Book Trade Information, 1984* (N.Y.: R.R. Bowker, 1984), p. 411.
6. Audrey Eaglen, "Too Many Books? Publishers' Problems and Collection Building," *Collection Building* 5 (Spring 1983): 40–42.
7. Norman B. Brown and Jane Phillips, "Price Indexes for 1984: U.S. Periodicals and Serial Services," *Library Journal* 109 (August 1984): 1422–1425. Similar data was included in previous reports.
8. *The Bowker Annual*, 1984, p.440.
9. *American Reference Books Annual* 1971 2nd ed. (Littleton, Colo.: Libraries Unlimited, 1971), p.xv.

10. *American Reference Books Annual* 1980–1985, v.11–16 (Littleton, Colo.: Libraries Unlimited, 1980–1985).
11. Kathryn A. Soupiset, "College Book Price Information, 1984." *Choice* 22 (April 1985): 1107–1111.
12. *Government Reference Books 68/69* (Littleton, Colo.: Libraries Unlimited, 1970), p. 5.
13. *Government Reference Books 82/83* (Littleton, Colo.: Libraries Unlimited, 1984), p.xvii.
14. Soupiset, "College Book Price Information, 1984," p.1107.
15. *CPI Detailed Report for December 1978*, (Washington, D.C.: U.S. Dept. of Labor, Bureau of Labor Statistics, Office of Prices and Living Conditions. Supt. of Docs. U.S.G.P.O., distributor), p. 3.
16. *CPI Detailed Report Data for December 1984*, (Washington, D.C.: U.S. Dept. of Labor, Bureau of Labor Statistics, Office of Prices and Living Conditions: Supt. of Docs. U.S.G.P.O., distributor), p 4.
17. Figures were computed from data published in the compilations entitled "Reference Books of 1978," *Library Journal* 104 (April 15, 1978), "Reference Sources of 1982," *Library Journal*, 108 (May 15, 1983), "Reference Books of 1983," *Library Journal*, 109 (April 15, 1984) and "Reference Books of 1984," *Library Journal* 110 (April 15, 1985).
18. Janet Fletcher et al., "*Reference Books of 1983*," *Library Journal* 109 (April 15, 1984), p. 781.
19. *The ALA Glossary*, p.203.
20. Nancy R. Posel, "Reference Book Costs: 'Pricing Us Out of the Market' Are Publishers Biting The Hand That Feeds Them?" *American Libraries* (July/Aug. 1985): 506–507.
21. *Ibid.*, p. 506.
22. *Ibid.*
23. Kathryn A. Soupiset, "College Book Price Information," *Choice* 21 (July–Aug.1984): 1577–1579.
24. Soupiset, "College Book Price Information, 1984," p.1108.
25. Steven G. Watkins, Michael Knee and Steven D. Atkinson, "The Osborne Executive for Indexing, Accounting, and Information Management," *Small Computers in Libraries* 5 (November 1985): 24–27.
26. Tina Roose, "Online Or Print: Comparing Costs," *Library Journal* 110 (September 15, 1985): 54–55.
27. Beth J. Shapiro, "Serials Resource Sharing and Public Services," *Serials Review* 11 (Summer 1985): 51–56.
28. "Cooperative Collection Development Said To Be Working in Colorado," *Library Hotline* 14 (October 21, 1985): 4.

Reference Publishing and Changing Distribution Techniques

Sharon C. Bonk

Three years ago, the *Reference Librarian* devoted an issue to reference services and the new technology.[1] Although video-text was discussed by two authors, the issue focused on one type of reference source—online bibliographic databases, accessed remotely through packet switched networks. Although most articles assumed the wide acceptance and use of this new technology, Stevens cautioned that much still needed to be rethought, refinanced, and relocated before new technology was truly integrated into effective and widely available reference service.[2] These concerns are also applicable to the technologies under consideration here. The existence and the potential of optical disks, videotext, satellite broadcast systems as distribution alternatives to print or centralized online systems are still a distance from being fingertip resources for the reference librarian. However, because of the same financial, intellectual, and psychological issues Stevens outlined, increased knowledge of these technologies as they apply to reference materials and reference service is needed by librarians to assist in changing attitudes, planning new services, using new capabilities, and imbibing old wine from new bottles.

This article will examine a variety of technologies in use or in development by traditional reference book publishers and information producers as alternatives to their current distribution systems or formats. Some of the technologies are already incorporated into many libraries' services: interactive bibliographic, numeric, and full text databases; electronic document delivery; electronic mail. Others, videotext, optical discs, direct broadcast systems, are operating in experimental modes. They offer tantalizing views of the future reference service along with potential problems that are based in the

---

The author is Assistant Director for Technical Services, University Libraries, State University of New York, Albany NY 12222.

intertwining of economic, social, and psychological factors for author, publisher, user, and intermediary. The technologies considered here were not selected as examples of technologies important in themselves, but as examples of developments in publishers' distribution systems.

Publishers have been concerned with improving distribution systems since Guttenberg. Although a generally behind-the-scenes and not highly glamorized activity in publishing, distribution activities and facilities represent a significant cost to publishers. Therefore, the adoption of technology to eliminate redundancy and inefficiency and to supply inventory control for the distribution of printed books was a natural evolution. Publishers use wholesalers, distributors, bookstores, and other retail outlets to distribute their materials. They also sell directly to individuals or their institutions. This multitude of centralized and decentralized approaches of publishers for print and some non print materials (audio disk, video tapes, video disks, microcomputer software) is fragmented and may even appear chaotic. The 1982 report of the Book Industry Study Group summarized the current situation:

> Distribution is a costly, frustrating and sensitive issue for every segment of the U.S. book industry. Problems associated with unique product characteristics—generally short life cycles and minimal item substitution possibilities—are compounded by continuing cost increases for freight, inventory carrying and clerical and warehouse personnel. Distribution issues have been debated for at least 50 years. Until recently, changes in industry practices have been slow to develop.
>
> Economics of book distribution have changed dramatically in recent years. The structure of the industry and its supporting technology also have undergone major changes. Physical distribution practices, however, have remained relatively static. Modification has been gradual and sometimes controversial, as could be expected when distribution policy actions within one industry segment quickly influence operating economics in other segments.
>
> In the last few years, the industry has seen the start of innovation in some elements of the distribution process. Examples include widespread use of the ten-year old uniform numbering scheme, transaction standards, upgraded data processing capabilities, combined shipments, and altered discount

and return policies. In most cases, these new practices are being adopted slowly, even after considerable effort. The cost and service pressures on physical distribution are intensifying faster than the industry's capacity to respond.[3]

One problem common to professional and trade publishers is the inadequacy of the existing distribution facilities and systems. Shatzkin has written extensively on the problems in marketing and distributing trade books.[4] He considers the publisher's sales force-bookstore method, "distribution-by-negotiation", horrendously expensive and resulting in lost sales and remainders. It reduces the special advantage the book has as a medium of communication. Dessauer discusses the use of expensive direct selling as the now preferred marketing tool for professional books in the context of the inadequacy of the number and quality retail outlets for selling professional books.[5] He also discusses the physical warehousing and delivery problems that exist for the whole industry and which slow the movement of materials and increase their cost.[6]

These issues are mentioned here because they are a major consideration in publishers' costs and an area ready for change and improvement—whether it be through nonprofit regional order processing and fulfillment centers, increased services from and reliance upon wholesalers, new technologies, or a combination of all three.

The publishers of important reference tools, indexes and abstracts, encouraged by database vendors (wholesalers), have been the first to use new distribution channels. As successful as bibliographic databases have become, they still present problems of availability, telecommunication lines and costs, methods of pricing the data to users, and methods of paying for the data. These have caused publishers to look into different forms or methods distribution for both the online and print products.

Paul Doebler, speaking as a representative of the reference and professional book publishers, outlined what is expected to remain constant and what will be changed from reference book publishers.[7] He posited that the basic content and purpose of reference source will not change dramatically. The format of the packaged information and the delivery channels will change. Online delivery via telephone lines will be joined by satellite transmissions (e.g., *Agri-data*, the agricultural data base providing an international audience information from USDA, commodity exchanges, Associated Press) or microwave systems for some publications that have a widely distributed audience and for whom timelessness and comprehensiveness are paramount considerations. Optical disks will be the low cost alternative to current online access for many databases, especially for the full text databases and the large retrospective files of indexes and abstracts. Prime candidates for optical disk format are directories, lexical products, statistical comprendia, encyclopedias, manuals, handbooks, standards, and images.

Corporate publications, not designed for general or library markets, but often acquired by libraries will eventually be printed on demand—byproducts of office automation of corporations, research institutes, and similar bodies. Doebler's views of the economics of production and inventory are such that he predicts that corporate publishers will not consider library and general consumer purchases significant enough to shape the systems and the output channels. This may make some information less accessible than it is now.

These production and output methods will speed up the availability of information by speeding the composition and production processes and by using "faster media" for distribution. It will allow the splitting-up or a customization of parts of products to specific audiences. Because of the high cost to publishers to rework their internal systems toward the totally electronic and toward the theoretically favorable economics of production and distribution equation, they must insure that the information in its new format will perform for the user. With the printed product there was at first little attention paid to the user of the book. Librarians' reviews of reference books, recommendations of change of format, and recommendations for new types of reference sources have been heeded, but basically the publisher did not have to teach the purchaser how to read. A variety of reference publishers now include hardware specialists as part of their customer services. This will be an important component in the transitional phase to different publication formats. The publisher will take on a responsibility for instructing the user/purchaser.

REFERENCE BOOKS

Library reference books are a very small portion of the total number of titles published each year. No industry figures or formal analyses are made at this specific level. Reference books, with the exception of multivolume general encyclopedias, are reported and discussed in industry literature as part of the professional books segment. This segment is further subdivided by the Association of American Publishers into technical and scientific, medical, business and other professional. It is the third category that contains general and subject oriented material produced primarily for the library market. However, since this category also includes law and business, it is not possible to isolate reference books in industry surveys, prediction, and statistical reports. It is necessary to consider market forecasts for all professional books and their subcategories because reference collections contain materials from all the categories that are published primarily for the professional and which find secondary sales to libraries.

Despite the economic ups and downs of the publishing industry, professional publishing is one of the most profitable categories in the industry.[8] The books are basic to the work of the purchaser. They supply standards, universally utilized data, reports of new developments, current statistics, biographical, and address information. Perhaps, the most important factor from a profitability view is the "almost totally predictable" markets based on the number of individuals practicing, teaching, and entering the profession, or on the number of companies active in a field, or the number of academic and special libraries supporting instruction and research in these subjects. Even the ever increasing specialization of researchers is comparatively easy to cope with for a publisher when compared to marketing trade books. Publishing technologies allow for short print runs and keep publishers from sustaining losses on specialized titles without placing the total burden of profitability on the individual or institutional purchasers. The market place indicates that professionals and libraries continue to be less price sensitive than general consumers.[9]

Market forecasts for the technical scientific, and medical publishing (TSM) through the eighties indicate that sales of scientific and medical books are expected to continue to be strong. However, sales will be affected adversely by any major reductions in funding of research and libraries, increasing competition from European publishers, and other forms of media. Medical books will see growth in specializations, but there will be a shakeout and reduction in the number of companies, leaving fewer high quality publishers with extensive financial resources.

Market dominance or market share is an important factor in the changing shape of distribution because relatively few companies can shape the majority of transactions. Although there are thousands of publishers, there are only a relatively few who produce the majority of our materials professional and library reference—large TSM publishers, international in scope, and professional societies. Six companies accounted for nearly one third of all scitech sales in 1982.[10] Eight medical companies accounted for more than 60% of the 1980 sales.[11] Most, if not all, of these publishers have in development or currently are developing materials in alternative formats—online full text journals, and instructional and continuing education materials in videodisk format. Duke concludes that the TSM information field

> will witness the continued conversion of information service from print to electronic media. As online service becomes more affordable, and as more professionals become familiar with, and, even more important, comfortable with their use, such services will become a more significant factor in the market.[12]

Reference books, as a subset of these professional books, have already become and will continue to be available in a variety of formats or product-services categories: broadcast and interactive services (viewdata, online databases); stand alone (video cassettes, optical disks, pc software); electronic journals, newsletters, news services. Table 1 groups publications or information services by distribution channel and lists the producer/publisher financial considerations on utilizing these forms of distributions.[13]

DISTRIBUTION TECHNOLOGIES

The use of the term "technology" in relation to publishers' utilization of automation encompasses a broad range of applications: editorial, financial, production, and distribution. The "old" technology, i.e., accepted by some as status quo, is the automation of the production of the physical book to make it more widely available and to reduce unit production costs. This includes production and editing of manuscripts, computer driven printing production control, and accounting inventory and physical distribution systems. Changes and enhancements continue to be made to various parts of the production process especially in manuscript-to-print and

TABLE 1.

Distribution Channel	Information Provider Financial Considerations	Advantages	Limitations	Market	Library Applications
Telephone	Common carrier Low cost data transmission	In place Reliable Friendly	Low speed Narrow band Costs rising Deregulation caused degradation of services	Universal Homes Institutions Commercial	Online databases Online journals Electronic mail Telefacsimile
Broadcast Television	High entry cost with existing frequency One-time purchase requirement 3rd party programming	Low marginal cost for additional markets In place Friendly	Limited channel capacity FCC regulation View data requires telephone technology	Approaching universality in household	Teletext news services Viewdata factual, interactive
Cable	Capital intensive Large cash flow High marginal profits User supported	No FCC regulations Friendly	Local regulatory complications	Urban/suburban Special interest	Library channels
Direct Broadcast Satellite	Low capital investment for information provided Large cash flow One-time purchase required of user User supported	Low marginal cost for additional markets Friendly	"Unknown" technology Limited channels Aiming of receiver	International Rural Large building complexes	Library as receiver site
Postal, truck Optical disk	Low capital investment to producer High user investment in hardware Requires new software for different products	User controlled No regulation Interactive potential Retrieval and display International standard for compact disks Friendly Low cost mass storage	Continued software costs High unit cost	Education Business Library/archive	Storage of large files Storage of graphic material Instructional materials Library catalog

distribution. Publishers will continue to enhance the "old" while developing the "new" technology, the use of which allows information to be stored electronically and accessed remotely, via a variety of paths for a variety of users without the need for the publisher to repackage the data for each user. In addition to the economies of production gained in the earlier stages, the potential economies made by changing the printing, packaging, fulfillment and physical distribution will be an essential part of the publisher's financial decision on whether to proceed with alternative formats. Currently, information is being distributed in print and online form. In some instances, online "publications" exist for which there are no printed counterparts.

Telephone Systems

Information distributed over telephone lines is the most common form of new reference technology. Because of extensive coverage in the literature of online bibliographic, statistical, and numeric databases, electronic document delivery systems, telefacsimilie, and electronic mail, no description is given here. Although far from universal in their inclusion in library reference services, they can be considered familiar tools.

Electronic Publications

Over the last several years there has been much written about the possibility of full text databases replacing traditional printed publications. Many printed reference books are now available as databases as well. Over 1000 newsletters and journals are available online.[14] Government funded research has been conducted in several countries to determine the viability of a totally electronic journal. Two close examinations have been conducted by university researchers who looked at the technological side and the human factors and scholarly communication issues.[15] Some discussions and explanations of cost of these systems have also been done.[16]

Less publicized are the private corporate examinations and market studies. Publishers too have been looking at the technological and economic feasibility of publications solely in electronic format.

An ambitious cooperative effort by a group of scientific, technical, and medical publishers to establish an electronic distribution system for journals and articles that would protect publishers' remuneration and explore the economics of production of journals without prepaid subscriptions was begun in 1980. For a number of reasons, including the high cost of the project, individual corporate strategies among the cooperating publishers and the requisite technology not yet available at a reasonable cost to produce high quality scientific illustrations and graphics, the ADONIS project is dormant.[17] Although the technology for mass distribution is not currently available to support the economic model, once reasonably priced equipment to handle large scale scanning into digital format, computer storage and production of illustrations and text, and rapid retrieval and distribution, the full potential of electronic publications will be realized. In the meantime several of the large multitype and multinational publishing groups continue to be involved in market tests designed to equip them for the future and to stimulate the market's acceptance of these products.

Wiley has had several of its journals available via data switched networks for several years. Elsevier offers an electronic medical journal to a selected audience. The American Chemical Society has its journals available in full text through data base vendors and is exploring with OCLC distribution in CD-ROM.

The Kluwer group based in the Netherlands has interests in mass market, medical, educations, and scholarly publishing. As such, it has been experimenting in each market. Under the name of Klunitel it operates a view data system offering public access to new, financial, and other timely reference information. The company has conducted market tests with video disks for special interest publications such as trade journals and handbooks. The professional academic markets are of principal interest in their plans for mounting full text databases. They have a Dutch legal database and an international medical database. Their aim is not only to provide access to printed counterparts online, but to add new material and restructure the database and access in such a way as to produce different and more useful products than the traditional printed journals, texts, or handbooks.[18]

Of concern to these publishers is market acceptance. In the development stage these new publications have to compete with existing printed products. The value of the new product and formats for users is difficult to access, but it is necessary in order that development continue in the right direction and that a price be fixed that will assure sales and return on investment.

The period for exploration of technical feasibility in regard to electronic publication is generally over. The publishers that have done extensive evaluation are in the process making a determination of what is most appropriate for each market and what is the most suitable or comfortable position in regard to leadership or following. They are identifying the real markets that are emerging or have emerged for specific types of media. They have begun strategies to recoup capital invested in the research and development, although profitability is expected only over intermediate or long term periods. The two areas identified as current and real markets are business and reference—where perishability of information, new, and tabular display of information is key to its use and which suits the electronic format.

Despite its seeming diversity, there has been a convergence of technology. Standardization is not universal. But, transparency to users and compatibility to increase sales potential are understood as basic marketing concepts. A wider variety of publishers are becoming aware of the special and new approaches to marketing electronic publications.[19]

Publishing industry seminars and courses now are a regular part of the trade literature. Several trade publications are focused on this type of publishing: *EPB* (Oryx), *Electronic Publishing News* (Mandarin), *Electronic Publishing Review* (Learned Information), and *Electronic Publisher* (Paul Kagan Associates). Successful production of telecommunication based or other digitally stored publications will require a vertically integrated corporate structure, a solid revenue base, capital investment, detailed market surveys, and the ability to act quickly to further technological developments and market opportunities.

Broadcast Services

Video text services were originally planned as consumer-home oriented services, but publishers have found special interest markets for videotext in businesses which can use the technology for both information gathering and fee based information delivery as well as for advertising. There are two types of videotext: teletext and viewdata.

Teletext is a one way communication medium which uses a portion of the conventional TV signal to transmit information in verbal or simple graphic form. This has been used to send newspaper or magazine type information. Examples of systems in use are primarily from European countries: Britain (Ceefax and Oracle); France (Antelope); and Sweden (Text-TV). Public libraries in Britain use these news services. Some Canadian and U.S. libraries offer the Canadian system, Telidon.[20]

Viewdata provides the user with the ability to interact with the system. Television and telephone technology are used to provide verbal and graphic information on frames selected by users. There is a wide variety of information and services available. They can be categorized as weather, schedules, financial, transportation and tourism, shopping, and banking services. Private databases exist for access by a restricted group of users. Several newspaper and communications companies have experimented with the use of these services, but use is more widespread in Europe where government controlled telecommunications and postal services have established the standards for hardware and telecommunications protocols: Britain (Prestel); France (Teletel); West Germany (Bildschmirtext); Netherlands (Viditel).

The potential of videotext services for public libraries were reported by Appleman.[21] She presented models and procedural concerns for two types of videotext services: videotext as a communication channel for provision of library services to the community; and videotext as a transmission channel for information transmitted to the library. In the first case the library plays the role of the information publisher or provider and uses videotext as its distribution system, similar to some libraries' cable television programming.[22] In the latter the library is a consumer.

In either case videotext best serves applications where information is computers generated, changes frequently, enhanced by color displays, and does not require the user to access too many frames to receive the information.[23]

Direct Broadcast Satellite

Direct broadcast satellite (DBS) technology was approved by the FCC in 1979, but is just now coming into use. One public library has reported on installation and use of the receiving disk in its programming.[24] Because DBS greatly extends the range of television signals over large geographic regions, a greater variety of educational, commercial, and governmental applications are possible than from standard or cable television.[25]

Optical Disks

Optical disks have the potential to become as major a distribution format and as widespread as online databases have become. Optical disks will provide some of the same "publications" and applications as online services with few incremental or usage costs, after hardware costs are ammortized. Reference sources currently available in this form are: bibliographic files (Bibliofile™; Library of Congress MARC files; Infotrak™ indexes; *British Books in Print*); full text databases (*Wall Street Journal*, McGraw Hill journals, American Chemical Society journals, *New England Journal of Medicine*, selected Bell and Howell and University Microfilms publications); statistical/business publications (Disclosure™; Predicasts™; *OECD World Outlook*).

Library applications will include the storage of their own archival and photographic collections. The public access catalog and scholars work stations will use the optical disk. Developments will include the capability of mixed media (textual graphic, audio), and nonlinear, interactive systems. Instructional materials for use by faculty and students and training material for library staff will benefit from this technology.

Reference services will continue to include information retrieval from printed books for the forseeable future. However, the number and variety of reference sources available in electronic format is increasing. Most libraries will probably be selective in their use and acceptance of the new formats, especially if print editions continue to be offered by the publishers. Those responsible for planning library services, including reference services, already face an array of local policy issues related to the alternative formats: acquisition and funding; bibliographic control; "physical" access; user assistance; maintenance; fees; and staff straining. The increasing number of publishers and information producers who are using or developing alternative methods for distribution of their products makes it imperative that the local plans and policies be formulated with a knowledge of the existence, potential, and probability of these information distribution technologies.

REFERENCES

1. *Reference Librarian*, 5/6, (Fall/Winter 1982).
2. Stevens, Norman D. "Skim Milk Masquerades as Cream: The Myth of Online Database Searching," *Reference Librarian*, 5/6, Fall/Winter 1982, pp. 77–81.

3. *Book Distribution in the United States: Issues and Perceptions.* New York, Book Industry Study Group, 1982 p. 2.1.
4. Shatzkin, Leonard, *In Cold Type; Overcoming the Book Crisis*, Boston, Houghton Mifflin, 1982.
5. Dessauer, John, *Book Publishing; What it is, What it Does*, 2nd ed. New York, R.R. Bowker, 1981, p. 55.
6. Ibid., pp. 152–154.
7. Doebler, Paul, "Book Publishing in the Electronic Age," Special Libraries Association 75th Anniversary Conference, 1984, New York, Audio Video Transcripts [1984].
8. Dessauer, p. 53.
9. Duke, Judith S., *The Technical Scientific and Medical Publishing Market*, White Plains, N.Y., Knowledge Industry Publications, 1985, p. 27.
10. Ibid., p. 18.
11. Ibid., p. 19.
12. Ibid., p. 169.
13. Chart adapted from Table 5.2, Some Characteristics of Residential and Small Business Electronic and Video Distribution Channels, prepared by the Program for Information Resources Policy, Harvard University, and published in *Understanding New Media*, ed. by Benjamin Companie, Cambridge, MA, Ballinger, 1984, pp. 132–133.
14. Aveney, Brian, "Electronic Publishing and the Information Transfer Process," *Special Libraries*, 74, October 1983, pp. 338.
15. Senders, John, "The Electronic Journal," *Eurim 4: A European Conference on Innovation in Primary Publications: Impact on Producers and Users*, London, Aslib, 1980, pp. 14–16. and Schackel, et al., "The BLEND-LINC Project in Electronic Journals After Two Years," *Aslib Proceedings*, 35, February 1983, pp. 77–91.
16. Singleton, A. and Pullinger, D.J., Ways of viewing costs of journals: Cost Evaluation of "The BLEND Experiment," *Electronic Publishing Review*, 46, March 1984, pp. 59–71.
17. Campbell, Robert M., Blackwell Scientific, personal communication.
18. *Kluwer's Policy on Unprinted Publishing*, Deventer, Netherlands, Kluwer, 1983.
19. Davis, Betty A., "Online Publishing: Marketing and Distribution Decisions," *EPB*, 2(3), May 1984, pp. 14–17, and "An Electronic Taste of the Future," *Bookseller*, June 29, 1985, pp. 2617–2618.
20. Mischo, Lare and Hegarty, Kevin. "Videotext—The Libarary of the Future," *Information Technology and Libraries*, 1(3), September 1982, pp. 276–277, and Toombs, Michelle and Wilson, Bob, "The Calgary Libraries Telidon Trial," *Information Technology and Libraries*, 1(4), December 1982, pp. 331–336.
21. Appleman, Merrie, *Videotex: Options for Libraries*, San Diego, CA, San Diego State University Center for Communications for the Electronic Text Consortion and the California State Library, (Electronic Text for Higher Education/The Anneberg/CPB Project), 1984.
22. Chepesiuk, Ron. "Information Around the Clock: Atlanta's Channel 16," *Wilson Library Bulletin*, 59(9), May 1985, pp. 597–599.
23. Saffady, William, *Video-based Information Systems; A Guide for Educational, Business, Library, and Home Use*, Chicago, American Library Association, 1985, pp. 142–143.
24. Amdursky, Saul J. "Dishing it out," *Library Journal*, 110(19), November 15, 1985, pp. 49–51.
25. Saffady, pp. 106–107.

The Effect of Publishing Policies on Reference Service in the Large Academic Library

Constance A. Fairchild

Publishers of reference books are in many ways responsible for the ease or difficulty experienced by reference librarians in their day-to-day quest for the elusive answer or the perfect source for the puzzled user. An index buried in the middle of a volume or a shelf of uncumulated supplements sometimes slows down the searching process to the point that the source may be rejected entirely in favor of something easier to use. The timing of publication dates, particularly for annuals, can be critical. Librarians and users learn to expect certain publications in certain months, and a late publication date can cause frustration, budget problems, and, in heavily used items, a binding that self-destructs before the new volume takes its place.

On the positive side, many publishers make a strong effort to improve the quality of their reference books by finding out how their books are used in libraries, and by keeping their publications up-to-date. Twentieth century reference librarians and users have a wealth of indexes, bibliographies, statistical sources, and abstracts that were completely unknown in previous centuries. Improvements in the indexes of non-fiction books are no doubt entirely the result of editorial policies of publishers, since good indexing is a concept foreign to many authors, as users of local history, genealogy books, and that mainstay of kitchen reference—the cookbook, are well aware.

Some publishers solicit opinions and suggestions from the users of their books by sending out questionnaires. Bowker and Gale Research do this periodically to get comments on proposed new reference books and also to get an idea of the possible market. Sometimes librarians are given a choice, as was the case with the

---

The author will be found in the Reference Department, University of Illinois Library, 1408 W. Gregory, Urbana, IL 61801.

© 1987 by The Haworth Press, Inc. All rights reserved.

Comprehensive Dissertation Index 1973–1982 cumulation. Early in 1984 University Microfilms International sent out a questionnaire giving librarians a choice of one of five options for the cumulation, covering several combinations of time period and author-subject. They followed up the questionnaire with a phone survey and found that over 50 percent of the respondents chose the 10-year subject and author cumulation. This became the cumulation that was published. This is a good example of direct publisher response to user opinion.

Cumulations or the lack of them present problems for both publisher and librarian. The publisher must decide when the market will bear the cost of an expensive cumulation, for librarians may be reluctant to pay for material that they already have just to get a more convenient format. On the other hand the tedium of going through a shelf full of annual supplements may make the cumulation welcome, especially if the supplements are also wearing out. From the librarian's point of view it makes more sense to make frequent cumulations of materials that aren't date oriented. An annual publication that includes only material published in a given year is not so difficult to use, assuming that the approximate date of the material wanted is known. A five-year cumulation of *Book Review Index* (Gale Research) might not be considered cost-effective, but the 20-year cumulation is very attractive. A heavily used publication such as *Biography and Genealogy Master Index*, (Gale Research) that has no date orientation, becomes inconvenient to use as soon as the second supplement is published. The tendency of microfiche publishers to replace each microfiche set with a completely new cumulation each time one comes out makes the microfiche easy to use, but no doubt contributes to the high cost of fiche subscriptions.

THE PROBLEM OF SPIN-OFFS

Computerization of information causes great temptations for publishers to issue spin-offs, or small sections of larger, previously-issued works. This in itself is not unethical, as long as it is clear where the material is coming from and how much of it is new, if any. The usual practice seems to be to use a specialized subject section of a larger, more general work and add enough new material to make it attractive to buyers. For small libraries that do not have the large work this presents no problem. For a large general reference library that already has, for example, the *New Grove*

Dictionary of Music and Musicians (Macmillan), the spin-offs on musical instruments and individual composers, attractive as they seem, will not get enough use to justify the expense.

Only by very carefully reading the Gale Research catalog can one sort out the maze of spin-offs of the *Biography and Genealogy Master Index*. The relation between BGMI and the *Bio-Base* microfiche is not spelled out in the catalog, but a comparison of the two shows them to be the same information cumulated somewhat differently. The Gale Biographical Index Series includes the BGMI and a number of direct and partial spin-offs in specialized subject fields. Gale has done the library world a great service in providing this monumental biographical index, but the unwary librarian could end up buying the same information in different packages.

A more confusing situation was pointed out in *Library Journal* (9/15/83, p. 1782) concerning Gale's *Periodical Title Abbreviations* and the *Acronyms, Initialism, and Abbreviations Dictionary*. In this case the PTA is incorporated into the AIAD, but the abbreviations are put into the PTA some 15 months sooner. However, it is unclear whether this advantage is worth the cost of subscribing to both sets.

The McGraw-Hill science dictionaries present a problem similar to the BGMI. There are a number of spin-offs of both the *McGraw-Hill Encyclopedia of Science and Technology* and the *MdGraw-Hill Dictionary of Scientific and Technical Terms*. Some are entirely extracted from the parent volumes and some have additional material, but it is not until one has the volume in hand that it is possible to determine how much material is new.

KEYWORD INDEXING VS. TRADITIONAL SUBJECT HEADINGS

Computerized periodical indexing has given rise to a new concept, that of the keyword index. The keyword technique uses only the important words in a periodical article title to access the article. In traditional subject heading indexing such as that used by the H.W. Wilson indexes, the subject is assigned to the article by the indexer, and may not appear in the title at all. The traditional method gathers many articles under a limited number of headings, and the user must become familar with the headings in order to use the index effectively. With keyword indexes, such as the Institute for Scientific Information's citation indexes, the user must use his or her own judgment as to whether the title is actually on the topic. Some keyword indexers find it necessary to add enhancements, since a title sometimes does not adequately describe an article's contents. Although the keyword approach requires more imagination on the part of the user in thinking of possible search terms, most users prefer the elimination of the pre-selected subject heading, and have good success with the terms that they select. When the keywords are grouped under broad subjects as in the *Cumulated Dissertation Index* the index is even easier to use, although this is actually a combination of the traditional and the keyword format. Keyword indexing is good example of computer technology causing changes for the better in reference publishing.

The computerized index is frequently tied in with an online database that has Boolean search capability. This gives rise to the question of the feasibility of discontinuing the paper index in favor of searching online. In theory there seem to be great advantages in using the online database for reference searching. Patterns of usage show the disadvantages. Since end user searching is not widespread, online searching is now done mainly by librarians. This means that most searches that patrons now do by themselves in the printed indexes would have to be performed by librarians, with all the concomitant problems of interviewing, interpreting search topics, scheduling searches, and billing for costs, that are entailed in online searching. Even with end user searching the cost to the searcher or the library mounts up very fast. Also the logistical problems of having several thousand freshman rhetoric students searching WILSONLINE instead of the *Reader's Guide* are mind-boggling. For the librarian looking up a quick answer or address the printed source is still faster. It takes longer just to log in to BRS or DIALOG than it does to look up an order number in *Cumulated Dissertation Index* or an address in the *Encyclopedia of Associations*. The online system becomes efficient only when it provides information not easily obtainable elsewhere. The best answer to the problem of economical use of online databases seems to be some combination of printed material and judicious use of the online system.

FORMAT PROBLEMS

An increasing problem with reference books is their annoying tendency to outgrow the convenient one volume format and become multi-volume monsters. From the information point of view this is wonderful—more information is always welcome. However a multi-volume directory with an index at the end of the last volume that must be consulted every time the work is used is an aggravation. If one of the volumes strays away the whole set is unusable. If the volumes are large and heavy the user will try to guess which section he needs, leave the rest, and invariably will have to make a second trip back to the shelf because the guess was wrong. There doesn't seem to be a good solution to this problem. Perhaps a revamping of multi-volume directories into straight alphabetical lists would help the situation.

Placement of indexes and bibliographies within volumes can create confusion. Users have become conditioned to find indexes at the ends of books. An index at the beginning or somewhere in the middle is likely to be missed. An appendix inserted after the index causes problems, and a reference book that is indexed in sections rather than as a whole may be abandoned altogether. Placement of lists of sources seems to be evenly divided, some appearing at the beginning of the book and some at the end. Users learn to cope with this, but some standardization would speed the searching process.

MICROFORMS

Microforms are space-saving and in some cases easier to use than print volumes because they are easier to handle. The most successful microform for reference use is the microfiche because it is in small sections and can be photocopied. The conversion of the *National Union Catalog* (Library of Congress) to microfiche has caused a tremendous saving of shelf space, and the fiche is actually easier to use than the large heavy volumes of the print sets. The addition of a title section where none was available before adds to its attractiveness.

Microfiche is most successful for works that are in short-entry dictionary format. Bibliographies, library catalogs, and alphabetical directories all work well in this form. Sometimes it is necessary to add searching aids to overcome inconveniences that occur in the conversion from print to fiche. The simple addition of the area code in the upper left hand corner of Bell & Howell's *Phonefiche* solved a major problem in the use of that set, since printed phone directories usually have the area code on the cover.

SUMMARY

Successful publishers of reference books use feedback from librarians and other users to improve their books. Cumulations, spin-offs, multi-volume formats, and placement of indexes are problem areas for both users and publishers. Publishers have been responsible for improvements in indexing and for making available large compilations of data through computerization. Microfiche is a space-saving and convenient alternative to large sets in print form.

REFERENCES

1. Bonta, Bruce and Cable, Frances. "The Gale Biography Series," *Reference Services Review* vol. 10 no. 1:25–33 (spring 1982).
2. Des Chene, Dorice. "Online Searching by End Users," *RQ* vol. 25:89–95 (fall 1985).
3. *Gale Catalog of Reference Books 1984–1985*. Detroit, Gale Research Company, 1984.
4. Katz, Bill. "The Cost of Repetition," *Library Journal* vol. 108:1782 (Sept. 15, 1983).
5. Kimble, Larry A. "The McGraw-Hill Encyclopedias and Dictionaries of Science: a Comparative Review," *Reference Services Review* vol. 10 no. 2:15–18 (summer 1982).
6. Malcolm, J. Parke. Letter dated 10 May 1984 concerning the *Comprehensive Dissertation Index* survey, sent to librarians participating in the survey.
7. Nitecki, Danuta A. "WILSONLINE," *American Libraries* vol. 16:804–809 (Dec. 1985).
8. Rettig, James. Review of *Performing Arts Biography Master Index*. *Wilson Library Bulletin* vol. 56:704 (May 1982).
9. Review of Brown, Maurice J.E., *The New Grove Schubert*; Dean, Winton, *The New Grove Handel*; Larson, Jens Peter, *The New Grove Haydn*; Sadie, Stanley, *The New Grove Mozart*. *Choice* vol. 20:1429–30 (June 1983).
10. University Microfilms International. Undated questionnaire "Comprehensive Dissertation Index Survey."

What Is Reference Publishing?
A Dialogue

Robert Franklin

We found the publisher chopping logs in his front yard—the Appalachian winter is not over until May and another begins in August. Splitting wood, he averred, is more definite than publishing books, but the two had several similarities. We chatted in this vein, with his maul resting between us, and I said we were interested today specifically in the experience of reference book publishing, and were glad to note that he considered himself a librarian as well. He knew six or seven libraries pretty well, he said, and was employed at the New Haven Free Public Library and in the cataloging department at Columbia. He went to library school, at Columbia, during the sixties. Inconclusively, he added. Our talk narrowed and we neared the central topic. I wanted to clear away one thing first.

What is reference?

Looking up. Looking "up." To authority. Only authorities are referred to—oneself, Chekhov, Strunk, Judith Martin. Authorities are quite fashionable, unfortunately, so there is a lot of impermanent, not to say downright wrong information lying in wait at the end of a reference reach . . .

Can you be more—

Look, "reference" means taking one's attention from the here-and-now and transferring it somewhere else. That somewhere else is any of thousands of consensus-reality, or sometimes just mildly vouched-for fact sources. One refers to them believing that most of the time they will as a class provide some degree of useful information with a generally reliable accuracy rate. One rarely does, but one ought also approach them knowing they might contain incorrect information. Given the explosion of data this society suffers—facts

---

Mr. Franklin is President and founder of the McFarland & Company, Inc. Publishers, Box 611, Jefferson, NC 28640.

© 1987 by The Haworth Press, Inc. All rights reserved.

streaming down like tickertape in a machine-driven hero's parade—the reliability of reference books as a class has no doubt proportionately gone down. All the Canute sycophants who wish may command the fact seas but the tide laps around us heedless. Mistakes are getting through, even frauds. Fact-checkers and proofreaders are one thing but the exceptionally well-informed, broad-minded, and detail-keen reference book compiler is quite another. Scarce, is what I mean. So, with "reference" we are talking not only about the generic activity of looking "up" to someone else's authority (and simultaneously *deferring* something—an action, a decision, an understanding—to a later time), but also about linking the information seeker into a chain of possible error we have no control over or knowledge of. Nor do we normally have firsthand ways of knowing the "authority" of the compiler(s) of the reference book we turn to—so we trust the review media and the passage of time.

My question was really not meant to be so abstract—

Reference is like algebra: simply "X" is what we tell each other hurriedly in the midst of conversation—A rose is a rose is a rose, we misquote—but in the *Columbia Encyclopedia* or *Bartlett's* or *Famous First Facts*, or their myriad fraternity, "X" is revealed in its fullness. ("Rose is a rose is a rose.") We may in fact turn to one of these sources, or we may pass onto something more important, secure in the knowledge that if we really had to, we *could* go back and check it out. In both occasions we have reference to the fact source; arguably the pass-up-using-it mode is the more significant use.

But, just taking the reference librarian—

People wander in with an enormous variety of questions—where's the men's room, who was the Dark Lady, was Polk born in the United States, how do you spell Armageddon? It is the perfect right and certainly the natural reaction of a librarian to "refer." Also, for us Americans and a few others, it's *very much* a democracy act. Eighteenth-century Irish peasants, for instance, were certainly not permitted by their English lords to "refer" to any information.

So—

So, what I'm getting at is, everyone involved in reference does the best they can, relying heavily on the judgment of others (often themselves relying on the judgment of others), achieving by accident, failing by accident, and very subject to elitism and prejudice.

What's that? You just said it was very democratic . . .

It is. And thereby having its elitist segments. Let me just put the idea into a frivolous mode for illustration. What baseball great is noted for saying "You could look it up"? In this democratic world, when this question is asked, or "referred," the answer will likely come up Casey Stengel. But how about who *actually* said it, the parallel to the "elitist" interest. Why, it was "Doc," baseball manager Squawks Magrew's pal, in James Thurber's 1941 *Saturday Evening Post* story, "You Could Look It Up." The point is, how often does the *real* answer or the *correct* answer become necessary? Much of current reference practice is filled with such examples, far less obvious of course. But anyway, reference is democratic and that includes some of the less clearly beneficial aspects . . .

How so?

Information authorities are viewed with a wide range of attitudes everywhere in the West, especially in the *n*th degree pluralistic United States. They are trusted or distrusted to widely varying degrees, and referred to by persons bearing enormously different standards of accuracy. A world of incorrect information, therefore, exists side-by-side a world of correct; each has legions of adherents because most people can't be bothered to try to come up with a way to certify all information—preposterous—and most people also do not have the savvy to satisfy themselves personally on the accuracy of a given item.

The disparities, the two kinds of "facts," never seem to matter much, cosmically speaking. Has Error slowed us down? One doubts. One even toys with making the case that Error, like genetic mishap, opens door to advancement that Rectitude passes by.

So, the reference publisher, to get back to our—

So, reference-book types—publishers *and* librarians—*do* make a difference in the quality of life over time but generally only the relatively elite information users can make short term "gains." Hoi polloi seem quantifiably more served, or informed, to the degree they are at all, by things like packaged-food labels, neighborly opinion, cold government flyers, than they are by reference books on library or even bookmobile shelves. I hate to say it. A beautifully crafted Oxford University Press tome of 1,850 pages, indexed by a world champion indexer and bearing $10,000 in proofreading costs alone, will never matter to almost everyone who lives or is to live.

That seems sort of bleak somehow. After all, you're not Oxford but you're in the business . . .

Well, the truth is, reference is not something that has characterized the race in its crowning moments. We are superb at fast-on-our-feet problem solving, plus learning-from-our-own-mistakes. We are creatures of courage and action and self-confidence. The world of referring (from here/now to when?/maybe?) is clearly not the central world of humankind.

So, what is the real value of reference?

Now that we know the Tonkin Gulf incident, which touched off the Vietnam War in 1964, never happened—no North Vietnamese gunboats (or anything else) attacked our ships out in the bay, as our government claimed (as a pretext for war)—what difference does it make? How many people, even those likely to lead us in the 1990s and 2000s, know what Congress' Tonkin Gulf Resolution was? Of those few who do know, how many know it was exposed as a lie? How many of the extremely few who have heard of the exposure nevertheless believe it is either partisan anti-LBJ rhetoric or commie-pinko turncoat talk? In short, using what "references" will what people to what end make use of the finding that there were no gunboat attacks? What is the value of this "fact"? Extremely little.

What is the (negative) value of a failure to "refer"? Kurt Waldheim, the Austrian former UN chief, was a ranking Nazi officer responsible in part of the mass murder of many thousands of Greeks. This information has existed for 40 years, yet few have ever "referred" to it, and those few unheard-from (until recently). What difference did this make? None, is the correct answer.

O.k., let's start over. You are a reference book publisher, living in majestically backward conditions in the Appalachians, with a happy and hardworking staff of 13, doing almost everything by mail and UPS, spending a good bit of your time passing judgment on things like authority, referenceability that counts, elitist and (one hopes) nonelitist information needs, and so on. You are full of "reference"; you told me you mercilessly beat all your authors to produce voluminous if not exhaustive indexes—to enhance the reference value of their books. I saw at your office piles of all manner of periodicals that review, dissect and theorize about reference materials and services. This is obviously all important to you, yet so far you poormouth the concept, and act like providing reference service is irrelevant in today's world . . .

The whole thing is in parts—the *referee* (or, the referred-to—i.e., the book or other material), the *referrer* (librarian), the *referral* (by which I mean the administrative-budgetary allowance for the act as a routine), and *reference*. I'm interested in the last-named. I mean it as the study of the whole matter not only of referring but of authority and how it is vouched for. I have both financial and intellectual-curiosity reasons for wanting to know how "reference" affects societies' interests, economics, needs, missions, and so on. I need to have a glimmer of how much reference should be going on, who should be doing it, for whom, at what real cost to "society," into what realms of information, not into what realms . . . I deal with all the rest, especially the first, the *referee*, whom we call "authors," but I find most interesting the larger questions.

Well, to get moving, shall I simply ask, What is reference book publishing?

Surely, "what is book?" is the easiest (though not at all simple); let's leave it for a while. We are left with two terms, "reference" and "publishing." I am embarked on the first question, "What is reference?"

But that's well established, it's a sizeable and especially honorable branch of librarianship—

And is not the name of the river as called by the Indians of that bank as interesting as the name called by the Indians of this?

You mean—

Publishing, we pretend, is a profession also. We have a view of "reference." The river of information you can dip a hook into and snag facts. We know what reference is, we feed the river. Yonder are reference librarians and information specialists. They know what reference is. They fish the river.

Is it the same "reference"?!

Aha, good point, if filched. Thus the expatiation on "What is reference?"

(Glancing at watch) Well . . .

I'll be terser. A little tendentious too, but I think if it's artful a little tendentiousness can be a locomotive. Let's see. Without a common understanding of seeker (library patron), referrer, or referee (*Famous* Joe Kane, say), or the act of referral—or, even more importantly, the critical overview and analysis of the above— without common understandings of reference, nothing a publisher would have to say on the subject of reference book publishing would mean a great deal.

Surely, common culture alone would—

So, ask Noam Chomsky to address this readership with a lecture on "reference"!

But there are limits on the amount of groundwork needed to spade over before planting a few simple answers—

It's catching, no? Yes, I only suggested that these subjects, the various turns on "refer," were all quite different and that I wanted to dilate on "reference" alone, from among them.

So, reference, the publisher might claim, is the big-picture, sociological feature of the "refer" continuum . . .

"Reference" is where the publisher's expertise is equivalent to the librarian's, where shelflist savvy meets printing risk, where cost-to-achieve-near-perfection meets nature-of-need, where tax bites on slow-moving inventory confront the deliberate trashing of knowledge-units. The economics of reference and scholarly publishing are an analogue (in well-managed companies) of public desire for information and public attitude toward "authority." (Current attitude? If a guy in the right tie said it on TV, it's true.) The balance sheet on bibliographies tells a lot also about governmental attitude toward scholarship, and a great people's real nature. Besides, the subjects of these books inflate the windsocks of intellectual trends for all to see.

But what's the practical meaning of all this?

There isn't any. It's expository. We, publishers and librarians, see and record somewhat different events on the two banks of the reference river. The publisher knows more dearly than the librarian, even the purchasing librarian, that certain literally invaluable, demonstrably useful sources of information would be so extremely difficult to publish profitably, or to publish at all, as to be virtual impossibilities. Detailed grammars and lexicons of all New World aboriginal languages. Comprehensive folk/pop words-and-music reference books. Complete works of only recently departed poets.

Yes, yes—

The publisher also knows more dearly about what the elitist world of seekers and referrers want and will pay for in the way of paper vs. cloth, perfect vs. sewn, modest vs. lavish, 10 pt. type vs. 9 pt., or 100 color phots vs. 40 B & W, and thus knows about 5000 vs. 750 print runs. These physical (that is to say, financial) considerations are key matters to "reference," in fact, arguably more significant than any other (the more so in market-driven cultures like ours). And of course it is the publisher astride the locks—

Catching back—?

Publishing Policies and Reference Sources 329

(Ignoring as it were, regulating—and, naturally, taxing—the safe flow of data from, say, the high excited Atlantic of ideas to the placid munching Pacific, or whatever. (See—there's "X"; if I *had* to I know I could look up *somewhere* which ocean is higher, at Panama.) Most ideas the publisher turns away. Apply elsewhere, go around the Horn, sorry no flammables. The rest we make demands of, then laboriously guide through the ways, in essentially 19th-century procedures, heavy in human labor.

From the mailbag's thousands upon thousands of would-be informants—all busily writing, for which society should no doubt nevertheless be thankful—the publishers (read, '"public'-makers") select the tens upon tens of products judged suitable for use by the people at large, or by library clientele, or librarians, or possibly by some other buyers somewhere at the right price.

And your thesis is, this is "Reference"?

First of all, can the "thesis." Next, I'd go so far as to say "reference librarianship" is a name for what was described just above. A publisher judges that an oversize, lavish, full-color, coffee-table, nostalgia wonderland tour of the career of Stepin Fetchit is not a product many will call for and that librarians know this and will not reward the competition for bringing it out after the publisher declines it. That the publisher's pudency may be involved is simply a bonus, a tertiary reason.

And so you have, as, shall we say, an adjunct librarian, predeaccessioned an information item, the above would-be book on a famous actor—denied "with prejudice," one could say, a future request for referral to it—

If you need a bad guy-good guy partner, that sort of image, I don't mind. So, o.k. But does my interlocuter suggest I simply forward all manuscripts and proposals as they are to reference librarians? *(Note—the publisher being interviewed does 60 books a year of general reference, scholarly monographs, cinema history and reference, librarianship, and some other stuff too.)*

I concede you have a useful function, but why pluck for yourself the title "librarian"?

Because we serve the same people in nearly the same way (we suffer them to use a book). Only the scale is different. And we do it for nearly the same reasons, are frequently cross-trained, share identical review media reading habits, stay equivalently abreast of fields within our purview and in similar ways, could easily be mistaken for each other on the street, and on and on. It's obvious.

But the publisher makes a buck! It's a big difference. Jackie Eubanks once told me—

Jackie told me too. Celeste out West is informative; one's own conscience is useful; in the B. Dalton Booksellers quarterlies can be glimpsed a growing picture. It's not worth our time here, the motives angle. Let me just say, the so-called scholarly, technical, and professional book buying world rewards fewer frauds than most buying worlds reward, and the finances of providing works that sell in the hundreds do not frequently support waste or overconsumption by the providers or encourage them to become a blight upon the culture. This behavior is left to the New York trade.

So—dare I ask—what is reference book publishing?

So, "reference" has these several facets, and the publishers bestride (they are "astride" only in repose, of course) the "locks" of knowledge, that's *their* facet, and thus they are participating fundamentally in "reference." "Referrals" are largely done by librarians, but "reference" is a different matter.

But you mentioned two sides of the river—

So the 'public'-maker/librarian reviews a proposal and sees it as, Does the field need this, Is it wastefully competitive, What would the market (libraries) pay for this and could we produce it for less, How many acquisitions librarians will view this as needed by their clientele, What kind of format would the librarian expect, or settle for?* The librarian/'public'-maker sees it in *Choice* or *WLB* or something and usually can decide in a flash—perhaps even along with "Gad, $38.50 and only 129 pp." or "Wow, they trashed Pudolfsky's other book too!"—whether to consider it or go on. This is clearly two views of the river of reference. And as I said, there is also the matter of scale. The librarian, say, must consider, in seconds each, the interesting reality of thousands of books (price, availability, statement of contents and length all known quantities), while the publisher lengthily, intimately creates the reality of a relative handful of books, simultaneously contemplating (forming, however briefly, in the mind) the often *un*interesting prospect of thousands of others. The librarian can work from desiderata, skimming over the print of possibilities, consuming hundreds

---

*Is it too dated, is the indexing too cumbersome, has the compiler *any* energy left, will she agree to change the arrangement from chronological to author's last names, can we drop the maps, will the author proofread all 1400 pages so diligently we can have our bright afterhours highschooler proof it at $5/hr., is Walt Whitman really enjoying a comeback . . . ?

quickly. The publisher must deliberate each possibility of user-need, once apprised of a plausible book.

Yet, the librarian has numerous individual requests for information, many of which are duplicated (over and over); the publisher contemplates each platonic Question but once. The two jobs are different and yet the same, each post accords certain kinds of expertise the holder of the other is then mostly only taught, by the mediating force of the market (the canoe across the river). By which I mean unpublished beautifully contrived reference works of interest to 55 purchasers abound.

My uncle indexed everything in all the newspapers in Wyoming published 1881–1886 by name and subject, including ads, weather, etc. Everybody said it was brilliant.

Right. Not counting your uncle, who could be eccentric and throw off the forecast, we could probably sell 55 copies (and spend 10 in review copies and 10 in dinged returns). Just winging it, I'd say, they'd go o.k. at $99.50 a pop. A crack publisher's loss could be held to $20,000 if your uncle refused any emolument. We'd have to leave "London" off the title page to save the expense of six depository copies in U.K. libraries. But if I was a librarian I'd roar that such a book demanded immediate publication! Get on it!

So, in sum, in answer to the question—

Anyway, that's part of what "reference" is. As for "publishing," that's the craft, the technique, the thing you can better *learn* (whereas "reference" is something I think you need a "feel" for). It's the people management, the invoice design, the type, the paper, the press, the brochure. I speak of the so-called scholarly and reference book world. Once one has decided go or no go on a manuscript, for instance, the basic format suggests itself. The concept "library" comes first: If a lot of people will use this book, some attention is due the binding. If they want to use it next week, but probably not after next year, publish it by photocopying the author's fairly crummy typescript and then adhesive-bind it. I just made this up (and it sounds rather extreme), but the point is, I wouldn't stop short of it if I thought the market could be maximized. After all, another way of saying *that* is: the information be put into the greatest number of hands (while still useful). Also, the basic marketing suggests itself: to libraries! Though we all are, by accident, still you don't have to be a genius to get "making-public" down.

So, "Publishing" is—

What you do after you've made your decision to initiate reference service. Once one has figured out pretty much, in this case, who's supposed to be referring to whom, for what purposes, in what detail, with what economies, with what expectations, with what ease, one "publishes"—which for us means pretty much cut it to a standard size (e.g., 6 x 9) make it sturdy, set a sharp editorial terrier to it, use good typography (help save the en-dash!), and design it carefully to maximize look-up usefulness. (You ought to be able to pick up a good reference book you've never seen before, open it randomly, and become familiar *instantly* with its general subject, specific subject, scope, nature, "level" and so on—how and when to use it, apparent in 10 seconds. The typography and layout should carry the burden.)

The librarians' view—

Is the same only more so—the scale of individual bits of questions being so much larger. Librarians want a book that is easy to understand—especially to understand its scope so they can figure out quickly if it's even this book they should have in their hands. Librarians find a well-*designed* reference book somewhat reassuring as to content. Often a book will inadvertently reveal by its design, or lack thereof, a fundamental ignorance of some important aspect of a subject and will thus turn away librarians, who have more needs than funds anyway.

So that's "reference" and "publishing"; what about "B—

That's extremely *little* about "publishing"! Why do some publishers fail? Should everything be on CD ROM? There's two questions of five thousand unaddressed.

But, for the record, "book" is part of my question. I'm sure even this ancient four-letter word is amenable to one of your exegetical skateboard numbers.

If you or any of your acquaintances think something is a book, it is. There *are* a few rules of thumb—we tell authors we'd surely prefer 200 or even 225+ double-spaced pages minimum when they think too small. (Too small a book has several advantages, all of which are overruled by too small a price tag.) We flag down the speedball movie book author who wants 225 full-page color photos. We reject the wider-than-tall, the spiral-bound, the update-every-six-months schemes, the pamphlet. "Books," to us, should have 150 to 1500 published pages, almost never need color, be typesettable in house, not require fold-out maps, be predominately in English, and be titleable such that a nonspecialist could recommend it to a specialist.

I guess I meant "what is a book" a little more philosophically— There isn't much distinction between book and nonbook and it's getting less distinct all the time. So the "philosophically" oriented remarks you request need to be fairly universal in scope. I'm not sure we have the time . . . What we, the scholarly publishers, consider in terms of "book" is market perception: 40 pp. at $29.95 is generally not possible; 400 pp. at $7.95 is equally unlikely. A very short work on a highly specialized subject is tough to handle. *Hungarian Irregular Verbs*, 35 pages. Who could publish this as a book? How about *Hungarian Irregular Verbs*, 1,350 pp. double column. Who again? Given the cost-plus-a-little-divided-by-number-of-customers (and allowing for things like royalties to authors and several or many tax years in inventory) equation, the first would need to cost perhaps $25, the second about $300 to $3000. Harvard and Yale, that's two copies; Budapest U., that's three . . .

All manuscripts tend toward "bookness," some from extreme distance, true, but knowing how to play them, one can bring a project to book with minimum pain or telltale bruising. Author wants each idea in his *How to Substitute Teach* book on a separate page with separate illustration—whoops, that's 412 pages, to sell at $40: Good luck!—mayhap we can convince him to run them in sequence, with illustrations scattered only here and there, plus drop the 58-page appendix on card tricks—voila! 176 pp. at $15.95. These are intrinsic matters in providing "reference service" but matters almost exclusively in the publisher's domain, and now I won't flog the fatal horse anymore except to say I believe to be well established the near-identity of reference book publishing and reference book librarianship.

Since you serve as a librarians' "screen" (my word, I realize, not yours) for books, do you also serve in some way on the behalf of all the rejected works, in order to pass through to the librarian whatever of value is to be gleaned from the vast numbers of rejects?

I can fulfill this function on these pages here and now, one of the rare times I have the chance to. The sea of unsolicited, rejected manuscripts is of late choked with end-of-the-world stuff, Revelation, the end times, apocalypse, proofs of the Second Coming based on Bible typography, and so on. I refer, as a body, to lengthy unpublishable mystico-religious works; I do *not* include o'er-aiming ecological speculations, Star Wars apologiae, postnuclear survivalist works or numerous other genres whose ends are bent coincidentally toward cataclysmic catastrophe. Adding them would double the numbers.

So, this is a tip—

Yes, get ready for the World is Ending action to pick up in the religion and philosophy sections of your libraries, as we press toward 2000. (Don't you for a moment believe the egghead nonsense about waiting until late December 31, 2000, before getting out the millennial balloons. The people like to note when their odometers read four or five digits the same, and they want "1999" to slip to "2000" and that's that.)

But you can't publish any of it?

Not and sell it. Actually, the biggest danger—forget loss of customer confidence—would be to enter into entangling relationship with people who believe Lincoln was a witch, JFK vegetates in the Caribbean, a secret band of *somethings* currently controls the U.S. Would *you* sign a contract for anything with such a one?

Surely other stuff comes along that's rejectable.

Well, the above is just the most entertaining—we're always polite and diligent in wrapping and returning—but it's small compared to what might be called Inappropriate Histories. These are 450-page documentations of ancillary minutiae to insignificant past events. They are so slight, so of-a-piece one is maddened by the temptation to write a form letter excoriating all history professors until one realizes it's the professors who write them. And besides these aren't as bad as the cinder block prose of quote-stackers. And still besides, they're all fun for the day's work.

We also get some—thankfully few—unannounced children's book proposals, and a few inspirational or self-help books, but most of our universe is scholarly and serious. We tend to reject books that compete with a known and respected book, that make up too small in size, that cover too exhaustively a subject of very modest interest, or too lightly one of major interest, that betray inaccuracy repeatedly in the most casual of inspection, that look unexpungeable of obtrusive racism or similar evil—there are many ways to fail to offer a good reference book (or scholarly monograph, which really is an extension of reference books insofar as it is indexed well). One of the more common ways is *not* the presentation of poorly written prose. This is editable.

So what is the ratio of proposals to acceptances? How fine is your screen? Do you represent your librarian-colleagues' interests faithfully?

McFarland selects perhaps 1 in 10; rejected are, say, 1 chileastic flying-saucer work, 1 exposé of how the IRS tried to screw one lone and valiant citizen, 1 work demonstrating that at the present rate of clear-cutting of Brazilian rain forest, ocean pollution, spray can sales, and the like, we will all hit the wall of oxygen deprivation in 15 years, 1 biography of a Minneapolis ward boss of the 20s (872 pp.), 1 Englished selection of Debussy's letters, 1 proposed anthology of criticism of male sexist verse, 1 critical bibliography of Kahlil Gibran—stop me—

Oh! Well—so what would you grab unquestionably?

Thank you. A 500-page (double spaced) typescript reference book exhaustively covering a manageable slice of a tremendously popular field without a shred of competition, by an acknowledged expert who realistically understands the publishing economics, has already alluded to the natural follow-up volume, proofreads superbly, and—

Well, I meant more what subject—

Oh, well, the subject is less important, don't you see. McFarland does not—or rarely—commission a book (dream up a subject, drum up an author), so our output, our service to libraries' clientele, is pretty well limited to (a) selecting among those that are offered, and (b) improving them and defining them as they move through our mills. So we have limited control over "subject."

But your list seems to have bulges in Soviet studies, chess, literature, women's studies—

Yes. Once you publish some good books in a field, you attract more manuscripts. As this begins to happen, as a pattern reveals itself before you, then it becomes worthwhile to arrange to bring out several together—spread costs of a special brochure, even review-copy mail-outs, over greater numbers. Now you're embarked on a program.

So your "reference-librarian" claim admits of much more personal taste or likes and dislikes in information handling than a practicing librarian would professionally tolerate.

I don't think that's true, in detail or in general. Because we so far have X number of books dealing with the Soviets does not mean I would reject a book on Democratic Kampuchea tomorrow. Perhaps by three years from now the list will be redefined, more as "international political science" than "Soviet." Developing expertise or repute in one area certainly cannot be said to slight another area.

So, o.k. you said "subject is less important"; first of all, less than what, and second, what do you really mean?

I'm serious: subject is less important than excellence of execution. If it's well-done, good-sized, unique, we want it for our library partners. There is no such thing as "rather have." Guy turns in a reference book to 20th century European women artists. If he's got the credentials, there's not already a good one out, and his job passes inspection, you go with it. You don't say we wanted women *composers*, or 19th *and* 20th centuries, or we consider Turkey part of Europe so it's not complete, or your cutoff date is 1983, we want it through 1985. If it's got *flaws* that's another matter—generally fixable, sometimes so bad it means reject, whatever the merits. But one must reject harshly if the quality is not there. Frequently, one author's mishandled subject will five years later see another's proper treatment of it.

Library collections grow not quite randomly but organically, according to the tastes of authors more than anything, which are today regulated by Harold Bloom, Doonesbury, television, the Zeitgeist, and things blowing in the wind, among other vectors. Publishers have realtively little effect upon this translation of grass-roots motive to library shelf. Except the ones that commission books. That's an interesting difference twixt us and others, incidentally. I would claim that by and large (and we *have* done it) books sought are at least not superior to books offered; the quality is now very high among some completed works offered out of the blue—why should the publisher add the labor of beating the bushes only to get—several years later—books of only comparable merit (and not as good, I'd argue).

One learns patience and long views. Full coverage of all subjects is not possible, is one dictum. If someone is interested enough to write it, X number of people are interested enough to want to read it, is another. Bird in hand, that's often useful. I've even heard of, This one's sort of . . . enh? . . . but we'd probably get that fabulous Index of Toll Booths in the Northeast she hinted she was going to do next, if we turn this one out decently for her. The most important thing to remember is, it's all a slender web, the information and reference world. It's gossamer, ephemeral, peripheral. Far apart from most people. It has at least one demerit. Every book published widens the unbridged chasm between the information rich and the information poor. When the poor come to "refer," as they do every 10 or 20 generations, they do so en masse, and their "referees" rarely have the right answer. But failures of "reference" are the stuff of which revolutions and renaissances are made.